THE GREAT BOOK OF
CLEVELAND SPORTS LISTS

THE GREAT BOOK OF CLEVELAND

SPORTS LISTS

BY **GREG BRINDA** AND **BILL LIVINGSTON**

RUNNING PRESS
PHILADELPHIA · LONDON

9 8 7 6 5 4 3 2 1

Digit on the right indicates the number of this printing

Library of Congress Control Number: 926939

ISBN 978-0-7624-3416-9

Cover Designed by Matthew Goodman
Interior Designed by Josh McDonald
Edited by Greg Jones

Running Press Book Publishers
2300 Chestnut Street
Philadelphia, PA 19103-4371

Visit us on the web!
www.runningpress.com

CONTENTS

Dedication

Greg: I would like to dedicate this book to the late David Halberstam and John Feinstein, who have written some of the greatest sports books and who inspired me to write at least one.

Bill: This book is for Marilyn, who:

3. keeps the family running by making lists and checking them twice.

2. put up with my complaints about Larry Hughes for years.

1. married me and made my life so much better.

Acknowledgments

Bill: Current and former *Plain Dealer* colleagues were incredibly generous with their time and expertise for this book. Multiple list contributors like Burt Graeff, Eddie Dwyer and the ever encouraging and encyclopedic Tom Feran were invaluable. No one helped more without a by-line than Chuck Murr. His local knowledge and readiness to share it helped make this book possible. Connie Schultz was always interested and upbeat about the project, which means a lot since she only won the Pulitzer Prize. Bob DiBiasio of the Indians solved many many problems for me, and Amanda Mercado of the Cavaliers and Amy Palcic of the Browns were the reasons LeBron James and Jim Brown contributed lists. All three have made my job much easier many times over the years, and I thank them for it.

Greg: I would add Geoff Sindelar, Chuck Murr, Jan Shanley, and Mark Procuk, and all the wonderful people I talked to along the way.

Introduction

Who were the toughest, fastest, and biggest opponents that Jim Brown faced? Bob Feller's toughest outs? LeBron James' favorite passers?

Who were the ten best Indians? Ten best Cavs? Ten best Browns?

What about the greatest villains in each sport? The most hapless Cleveland team owners and executives?

The best and worst trades, draft choices, and free agent signings?

The most galling defeats? The most glorious victories? The most despised Steelers?

Who fought over Jeff Garcia and at what appropriately named night spot? (Hint: It wasn't his teammates, out of deep love for the quarterback). Who was Lily Miller? How about Karen Panek?

We set out to answer these questions and raise some more, selecting, for example, an All-Time Cleveland Area Ohio State Football Team. And an All-Time Cleveland Area Track Team.

We didn't neglect the preps, either. Our panel of experts picked the best football players ever from St. Ignatius, St. Edward, Benedictine and Glenville.

We also re-visited midge infestations, blizzards and beer riots. We asked irreverent questions about some local sports bigwigs and we share our radio memories of others we loved. We tried to cover most of what area sports fans care about. So we included lists on the Mid-American Conference basketball standouts since the conference tournament came to The Q, indoor soccer stars, Cleveland State worthies, the top golfers, boxers and bowlers, as well as the race car drivers who brought thunder to the lakefront.

We discuss the city's mostly glorious hockey history—and its uneven experience with several soccer teams.

We asked people you know from your TV screen or sports page to help us out. Current or former play-by-play men from the three major pro teams chipped in lists of their top memories. So did some of the city's most famous athletes. Let's just say that the three guys in the first paragraph on this page contributed lists. So did Drew Carey, U.S. Senator Sherrod Brown, Iron Chef Michael Symon, Bernie Kosar and a lot more—including three Cleveland-born or Cleveland-based Olympic gold medalists.

Because man does not live by ESPN alone, we got a little help from our friends in the newspaper and radio business in town who laid out their ideas of the best local comedians, actresses, songs and movies either set or shot here. We also came up with lists of the top area eateries and places to get a good hot dog.

We would like this book to be definitive, but we realize that's not the way subjective opinions work. Still, we wouldn't want to order a drink in any bar that couldn't settle a sports argument with our book. (We also rate the top area sports bars).

We rated just about everything we could think of, except the fans. Because for passion and for perseverance without a whole lot of payoff, Cleveland fans have to be No. 1.

Bill and Greg

"Super" Joe Charboneau's 1980 American League Rookie of the Year season doesn't even make the honorable mention category on this list. It just wasn't good enough to compete with the seasons these guys enjoyed coming out of the gate. Injuries and a downturn in team fortunes stunted some of their careers. Others went on to establish themselves as among the best to ever play their respective games.

10. Zydrunas Ilgauskas, Cavs, 1997–98. Z scored 13.9 points, averaged 8.1 rebounds and was the MVP of the Rookie Game at the All-Star weekend. Provided a sneak preview of great things to come, at least after he recovered from his foot injuries.

9. Eric Metcalf, Browns, 1989. The big-play scatback from Texas scored 10 touchdowns, injecting new life into a fading Browns team that had one last title run in them. On the Monday night game in Cincinnati, his hopscotch through the Bengals' defense made you think the play was called "Abracadabra."

8. Kenny Lofton, Indians, 1992. "We have acquired an impactful center fielder," predicted General Manager John Hart. Had they ever! Lofton was a throwback to the '60s when superior black athletes transformed baseball, especially the National League. He stole 66 bases in 78 tries, hit .285 and played the outfield with the athleticism of the sixth man on one of University of Arizona's Final Four basketball teams, which he had been before baseball.

7. Al Rosen, Indians, 1950. Thirty-seven homers, 116 RBI, a .287 batting average. Some critics claim Rosen is overvalued because there weren't that many top third basemen in his day. Not with those numbers, he isn't.

6. Herb Score, Indians, 1955. What might have been? Herbie threw $227^{1/3}$ innings, went 16-10 with a 2.85 ERA and flame-broiled 245 hitters with his fastball.

5. Jim Brown, Browns, 1957. What kind of a list is this when 942 yards (in only 12 games, remember) and 10 touchdowns, nine of them rushing, only rates #5? A damn impressive list, that's what.

4. Marion Motley, Browns, 1946. We know now that Paul Brown's presence on the sidelines assured that the top team in the All-America Football Conference was ahead of its NFL brethren. But having Motley on the field nearly every play of the game didn't hurt. Playing both offense and defense, Motley averaged a breathtaking 8.2 yards on his 73 carries, scored six touchdowns, intercepted a pass while making the prospect of colliding with him an eventuality to be avoided. And he accomplished all that while coping with the era's racist Jim Crow rules that forced him and fellow black teammate Bill Willis to sit out a game at Miami.

3. LeBron James, Cavs, 2003-04. The first overall pick in the draft, LeBron inspired hope for the future of a Cavs franchise that had fallen on hard times. But considering that he was coming into the NBA at the age of 18 with only high school experience, even the giddiest only hoped LeBron might develop enough over the season to reach double-figures in scoring average. LeBron opened the season with 25 points in Sacramento on national television. Then in March, he poured in a franchise-record 56 points against Toronto. For the season, he averaged 20.9 points per game and added enough assists and rebounds and dazzling plays to justify comparisons to Oscar Robertson—along with the giddiest predictions about even greater things to come.

2. Hal Trosky, Indians, 1934. How do 35 homers, 142 RBI and a .339 batting average sound? Even in the MLB's batter-friendly era of the '30s, these were startling numbers.

1. Gene Bearden, Indians, 1948. He appears elsewhere in this book, but the knuckleballer from nowhere has to top any list of rookie excellence. He went 20-7, won the sudden-death playoff game, had a 2.43 ERA, pitched on short rest and established himself as the original "Mr. October" before Reggie Jackson was even born.

Honorable Mention/Didn't Quite Make the Final Cut: Sandy Alomar Jr. (Indians, 1990), Brad Daugherty (Cavs, 1986), Addie Joss (Bronchos, 1901), Ron Harper (Cavs, 1986), Kevin Johnson (Cavs, 1987).

Not every player or coach brought in to revive a Cleveland franchise turned out to be LeBron James. Some turned out to be more like Frank and Jesse James, robbing fans and teams for big paychecks in return for little effort or results. Some lied and cheated, in addition to stealing. Some didn't give enough of a damn to do even that. And some just hung around and ate.

10. The "Quiet Storm" himself, the oft-injured, seldom-double-teamed, sackmaster-who-wasn't, Courtney Brown. But, hey, he only cost the Browns a #1 overall pick in the draft.

9. Mike Phipps. He wasn't the #1 overall, but many still consider this QB bust the worst selection in the history of the Browns—not only because of Phipps' performance, but because of what the team gave up to get him (future Hall of Fame WR Paul Warfield). Phipps ended up with the lowest starting QB rating ever for a Brown. Just think about some of the stiffs he had to beat out to claim that distinction. For instance . . .

8. Tim Couch. Another NFL #1 overall draft pick who looked more like a midseason pickup from NFL Europe. Couch matched a weak, inaccurate arm with a lame work ethic and utter lack of passion. If told to show up at 9 a.m., Timmy showed at 8:59. If the day was over at 6 p.m., he left at 6. The young quarterback also spurned Bernie Kosar's offer to become his personal mentor, even though Bernie, far less emotionally fragile, had been through the same welter of experiences—adulation, scorn, injury, booing, being cut. But, hey, Bernie might have urged him to stay late some days to work on improving. To make it in the NFL, you have to have Vinny Testaverde's arm or Bernie's brain or a movie critic's enthusiasm to analyzing film. It became cute, as Couch continued to scattershot the ball around the field behind his expansion-team o-line, to spell it "Ouch." Unfortunately, Browns fans were the only ones feeling the pain.

7. Rollie Massimino. He simply lacked the local contacts, the energy, the interest and the panache to rebuild a downtrodden program like Cleveland State's. Kevin Mackey cut corners and sold the sizzle of the Run 'n' Stun before his player's discipline problems (and his own) caught up with him. Massimino had troubles with the youth, too (his best player, Damon Stringer, a transfer from Ohio State, wound up in prison for his part in an armed robbery of Indians pitcher C.C. Sabathia). But the coach who had guided Villanova to the NCAA championship in 1985 lacked Mackey's crowd-pleasing style, victories and roguish charm. You quickly got the feeling that Rollie was yesterday's news today. During his last season in 2002-03, Rollie rivaled Keith Hernandez for sheer lack of pride and effort.

6. Keith Hernandez. Signed as a free agent to a two-year, $7 million deal. "That," owner Dick Jacobs observed, "is a lot of nachos." Or one giant bag of chihuahua dung. Played 43 games in 1990 for the Tribe, hitting .200 with 8 RBI and 1 HR. But he did have a lusty .287 OBP. He was a jerk with the media, as well, once making Bill Livingston wait for two hours for an interview while Hernandez did a crossword puzzle in the trainer's room that was his private lounge. Hmmm, what's a nine-letter word beginning with "H" and ending in "z" for money-grubbing, malingering fraud?

5. Andre Rison. Art Modell's last, dingbat idea in Cleveland was to bring in this loud-mouthed, high-cost, low-production management toady. After pocketing a $17 million signing bonus that turned Modell's pockets inside-out, Rison produced 17 million reasons to think he was as useless a loogie as Uncle Artie in his desperation ever coughed up. Rison flexed his gratitude and class by ripping the old Stadium ("Look at this raggedy-assed place") when he should have been looking at his own raggedy Andre play.

4. Danny Ferry. The Cavs were finally developing into a perennial title contender with an even brighter future. Until they pulled the trigger on the gun owner Gordon Gund put to GM Wayne Embry's head to make this 1990 deal. Ron Harper and two No. 1s for 7.8 points per game, dipping to 4.5 in the playoffs, over ten years of a stunning-for-its-time $26 million contract. Biggest shot of his career: Third game, 1994 first round playoffs vs. the Knicks, tied 1-1. Cavs down two. Mark Price's pass out of a double team finds Ferry open in the final seconds at the middle of the three-point arc. Ferry, in the long view, was destined for the shortlist of candidates for the biggest mega-bust trade of all-time in pro basketball. But this shot at a winning trey provided one brief moment when he could choose, for 24 hours anyway, to become hero instead of goat, saved over damned, make not miss. Clang! Short.

3. Butch Davis. This drawling Baghdad Bob o' Berea ended up with even less credibility than his Iraqi counterpart. Before a panic attack sent Davis out of the league in a Brink's truck full of Little Lerner's money, he built a draft legacy (e.g. Gerard "Big Money" Warren instead of LaDanian Tomlinson; William Green; Ryan Pontbriand; a long snapper in the fifth round) that sits at least in the suburbs of Stepientown. He was so, um, creative with the facts that Davis' nose was conservatively estimated to reach from Berea to Bombay by the end of his tenure. And by almost any measure, the Browns were worse for his time here—and they were an expansion team when he arrived.

2. Shawn Kemp. Pretty much the anti-LeBron as Cavs' superstars went. Showed up as bloated as his contract, then had a third piece of pie every night. Made the worst series of faces until LeBron after key baskets, too. In Kemp's case, the expressions simply mirrored the scowls of Cavs fans watching him blow up from merely fat into a Macy's parade float.

1. Al Lerner/Carmen Policy. Whoever was granted ownership of the new Browns in 1999 was going to be the Messiah of the next millennium, because Cleveland wanted pro football back in the worst way. Which is exactly what NFL Commissioner Paul Tagliabue gave us when he made the lamest match since Julia Roberts fell for Lyle Lovett. What was he thinking when he put Big Al, the man who helped hijack the original Browns to Baltimore, in Carm's way and all the sleazy bluster that made up Lerner's straw-man lieutenant? Or here's another one: Quick. Who was responsible for more spin than Policy? That wheel Blood, Sweat and Tears sang about? Charlotte, whipping up the web to market her favorite pig's supernatural abilities? The group responsible for "Rubber Band Man" and "They Just Can't Stop It (Games People Play)"? Rumplestiltskin? Meadowlark Lemon's finger and a basketball?

As Bogey told Bergman in Casablanca: "We'll always have Paris." Against all odds (and they were often high) and under various names, we've always had a baseball team in Cleveland. Or at least we've had one since 1870, along with plenty of other clubs playing a variety of sports. The Browns have now played 59 full seasons in Cleveland. (By the Browns tally, they hit 60 years in pro football in 2006, counting the 0-0 records from 1996-98. As Bill told Ted, "Whatever.")

Baseball

Forest Citys (National Association, 1871; National League, 1879-84; American Association, 1870-88).
Spiders, (National League,1889-1899).
Blues (American League, 1900-01).
Bronchos (AL, 1902).
Naps (AL, 1903-14).
Indians (AL, 1915-).

Basketball

Rebels (BAA, forerunner to the NBA, 1947).
Pipers (ABL, 1961-62).
Cavaliers (NBA, 1970-).
Rockers (WNBA, 1997-2003).

Hockey

Barons (AHL, 1936-73).
Crusaders (WHA, 1972-76)
Barons (NHL, 1977-78).
Lumberjacks (IHL, 1992-2001).
Barons (AHL, 2001-06).
Lake Erie Monsters (AHL, 2007-).

Soccer
Stokers (United Soccer League, 1967).
Stokers (NASL, 1968).
Cleveland Stars (American Soccer League, 1972-73).
Cleveland Cobras (ASL, 1974—81).
Cobras (ASL, 1976-81).
Force (MISL, 1978-88).
Crunch (MISL/NPSL, 1989-2002).
Force (MISL, 2002-05).

Tennis
Nets (World Team Tennis, 1974-77).

Football
Tigers (NFL, 1920-21).
Indians (NFL, 1923, 1931).
Bulldogs (NFL, 1924-25).
Rams (NFL, 1937-42, 1944-45).
Browns (AAFC) 1946-49).
Browns (NFL, 1950-95, 1999-).
Thunderbolts (Arena 1992-94).
Fusion (Women's Football Asscociation, 2002-).
Gladiators (Arena, 2008).

Note: LeBron James . . . does he really require an introduction in a book customized for the Cleveland sports market? Let's just say the Cavaliers' superstar understands passing and practices it readily enough to squelch any talk of incipient Kobe-ism. A student of the game's history, LeBron also dishes stylishly enough to be compared more often to Magic than to Mike. LeBron, who prefers to let his play do the talking, did not add commentary on his top five, but we will.

5. Magic Johnson. Height that allowed him to pass over double teams, strength that let him play power forward as well as point guard, no-look passes that made Sports Center viewers drool, precocious audacity that inspired teammates to greater things. . . . Nah, there aren't too many similarities between Magic's game and LeBron's game.

4. John Stockton. The ultimate triggerman on the game's ultimate pick-and-roll, Stockton came out of nowhere (Gonzaga, actually, but that was pretty much nowhere back then) to become the NBA's all-time assists leader. James and Gooden or James and Varejao will never be joined at the hip in history like Stockton and Karl Malone are linked. But Mike Brown's entire set-offense seemed to consist of that Old School play in the 2006 playoffs. Stockton and Malone were sometimes predictable, but they were also as close to unstoppable as anyone has been in basketball since Wilt.

3. Oscar Robertson. The James role model for season-long triple-doubles, Oscar actually had the ball in his hands even more than James does. And "The Big O" spent much of that time backing down opponents for an eight-footer instead of a ten-footer, or to put it up from ten instead of a dozen. Effective as he was, Oscar was nowhere near as aesthetically pleasing to watch as James can be. LeBron has, however, picked up on Oscar's habit of racking up assists in the first quarter to get his teammates involved early and keep defenders guessing the rest of the game.

2. Steve Nash. When asked once about the legendary "Pistol" Pete Maravich, James, revealingly and effusively said, "Pistol was like Steve Nash. A little white guy who didn't look like he could do much, but he was amazing." Pistol was and Steve still is amazing. And unlike Maravich, Nash makes his teammates and his team a lot better with his passing.

1. Jason Kidd. One of James' favorite rivals and a player LeBron actively recruited to come to Cleveland, Kidd never made it here because the Cavs just didn't have enough quality, expendable players to offer in return. James did get to team with Kidd on the United States' 2007 World Championship gold medal squad. The active leader in triple doubles, Kidd ranks as one of the great rebounding guards ever and he's still able to direct a fast break the way Busby Berkeley choreographed musicals.

Only Peyton Manning's ads can compare to LeBron's. And, as James once said, when asked whose were better: "Mine. I play four characters. He just plays one." Admittedly, he doesn't play the "Four LeBrons" all the time. But it's what he will be remembered for, along with triple-doubles, reviving the Cavs and precocity to rival anyone outside Mozart. These ads warrant a few fond memories and reruns, too.

14. Chamber of Fear (Nike). James faces his deepest fears in a spot filmed to look like a Bruce Lee movie. The fears are each written in Chinese letters and then translated into English: "Hype," "Temptation," "Haters," "Complacency" and "Self-doubt." When he dunks in the face of two fire-breathing Chinese dragons, causing them to explode, he also immolates the commercial's chance to be seen by its target audience. The Chinese government deemed it disrespectful to the country's history and banned the ad.

13. Glory Days (Nike). Over a family dinner he made, "Wise" LeBron tells "Athlete" LeBron he's not so hot. Actor James captures an old, proud man's mannerisms, as Wise says: "In the state championship game, I scored 35 points, with 15 rebounds, 12 assists." Pause . . . "and 12 assists!" Longer pause. "That's a quadruple-double, boy."

12. He Passed? (Nike). Meant as a YouTube spoof of an earlier Steve Nash spot, it turns out to be an exquisite answer to the media chorus that criticized James' drive-and-dish in the first game of the Eastern Conference Finals. There is no voice-over in this commercial, just music with white print over action shots. LeBron James," it reads, "27.3 points per game during the regular season." As the game begins, it continues: "The second-most decorated NBA player behind Michael Jordan." It ends: "Even with the spotlight all to himself." And here the fateful play repeats: The drive, the left-hand pass to an open Donyell Marshall, the miss. "He passed?" A resolute James then walks off the court with only the Nike swoosh showing in the background. In the context of Game 5, when James scored a critical basket in his 48-point extravaganza because Rasheed Wallace would not leave Marshall a second time to help out on James, it becomes an ode to unselfishness.

11. Pressure (Nike). The rookie James gets the ball for the first time in his first game, then literally freezes. A lone voice yells "Jerk!" from the stands. A bobbing sign reads: "All hype." Sitting on the bench, George Gervin murmurs: "C'mon, young fella." Suddenly, a derisive laugh booms from James and he roars to the basket.

10. Bursting His Own Bubble (Bubblicious). Much the same theme. A voice-over says: "So much hype, so much pressure" as James chomps on the gum, then blows a bubble that expands to cover one-quarter of his face. It pops into splattery goo as the voice says: "So much for letting it affect you."

9. 2007 ESPYS co-host (ESPN). Another self-inflicted needle prick to deflate the Jamesian ego. Co-host Jimmy Kimmel tells LeBron he has to do better the next time he reaches The Finals. "You don't want to be that guy who didn't win the Super Bowl," the talk show host says. "Jimmy, I can't win the Super Bowl," James replies. "Because that will follow you if you're that guy who didn't win the Super Bowl," Kimmel continues. "Jimmy, you don't understand. I CAN'T win the Super Bowl," James says. "Well, not with THAT attitude," sniffs Kimmel.

8. Full-court Shots (Powerade). James squares up and drains a series of 90-footers at practice as if they were free throws as a TV anchorman says in an excited gabble to his camera crew: "You ARE getting that, right?" Life imitates art. James hit an 84-footer at the end of the third quarter against Boston during the 2006-07 season. A 90-footer he made while fooling around at practice before The Finals convinced the Spurs to double-team him even on no-hopers.

7. Paper Reject (Cub Cadet). James, in pajamas and a bathrobe, walks out to pick up his paper (obviously, *The Plain Dealer*). A neighbor mowing his lawn next door begins taunting James about the maneuverability of the mower, crying: "Hey, Mr. All-Star! Look at my moves!" Later, the neighbor dribbles a basketball near the hoop attached to James' garage. LeBron, poker-faced, watches as he says, "He goes right, he goes left," then shoots. LeBron REJECTS him—with the hand still holding the newspaper! Bill Livingston's column presumably survives the impact.

6. Book of Dimes (Nike). Anticipated the "Rise up!" ad campaign that anointed James a basketball messiah. Bernie Mac plays the sweatsuit-clad preacher. George Gervin and Dr. J serve as witnesses in the congregation. The High Church of Sports had found a new idol to worship.

5. Paper Jam (ESPN). More admirable self-deprecation from King James. Kneeling, he struggles to unsnarl a paper jam in an office copier. Anchorman Stuart Scott wanders by and snorts: "Chosen One, huh?"

4. Royal Chair (ESPN). Plopping into an office chair whose back bends and groans under the burden, James frowns, then clambers out. He walks into the next cubicle where he asks anchorman Scott Van Pelt if he took his chair. Seated on a throne with a red velvet back and intricate carved woodwork, an ermine cape spread over his legs, Van Pelt denies doing so.

3. 2007 Playoff Promotion (TNT). Alone on the Cavs' practice court, James flings the ball off a wall, catches it, mutters a pretend broadcaster's play-by-play ("Cavs down by one, seconds left . . . "). He cuts and weaves downcourt while continuing the commentary ("Oh, behind the back!..."), He gets to the paint ("Backs him down, backs him down . . . "). Then turns and shoots ("Ohhh, it's good! The Cavs win! And the crowd goes wild!"). It's Russ Hodges' famous "The Giants win the pennant!" call recast in the setting of every kid's playground dreams. An absolutely perfect fantasy. And because it's LeBron playing it out, it assures you that dreams really do come true.

2. Pool (Nike). The best of the "Four LeBrons" genre. Literally baptized in battle the year before his first playoff appearance, "Athlete" James jogs in a swimming pool to prepare for The Finals run. "Wise" LeBron, the crotchety old man, says: "You think Michael trained in a pool? You think you're going to get through Detroit in a pool?" Wearing an immaculate white linen suit, the "Business" LeBron then dives off the high board with a twisting somersault from the pike position, then smiling through the air bubbles, prepares to "rise up" to the surface.

1. Better Than Me (Nike). A montage shows LeBron progressing from childhood through high school (complete with the St. Vincent St. Mary-mandated bandages to cover his arm tattoos). Then some quick glimpses of Draft Day with NBA Commissioner David Stern, of cheering crowds, and then of James holding aloft the Eastern Conference trophy. Only the SVSM and Cavs shots are actually of James. Actors fill the other roles. In one of them, a kid playing James wears a purple uniform with "Soldiers" written across the chest in white. A reference only serious LeBroniacs will catch, the uniform pays homage to the Oakland (Calif.) Soldiers, an AAU team James played for when he was 15 to get some experience against West Coast competition. It led to the so-called "LeBron Rule," which prohibits kids from playing for teams more than 100 miles from their hometowns. In the commercial, a surprisingly subdued King James says: "I can't inspire you. Nothing about my game is great yet." He promises to keep working. As James floats into a dunk, he repeats the opening phrase of the Nike commercial. "You don't want to be LeBron James." The surf-like sound of a crowd's roar grows to a crescendo. The screen goes black with only the Nike swoosh showing. "You want to be better than me," concludes James in voiceover. He has done "Be Like Mike" one better. The commercial serves as both a challenge and blessing to the next generation.

Note: Toughness was required just to take the field against the Browns in the days of Jim Brown, because No. 32 was Cleveland's warrior-in-chief and maybe the toughest guy to ever play the game. He was also, no maybes, the greatest running back there ever was, boasting the speed and power of LeBron James, plus the durability to take anything the opponent could dish out and give it back to him, at a record 5.2 yards per carry. Brown's offers his list of the toughest guys he came up against in no particular order.

7. Gene "Big Daddy" Lipscomb, Los Angeles Rams and Baltimore Colts defensive lineman. Died too young of a heroin overdose. Gene was big, fast and agile. He was very tough, physically. He was the strongest player in the league.

6. Larry Wilson, St. Louis Cardinals safety, Pro Football Hall of Fame member. He was very smart and a great tackler. Everybody I would put on my list was a sure tackler.

5. Mel Renfro, Dallas Cowboys defensive back, Pro Football Hall of Fame member. I put him on here because you asked who was the fastest guy I played against. He caught my ass from behind once, when I thought I was gone. There were other fast guys, but Mel could fly.

4. Dick "Night Train" Lane, Detroit Lions defensive back, Pro Football Hall of Fame member. He was fast, quick, and he would tear your head off. Players could do all kinds of things they can't do now. He would club you in the head with his forearm.

3. Sam Huff, New York Giants linebacker, Pro Football Hall of Fame member. He played on some great Giant defenses. Without question, he was the smartest player of his time.

2. Joe Schmidt, Detroit Lions linebacker, Pro Football Hall of Fame member. He's not remembered as well as he should be now. He was a very sure tackler and very smart.

1. Dick Butkus, Chicago Bears linebacker, Pro Football Hall of Fame member. I only played against him in the (College) All-Star Game in 1965. But he was the meanest and the toughest guy I ever played against. He and LT (the Giants' 1980s-90s linebacker, Lawrence Taylor) are my all-time 1-2 at linebacker.

Note: Diek appears in this book in other places. But nowhere is his humor more pointed than when the long-time Browns' left tackle ponders our rivals down I-76. His prime coincided with the prime of the Steelers' franchise, when they won four Super Bowls in six years and put some of the most highly regarded teams and players in league history on the field. Diek gets beyond the hype to tell you what these guys were really like to play against.

10. L.C. Greenwood. Looked like a badly dressed pimp with his gold shoes. His arms were so big, it was tough to get close enough to grab him.

9. Mel Blount. Didn't talk much, but would stick you like a linebacker. Heck, he was as big as our linebackers. Didn't talk like Erich Barnes, but patterned his physical style of play after him.

8. Lynn Swann. The finesse part of their offense, he was smooth and always good for one big play. When he accused Ron Bolton of spitting, it was clear he had political aspirations.

7. Ernie Holmes. As wide as he was tall. He never said squat, and had that scary look. I think even his teammates were afraid of him. Ate blockers instead of steroids.

6. Franco Harris. Nice guy who ran faster than it looked like his body was capable of going. Unlike Jim Brown, he ran out of bounds, too. But that conserved energy to beat you with later. Nothing too flashy, but very steady.

5. Dwight White. The ultimate example of diarrhea of the mouth. He would flop the whole game, slobbering and spitting the whole time. He still sends me Mother's Day cards.

4. Rocky Bleier. Anytime a white running back with lead bullets still in his foot from Viet Nam outruns your secondary, it's demoralizing. Rocky brought toughness to their offense.

3. "Mean Joe" Greene. Tried to kick a field goal with Bob McKay's groin, and then had the guts to blame it on Dwight White and me for screaming at each other. A disruptive force on the defensive line.

2. Terry Bradshaw. Big old country boy who took apart your secondary like a corn picker on the back 40. It's a shame Joe "Turkey" Jones couldn't have planted him a little deeper. Made big plays at critical times.

1. Jack Lambert. The straw that stirred the drink on defense. If you were having success against the Steelers, Lambert would have a hissy fit, start foaming through his remaining teeth, and it would be a signal to the rest of the defense to bring out the brass knuckles.

Top Ten Glenville High School Football Players
:: Eddie Dwyer

Note: Our resident prep expert Eddie Dwyer turns his discerning eye to the area's flagship public school football program. Glenville is a source of great pride to inner-city Clevelanders. Under coach Ted Ginn, Sr., the school's football program has provided a way to a better life for many disadvantaged young men. Ginn has mentored a number of fine players over the years, helping them gain college scholarships and even pro stardom. Dwyer picks the cream of the Glenville Tarblooders crop.

10. Troy Smith, quarterback. Impact season was 2001. Troy would be higher on the Glenville list if he hadn't played the majority of his high school football career at St. Edward. He drew the attention of college recruiters at numerous summer camps, went on to a Heisman Trophy season at Ohio State in 2006, then was selected by the Baltimore Ravens in the fifth round of the NFL draft.

9. Dareus Hiley, defensive back/quarterback/tailback/wideout/kick returner. Impact seasons were 2000, 2001 and 2002. Nicknamed "Superman" for his all-around skills, Hiley helped Glenville become the first football program from the Cleveland Public Schools to win an OHSAA playoff game (Nov. 2000 at Shaker Heights). In what was probably the most memorable scene of the 2000 season, Hiley was lifted in the air and carried off the field by a throng of fans, neighbors and teammates after his last-minute heroics against Shaker Heights. The brisk, but sunny Saturday afternoon encounter drew the largest attendance in the history of Shaker's Russell H. Rupp Field. Truly an exceptional athlete, academics and other personal issues sidelined Hiley's college career. This two-time All-State honoree could have played on Sundays.

8. Robert Rose, defensive tackle. Impact seasons were 2004 and 2005. Big Rob (6-5, 265 pounds) started his athletic career at Cleveland Central Catholic before becoming a defensive force for the Tarblooders. He garnered All-Ohio and All-American honors his senior season (2005) and chose Ohio State from a Who's Who list of college football programs that offered him scholarships. Rose also was an inside force on Glenville's varsity basketball team.

7. Ray Small, running back/kick returner/defensive back Impact seasons were 2004 and 2005. A game-changer, the lightning-quick Small put the opposing defense on its heels throughout his high school career, which started as a promising freshman at St. Edward. Now a member of the Ohio State Buckeyes, he earned All-State and All-American recognition as a high school senior. This kid has a range of talent as wide as his smile.

6. Freddie Lennix, wide receiver/running back. Impact seasons were 2003 and 2004. A dominant linebacker, Lenix won Ohio's Division I Defensive Player of the Year award in 2004. His field awareness, pursuit and pad-rattling hits earned him All-American honors at linebacker and he was no slouch when asked to carry the ball on offense. He put on defensive clinics against St. Edward and St. Ignatius in the 2004 regional playoffs.

5. Richard Bishop, two-way lineman. Impact seasons came in the late 1960s. After an impressive senior season, Bishop was recruited by Lee Corso at Louisville and went on to become a mainstay for the Cardinals. He played in the NFL with Los Angeles, Miami and New England, and also played in the Canadian Football League. Bishop is often overlooked when the discussion of Glenville standouts comes up, but he should be remembered as one of the greats.

4. Pierre Woods, defensive lineman/punter/tight end/wide out. Impact seasons were 1999 and 2000. Woods was the emotional and physical leader on the Tarblooders' history-making squads of 1999 and 2000. Possessing cat-like quickness and a relentless, aggressive attitude, he totaled 42 sacks in his junior and senior seasons. An All-Ohio and All-American honoree as a senior, he went on to a solid career as a linebacker for the University of Michigan and signed as a free agent with the New England Patriots.

3. Donte Whitner, defensive back/all-purpose player. Impact seasons were 2001 and 2002. Whitner's defensive skills were evident from the get-go, and he also could contribute on the other side of the ball. He was rated among the nation's top defensive prospects during his senior season at Glenville and didn't disappoint, earning a scholarship to Ohio State. After an outstanding career at safety for the Buckeyes, he passed up his senior season and was selected by the Buffalo Bills as the eighth overall pick in the NFL draft (April 2006). He had an All-Rookie season for the Bills in the fall of 2006.

2. Benny Friedman, running back/quarterback/all-purpose player. Impact made in early 1920s. In 1920, Friedman was a relatively small running back on East Tech's reserve team. East Tech's coach at the time, Sam Willaman, told Friedman he was too light for the East Tech varsity and advised him to transfer to Friedman's neighborhood school, Glenville, if he intended to keep playing football. The rest is history as Friedman helped put Glenville on the area high school football map, went on to an All-American and Big Ten championship career at Michigan, then a legendary professional career. The son of a tailor, the late Friedman is enshrined in both the National Collegiate Football and Pro Football Halls of Fame.

1. Ted Ginn Jr., quarterback/defensive back/wideout/kick returner. Impact seasons were 2001, 2002 and 2003. Ginn Jr., the son of Tarblooders head football coach Ted Ginn Sr., was one of the most exciting players in the rich history of Northeast Ohio high school football. After a senior season that saw him garner a spot on every All-Area and All-State team, Ginn Jr. was chosen as USA Today's national player of the year on defense. He earned high school All-American honors in football and track and, after seriously considering Pete Carroll's USC Trojans, he decided to stay in Ohio and play for the Buckeyes. An All-Big Ten selection as a wide receiver/kick-return specialist, Ginn, Jr. was selected by the Miami Dolphins as the ninth pick in the first round of last spring's NFL draft. St. Ignatius' 25-year head football coach Chuck Kyle lists Ginn Jr. among the toughest three opponents he has ever had to prepare for.

Note: A Benedictine grad from the Class of '71, Wally has followed the "Home of Champions" football team since the early 1960s. He can still recall the jersey numbers of many of their players. Just ask the next time you see him. Since 1977, Mieskoski has handled the Bengals football publicity and serves as the Benedictine football historian. He still works the Bengals football stats from the press box with his sidekick, Andy Hudak (Class of '60), who has been helping Wally for over 20 years. He lists his top Benedictine football players alphabetically.

Honorable Mention: Chuck Noll (Class of 1949). Noll played on Benedictine's first undefeated, untied team that posted a record of 10-0 in 1948 on its way to winning the Cleveland city title game 7-0 over South High at Cleveland Stadium. The lineman was named to the All-Catholic Universe Bulletin team by the Diocese of Cleveland newspaper as a Benedictine senior. But Noll's feats on the Bengals' playing field were not enough to gain a place on this list. He did develop his game enough to become an NFL linebacker and messenger guard for the Cleveland Browns in the 1950s. Nicknamed "The Pope," Noll then entered the NFL coaching ranks and guided the Pittsburgh Steelers to four Super Bowl titles, establishing himself as one of football's greatest all-time coaches and winning entry into the Pro Football Hall of Fame in Canton. So we give him at least an honorable mention here.

13. Bob Clark (Class of '87). A three-year starter at wide receiver, Clark set school career marks with 145 pass receptions for 2,469 yards. He also established the school record for the longest pass reception, a 93-yard TD catch from quarterback Larry Wanke in 1985 vs. Padua, and tied for another Benedictine mark with 10 catches in a game vs. Padua the following season. Clark still ranks seventh on the school's all-time scoring list with 204 points on 34 touchdowns. He caught four touchdown passes in a 27-0 victory over St. Ignatius in 1986.

12. Jack Glowik (Class of '74). At the conclusion of the 1973 Benedictine Class AA state championship season, Glowik earned first-team All-Ohio honors from United Press International as a center on offense and as a defensive tackle, along with the "Lineman of the Year" award from the Associated Press. A co-captain of that '73 state title, Glowik was a three-year starter. He went on to play for Miami (Ohio) University and win the Mid-American Conference "Defensive Player of the Year" Award.

11. Mike Griffin (Class of '83). Combining quickness with strength and size, Griffin became one of the most dominating linemen in Benedictine history. A three-year starter, he played on the 1980 Division III state title team and the 1981 Division II state title team. An All-Ohio choice as a junior and a senior, the 6-5, 235 pound Griffin also earned a spot on the Adidas/Scholastic Coach prep All-America team. Before enrolling at Notre Dame, Griffin was ranked as one of the Top 100 incoming freshmen by Football News.

10. (tie) Gary Hansley and George Sefcik (Class of '58). During their state championship 1957 season, the Benedictine student newspaper The Bennet dubbed Gary Hansley as "Mr. Inside" and George Sefcik as "Mr. Outside." The backs finished their careers as the top two scorers in school history. Today, Sefcik still ranks fourth all-time with 233 points, while Hansley ranks sixth with 216. Both played on three straight city title teams that defeated St. Ignatius in 1955, '56 and '57. Hansley was voted the Charity Game MVP in the 27-3 win to clinch the state title.

8. Mike Krak (Class of '31). A member of the first Benedictine graduating class of 31 students in 1931, Mike Krak was also Benedictine's first football superstar. After a winless three-game inaugural season in 1929, Benedictine rebounded with a 4-2 record the following year. Krak, a running back, scored the first points in school history on a touchdown run in the school's first victory on September 26, 1930 over Lorain St. Mary 38-0. His 72 points that season placed him at the top of the all-time scoring list until 1947 and he continued to hold the single-season mark until 1955.

7. Pat Minnillo (Class of '97). A special teams specialist, Minnillo scored eight special team touchdowns on 6 punt returns and 2 kick-off returns to help the Bengals win the 1996 Division III state title. His most impressive performance may have been in the state playoff game against Olmsted Falls. He returned the opening kick-off 90 yards to give the Bengals a 7-0 lead. After Olmsted Falls was forced to punt on the next series, Minnillo returned that kick 70 yards for a TD to give Benedictine a 14-0 lead before the Bengals had run a play from scrimmage.

6. Ron Skufca (Class of '58). Skufca became the first Benedictine lineman to earn national honors when he was selected to *Teen* magazine and *The Sporting News* All-American team in 1957. Skufca, who also earned Ohio's Top Lineman honors for the year, was flown to Hollywood to appear on NBC-TV's *Eddie Fisher Show* with the other *Teen* All-Americans. The 6-4, 240-pounder cleared the line of scrimmage for running backs Gary Hansley and George Sefcik during the state title year of 1957. He was recruited by Purdue University by the man who would eventually become the owner of the New York Yankees, George Steinbrenner.

5. Larry Wanke (Class of '86). Wanke rewrote the school's record book by throwing for 5,480 yards completing 386 of 736 passes and 50 career TD passes in his Bengals career. The 6-2, 198-pound QB also holds the Bengals' single-game mark with 344 passing yards. In 1985, he threw for 3,045 yards and 34 touchdown passes. As a senior, Wanke was selected as the first-team quarterback on the Catholic Preparatory All-American team. He was the last selection ("Mr. Irrelevant") in the 1991 National Football League draft by the Super Bowl champion New York Giants.

4. Raymond Williams (Class of '03). He became the school's all-time scoring leader in 2003 with 538 points topping what was once thought to be the unbreakable mark of 416 points set by Larry Zelina in 1966. Williams won Ohio's "Mr. Football" award for the 2003 season and was the runner-up in 2002. The 5-11, 185 running back finished his career with 7,045 rushing yards and 89 touchdowns. As a junior, Williams gained 3,250 yards rushing. In back-to-back weeks in 2002, Williams rushed for school record totals of 324 and then 337 yards. Some of his single-season and career totals rank among the all-time bests in the entire state.

3. Mike Woods (Class of '73). Possibly the most physically talented player to ever wear a Bengals jersey, Woods sacrificed personal stats to help his team by playing multiple positions on both offense and defense in his senior season. He led the 1972 Bengals in their 14-0 upset victory over highly-touted Cathedral Latin, scoring on a 55-yard pass play early in the game to give the Bengals the only points they needed. Woods and his teammates prevented the Lions from crossing midfield for the entire game. On defense, he could cover sideline-to-sideline as well as anyone. In 1977, he became Benedictine's first collegiate All-American as a linebacker at the University of Cincinnati.

2. Jim Yacknow (Class of '64). Yacknow is best remembered for his MVP performance in the 1963 Charity Game 30-16 upset win over St. Ignatius when he dismantled the Wildcats on offense and defense. The 6-2, 215-pound senior end caught a 46-yard TD pass, grabbed a two-point conversion pass and pulled in a key third-down pass. Playing inspired defense, Yacknow blocked a St. Ignatius punt and recovered a Wildcat fumble. Yacknow earned All-Ohio honors in football and in baseball and was also a two-time selection to *The Plain Dealer* All-Scholastic team.

1. Larry Zelina (Class of '67). Widely acknowledged as the best player in school history, Zelina remains the only two-time Charity Game MVP and the only Benedictine player to have his jersey number (44) retired. A three-year letterman, Zelina used speed and power as a running back to become the school's all-time scoring leader with 416 points. As a junior, he led the state of Ohio in scoring with 210 points. He also handled the Bengals punting and place-kicking duties. While at Ohio State, Zelina was a starter at wingback on the Buckeyes 1968 national championship team.

Coaches

2. Joe Rufus. Rufus put the growl in the Bengals Roar. The cornerstone of football success at the school was placed when Joe Rufus first arrived on the Benedictine campus in September 1945. In his first season, he led the Bengals to their first football crown of any kind—an East Senate co-championship with archrival Cathedral Latin. He won more games (61) in nine years as head coach than the school did in the previous 16 seasons.

1. Augie Bossu. By almost any standard, there is no better coach in high school sports than Augie Bossu. He's one of the few men to coach in seven different decades, beginning in the 1940s. When he stepped down as varsity coach on March 1, 1994, Bossu ranked as Ohio's winningest football coach. From 1955 to 1993, Bossu compiled a 275-105-15 mark at Benedictine and added to his overall mark of 310-130-20. He was also the Bengals baseball coach finishing with a 681-300 record. In 1988, Bossu gained induction into the National High School Sports Hall of Fame in Kansas City. From the 1994 through 2005, Bossu coached the Bengals freshman football teams. He died January 1, 2008 at the age of 91.

The Best Players At Each Position That I Ever Saw
:: Mike Hargrove

Note: The Indians skipper won two pennants and five straight division titles in the 1990s. An accomplished and respected player before that, Hargrove took home 1974 AL Rookie of the Year honors (with the Texas Rangers) to jumpstart a 12-year playing career that included over 1600 hits and an All-Star Game appearance in 1975. Hargrove remains one of the most popular Cleveland Indians of all time.

Catcher. Carlton Fisk. Thurman Munson was right there with him, but Fisk hit for more power. I considered Pudge Rodriguez. I never saw Johnny Bench play, but I can't imagine anybody had a better arm than Pudge. On a one-to-eight scale for arms, he was an eight. The drawback is I heard a lot of pitchers complained about Pudge's game-calling in Texas. They might have just been poor pitchers being bitchy.

First base. Jim Thome. Jimmy made the switch pretty well from third to first. Over the years, he became much better at picking the ball out of the dirt. He had good hands and he had big power numbers at an offensive position. First base is a much tougher position defensively than people think. You can stick anybody over there and he can catch throws, but there is a lot more to it. The hardest thing to me when I played first was knowing when to go to the hole and when to cover the bag. A smart first baseman will check where his second baseman is positioned before the pitch and will know what pitch is coming. But your primary responsibility is to get to first base.

Second base. Roberto Alomar. It's hard for me to imagine anybody would be better than Robbie. Now, like anyone who's great at what he does, he had some idiosyncrasies and eccentricities. But 99 percent of the time he was into the game and was a smart, exceptional player. He could just dominate with his glove, with his legs, and with his arm. And he didn't have to play 40 feet out in right field like (Ronnie) Belliard did.

Third base. Buddy Bell. We had some good ones when I managed in Travis Fryman and Matt Williams. Anybody of a certain age will say Brooks Robinson and possibly, anybody in his right mind should say Brooks Robinson anyway. But I didn't see Brooks at his best by the time I was in the big leagues. I'd say Buddy Bell. He had great hands, great athletic ability. Buddy had good feet, and that leads to balance and quickness. He was not a power hitter and third is a power position, but he could hit it out if he got his pitch. The biggest thing was players gravitated to him as a leader. On any good team, you have one or two players who don't even have to say they're leaders, everyone just knows.

Shortstop. Omar Vizquel. If Ozzie Smith is in the Hall of Fame there Omar should be, too. He is the best shortstop I ever saw. He was charismatic and he had the guts of a burglar. Omar was such a risk taker that sometimes he tried to steal in the wrong situation and would get thrown out, and I'd have to bite my tongue. If that was the worst thing, we were all still way ahead with him. He made more barehanded plays than I ever saw anyone else attempt. And when he turned his back to the infield on pop-ups, well, when you thought about it, he was shielding the sun with the bill of his cap, but only Omar would have had the guts to try it.

Left field. Albert Belle. Albert was such an impact player. When he got hot, he could absolutely carry a team—and I mean for two or three weeks. When he was not hot, he was still good. He had personality issues that detracted from the ability of his teammates—and even his coaches and managers—to relate to him. But when he came to the ballpark in Jacobs Field, he was a player who played hard from the first out to the last. That stuff about not running out balls was pretty much over by then.

Center field. Ken Griffey, Jr. I just saw so many great center fielders that this is tough. People say Mickey Mantle. Well, I didn't play against Mickey Mantle or manage when he played, though I've played golf with Mickey Mantle. Torii Hunter is one who comes to mind. But I go with Griffey Jr. He is a five-tool player who, if he hadn't started getting hurt when he went to Cincinnati, would be getting some of that love that goes to A-Rod now, in terms of his place in baseball history. I would consider Kenny Lofton, too, except for the power. People tell me all the time that when he scored from second base in Game 6 against the Mariners, it was the most amazing things they ever saw. One thing I noticed with Griffey Jr., though, is fans gravitated to him at all ballparks. Baseball isn't like the NBA, where LeBron (James) has fans in every city. Baseball is local. But fans everywhere loved Griffey.

Right field. Manny Ramirez. Manny could play left, too, because that's where he plays in Boston. He had a very quick release, which wasn't always appreciated enough. That's how he plays the Green Monster. He just gets it out of there fast. He is the best hitter I ever saw, but then, I didn't see Ted Williams. He has the most natural right-handed swing of any player I ever saw. He is unpretentious to the point of being naïve, but underneath that exterior ("Manny being Manny," as everybody says) is a smart baseball player. Watch in batting practice. He doesn't try to hit the ball 500 feet. He's working on things. As he's gotten older and heavier, he doesn't run the way he used to. But he could go from first to third and probably had average speed when he played here.

Right-handed pitcher. Pedro Martinez. It just kills me to say him. I didn't much care for him. But for consistently competing at a very high level, it would have to be Martinez. He had great stats, compared to the era in which he pitched, but he didn't have to have great stuff to beat you. He never threw more than 85 mph in Game 5 in 1999, but he shoved it right up our ass by changing speeds and by having great location.

Left-handed pitcher. Randy Johnson. It's a tough call between him and Steve Carlton. One of the things that made the "Big Unit" so tough was he had that wild look in his eye. He sure wasn't afraid to pitch inside on you. He and Kenny Lofton had a thing going. Kenny hated hitting against him, but he usually did something in the game to hurt Randy. He threw three-quarter arm, not over the top. When I played, Frank Tanana would come in at you that way, throwing 94-95 mph. If you're a lefty, it is just an amazing, terrifying sensation. He appears to be throwing from behind you. Remember how John Kruk didn't want any part of the Big Unit in the All-Star Game? He had that effect on people, especially as tall as he is.

Relief pitcher. Mariano Rivera. I thought Bruce Sutter, Rollie Fingers and Goose Gossage were all great at the start of the closer era. Some people would say Dennis Eckersley, too. But for consistency, Mariano Rivera has to be the pick. He's done it for years and years. And he's basically a one-pitch pitcher. The funny thing was right-handers hit him better than lefties because the ball ran in on them. Sandy Alomar, Jr. hit that homer off him late in the game in Game 4 in 1995. I had Brook Fordyce in Baltimore and Brook didn't hit anybody, but he was 12-of-15 off Rivera. Mariano threw 94-95 mph, but like all the really great relievers, he had such great command.

Ten is a nice round number and serves as a logical end point for a list. But ten just isn't enough when it comes to highlighting the most illogical and damaging trades of the Cleveland Indians, even if you only cover those made after WWII.

11. Brandon Phillips to Reds for a player to be named later, April 2006.

We're predicting the future here. But Phillips seems on his way to a terrific career. The Indians got the young second baseman, along with Grady Sizemore and Cliff Lee, for Bartolo Colon in June 2002 from the Expos. Despite three-and–a-half years of trying, Phillips never quite fit in with the Tribe. In 2003, he played in 112 games, but batted just .208. What you did see was a terrific fielder and a ton of potential. That wasn't enough for the Indians, who dealt Phillips to Cincinnati at the beginning of the 2006 season. In his first two years with the Reds, Phillips batted .276 and .288 with 47 home runs and 169 RBI. Last season, he joined Barry Larkin and Eric Davis as the only Reds players to hit 30 homers and steal 30 bases in a season. At the age of 27, Phillips promises even better things to come. In February 2008, Phillips signed a four-year contract for $27 million. The "player to be named later" turned into reliever Jeff Stevens, who failed to turn into a Major Leaguer in his first two years with the Tribe.

10. Brian Giles to Pittsburgh for Ricardo Rincon, November 1998.

Looking for a southpaw to shore up their bullpen, Indians General Manager John Hart traded Giles, owner of one of the greatest tans this side of George Hamilton, for Rincon. The Indians had an excess of outfielders and Giles was deemed expendable. Although Hart had good and logical intentions, the deal bombed as badly as anything this side of a George Hamilton movie. Giles batted .298 or higher in each of the following six years, collecting over 100 RBI and scoring over 100 runs in two of those seasons. Now closing in on the 2000 hits and 300 home runs for his career, the two-time All Star continues to show up regularly in the top ten of many offensive categories. Plus, since the Pirates traded him to San Diego, Giles' tan has gotten even better. Rincon was decent in Cleveland for three-and-a-half seasons as a set-up guy, then got shipped to Oakland.

9. Sonny Siebert, Joe Azcue and Vicente Romo to Red Sox for Ken Harrelson, Juan Pizaro and Dick Ellsworth, April 1969. The Summer of

Love was approaching and the Indians weren't receiving any from fans still angry with their poor play and all the bad trades they'd made over the previous decade. So they decided to make another bad trade. Harrelson had hit 35 homers the previous season for Boston and the Indians were looking for a gate attraction, as well as some power to beef up the lineup. Harrelson did hit 27 homers in 1969, but he broke his ankle in spring training the next year. He was done by 1971. Siebert won 79 games over the next five seasons for Boston, while Romo went on to save 40 games for them before he retired. Ellsworth and Pizaro did little for the Indians.

8. Julio Franco to Rangers for Oddibe McDowell, Jerry Browne and

Pete O'Brien, December 1988. It seems like a hundred years ago when the Tribe shipped Franco to the Texas Rangers. Or maybe that's just wishful thinking because it means he would have retired in the 1930s, instead of continuing to haunt us with a fine career that has continued into the 21st century. The Indians moved the talented

Franco, in part because he refused to play second base. He played there for Texas, though, and filled in at DH. And he played well, batting .316 and adding 92 RBI for the Rangers in 1989. Two seasons later, he won the AL batting title, hitting .341. Franco made three All Star Game appearances while playing for the Rangers, who traded him to the White Sox in '94. Franco, almost two decades after the Indians dealt him, at the age of 48, became the oldest player in MLB history to hit a home run in 2007. The "Governor," as Browne was called had a couple of decent campaigns, batting .278 over three seasons here. O'Brien and McDowell did nothing in Cleveland.

7. Pedro Guerrero to Dodgers for Bruce Ellingsen, April 1974. Guerrero lacked a natural fielding position and never really did learn to slide. But could he hit. The Indians must have recognized his batting talent when they signed the Dominican Republic native as a free agent, but then forgotten about it when they dealt him to the Dodgers for Ellingsen, a journeyman pitcher whose career with the Tribe lasted less than three months. Guerrero went on to bat .300 during 15 seasons with Los Angeles and St. Louis. The five-time All-Star also claimed MVP honors in the 1981 World Series. Baseball guru Bill James called Guerrero, "the best hitter God has made in a long time." It would be nice if we could call trading him the worst deal the Indians made in a long time. But there were others, some even worse.

6. Rocky Colavito to Indians for Tommy John, Tommy Agee and John Romano, January 1965. Trying to make up for the mistakes of the past can sometimes be as damaging as repeating them. In an effort to undo some of the harm done by his predecessor Frank "Trader" Lane and reverse "The Curse of Rocky Colavito" before it had a chance to dig in, Indians GM Gabe Paul brought the popular outfield slugger back to Cleveland as part of this three-way deal with the White Sox and Kansas City. The problem: Colavito was nearing the end of his career while John and Agee's careers were just about to take off. John went on to pitch 20 years in the majors, winning 288 games and playing in three World Series and four All-Star games. He even had a famous surgery named after him. Agee starred for the World Champion 1969 Mets, batting .354 and clocking two home runs in the NLCS. Colavito played just over two seasons with the Indians. He reminded Cleveland fans of what we'd been missing out on since trading him to Detroit after the 1959 season by smashing 56 homers in 1965 and 1966. But Rocky II began to peter out by 1967, when Colavito was demoted to a platoon player, then traded in July to the White Sox for Jim King and Marv Staehle. You remember those two guys. Don't you?

5. Chris Chambliss, Dick Tidrow and Cecil Upshaw to Yankees for Fred Beene, Tom Buskey, Steve Kline and Fritz Peterson, April 1974. The Tribe continued the tradition of trading away their best young players into the next generation with this stinker. The first overall pick in the 1970 MLB draft and 1971 AL Rookie of the Year, Chambliss went on to play 13 more seasons for the Yankees and Braves. As for the four pitchers Cleveland got in return, they didn't exactly turn into the Four Horseman of the Apocalypse for opposing batters. Kline had arm problems and retired shortly after arriving here. Beene and Buskey were mediocre, at best, winning a combined 17 games in four seasons. Peterson was slightly better, winning 23 games in two-plus seasons. In the mean time, Chambliss won two World Series with New York,

appeared in the 1976 All-Star game and picked up a Gold Glove at first base in 1978. He put in one of the great playoff series performances of all time in 1976, leading the Yanks past the Royals by hitting .526 with eight RBI and two home runs, the second a walk-off, ninth-inning shot that won Game 5 and the series for the Yankees.

4. Graig Nettles and Jerry Moses to Yankees for Charlie Spikes, Jerry Kenney, John Ellis and Rusty Torres, November 1972.
The original install-ment of "Escape to New York" for young Tribe players starred Graig Nettles, who went on to play 22 seasons in the bigs, 11 with the Yankees. Still considered one of the best-fielding third baseman ever, Nettles also banged out 390 home runs and knocked in 1,314 runs while appearing in six All-Star games and picking up the 1981 ALCS MVP award. With Buddy Bell replacing Nettles at third, this trade still could have worked out for the Indians had Spikes lived up to his advanced billing of being a great power hit-ter. But he didn't. "The Bogalusa Bomber" banged out 45 homers his first two years, but just 17 the next two-and-a-half seasons. Ellis was a decent catcher for a couple of years, while Kenney and Torres were awful.

3. Dennis Eckersley and Fred Kendall to Red Sox for Rick Wise, Mike Paxton, Bo Diaz and Ted Cox, March 1978.
A bold move designed to jump start the Indians into the regular season, GM Phil Seghi saw this deal instead backfire in his face like a 50s jalopy. Although Paxton and Wise were serviceable pitchers and Diaz a decent catcher for a couple of seasons, Cox was awful. He might have had the slowest bat in the majors and eventually found his calling as a softball player. Eckersley, who threw a no-hitter with the Tribe, won 20 games in his first season for the Red Sox. He found even greater success as a closer, winning a Cy Young Award in 1992, saving 390 games and gaining entry into the Hall of Fame on his first ballot in 2004. So maybe the deal didn't backfire on Seghi and the Indians so much as it blew up in their faces.

2. Early Wynn and Al Smith to White Sox for Minnie Minoso and Fred Hatfield, December 1957.
The Lord giveth, the Lord taketh away. But when it comes to Indians' trades, the "taketh" side of the ledger always seems to come out heavier. Wynn won 163 games for the Tribe in the 40s and 50s and helped them to the pennant in 1954. A season after the trade, the flame-throwing righthander won 22 games and the Cy Young Award while leading Chicago to a narrow win in the 1959 AL title race over—you guessed it, the Indians. Minoso enjoyed two fine seasons with the Tribe in left field, then had a career year in 1960, batting .311 with 20 homers and 105 RBI. Unfortunately, by then, the Tribe had dealt him back to the White Sox.

1. Rocky Colavito to the Tigers for Harvey Kuenn, April 17, 1960.
If you are an Indians fan, you probably already know all about this trade and would rather not read another word about it. But for anyone else, here's what happened on that fateful day in 1960: Indians GM Frank Lane ripped the hearts out of the franchise and its fans by trading the beloved "Rock" to Detroit for Harvey Kuenn. Colavito went on to smack 173 home runs over the next five seasons, putting him in the class of Aaron, Mays and Mantle, while Kuenn was gone from Cleveland after just one season. The trade is so infamous, it inspired a book, *The Curse of Rocky Colavito* by former *Plain Dealer* sports writer Terry Pluto, who hypothesized that the Colavito trade doomed the Indians to decades without a pennant.

Note: In many ways, Drew Carey was Cleveland during his hit sitcom's 1995-2004 run on ABC. With his Marine Corps crewcut and thick, black-rimmed glasses, the actor-comedian embodied our civic hopes and shattered sports dreams while displaying the humor that helps Clevelanders not only endure, but enjoy ourselves while doing it. During one episode of The Drew Carey Show, broadcast live, he popped out of the bathroom at his house and, smirking, said: "Sorry. I had to take a Modell." Carey is a passionate soccer fan. But we will have none of that here (or, only a little, and later). Instead, Drew offers his fondest memories on maybe the best thing about living in Cleveland: being a fan. Like the comedian himself, the list is often irreverent and funny as hell:

10. The Indians' Ten-Cent Beer Night in 1974. Some might consider the riot started by drunken fans as a black eye for the city. But one of my friends was there and got hit in the head with a bottle and bragged about it for years.

9. Let it snow, let it snow, let it snow. The real-life version of the 1962 film *The Fortune Cookie* occurred in 1988 when an Erie, PA. TV cameraman was knocked out at a Browns game. I think we were playing the Oilers. Everybody was yelling and throwing snowballs at the paramedics. Shows how the fans get worked up around here.

8. Frank Robinson's home run on Opening Day as the first black manager in baseball. Maybe it was a set-up by the pitcher? (Author's Note: Carey was kidding, of course. The racially progressive history of the Indians has led Carey, often a critic of political correctness as a Libertarian, to reluctantly admit Chief Wahoo should go. "Indians is fine as a nickname. I work a lot of Indian casinos. They have no problem with Indians. They have a problem with Chief Wahoo. I used to wear a Wahoo hat all the time. But if it hurts so many people, they probably ought to get rid of it," he concluded.)

7. Dennis Eckersley's no-hitter at Cleveland Stadium. I was at that game. It's the only no-hitter I ever saw. Had great seats because few people bothered going to Indians games in those days. But I guess it and Len Barker's perfect game were now attended by 100,000 fans. It's like how I found out I had so many friends in high school when the TV show became a hit.

6. Playing one-on-one football in the side yard with my friend Rickey Martin. Rickey was Jim Brown; I was Mercury Morris. I loved Mercury Morris. He later went to prison for distributing cocaine. If I ever see him, I'll say, "I used to be you as a kid."

5. Beating Tommy John. All I remember was sitting in the bleachers at the old stadium with all my friends and relaxing. No Indians games were important then. You could sit in the sun and have a good time. I thought, 'Hey, the Indians finally beat somebody decent.'

4. Steelers beat Browns, 16-13, 2002, overtime. So I'm sitting with Franco Harris in a box seat. I walk in, and this guy with Coke-bottle glasses sitting in a wheelchair takes my ticket. "Heyyyyy, Drew. You're going to lose." And we did. We always do to Pittsburgh. So we miss a field goal at the end of the game. Then in overtime, we block their field goal (it hit Orpehus Roye's helmet), and the Steelers get it back and get to try it again. I'm thinking the refs must have blown the rule, and on the next play they kick the winning field goal. I'm walking out, totally depressed, and the same guy goes, "Heyyyyy, Drew. What happened?" I thought, "Oh, I guess you think those Coke-bottle glasses and wheelchair are going to protect you? Well, you're wrong!" I'm in the parking lot and people recognize me. A guy yells, "Hey, Drew. You're a fag! And your show sucks." Thank you, Pittsburgh.

3. Red Right 88, playoff game vs. the Raiders in 1982. I'm at the Union Plaza Hotel in downtown Las Vegas. The Browns had done a great job covering the point spread all year. I didn't have much money in those days, but what little I did have went on this game. It's 15-13, Oakland, when Sipe throws the interception. You should have heard the screaming in outrage and shock. Everybody thought we were going to kick a field goal. I took losing hard then, and I took it hard all the way through "The Drive" in 87. That was the last time I got so upset I cried after a game.

2. Spurs sweep Cavs, 2007 NBA Finals. I'm at the fourth game. The Cavs got three points in the spread. A guy sitting in my section had a $50,000 bet on the Cavs, plus three. The deficit is four, then five, then four, then five, all the way to the end. The horn is sounding, the Spurs are celebrating and the Cavs' Damon Jones hits a junk 3-pointer to make it a one-point loss. Our whole section started high-fiving.

1. The Browns return, Pittsburgh at Cleveland, 1999. I got to introduce the starting lineups. It was the greatest day of my life. So we lost, 43-0? So what?

Five Reasons to Like Soccer :: Drew Carey

Note: Not only did Carey travel to Germany for the 2006 World Cup, he is a fervent booster of American soccer, making him the informal chief of one of our nation's smallest sports subcultures. He was prominent at the fizzle of David Beckham's 2007 debut with the Los Angeles Galaxy. Though Livingston will question his reasoning for liking the game, no one can question Carey's dedication to soccer.

5. Big deal on 1-to-nil. You don't complain about a 14-7 football game or a 2-0 baseball game, do you?

4. Foreplay. You have to realize how much goes into scoring one goal. It's a long string of 'what if's' and 'almosts.'

3. Hands off. You can't touch the ball with your hands unless you're the goalie. Try that sometime.

2. Freedom of expression. I hate going to NBA games because they're always telling you what to do—when to scream, when to clap. Soccer fans do what they want to when they want to.

1. Just rewards. You actually have to do something in soccer to get a response from the fans. How novel is that?

Bill's Five Dumb Things About Soccer

By admitting a fondness for the World Cup, Livingston can still be friends with Drew Carey, right? Drew not only loves soccer, he loves North American soccer. Which has to be as funny as anything that happened at the Winfred Lauder store.

5. World Cup penalty kicks. Let's play Putt-Putt to decide the Masters.

4. The end of the Golden Goal. After 90 minutes, sudden death is too quick for them?

3. More flops by guys trying to get a penalty kick than by Anderson Varejao or Kevin Costner.

2. 1-to-nil.

1. No wonder that "Goooooooooaaaalllllll!" guy on TV sounds like he just stepped into the Orgasmatron with Brandi Chastain after she stripped down to the sports bra.

Note: Burt Graeff covered the Cleveland Cavaliers from their inception in 1970 through 1981 for the Cleveland Press, then returned for another tour of duty from 1987-'93 with *The Plain Dealer*. He continued covering the team in the years following through off-day stories, long features and sidebars. Graeff co-authored the book *The Cavs From Fitch to Fratello: The Sometimes Miraculous, Often Hilarious Wild Ride of the Cleveland Cavaliers* with Jon Menzer in 1994. With the exception of a longtime Los Angeles Clippers beat man, no one might have seen more bad basketball than Graeff. Absolutely no one wrote more perceptively about the good, the bad, and the ugly of the Cavs than he did.

Final Cuts: World B. Free, Campy Russell, John (Hot Rod) Williams, Phil Hubbard, Wesley Person.

10. Jim Chones. A 6-11, 230-pound center, Chones ran the court as well as any big man to ever play for the Cavaliers. He was good for 15 points and 10 rebounds a game and held down the middle for the Cavaliers Miracle of Richfield team in 1975-76. A case can be made for that team winning an NBA title had Chones not broken his foot during a practice prior to the Eastern Conference finals.

9. Mike Mitchell. He was a virtual scoring machine from the small forward spot, where his corner jumper was as good as any in the game in the late 1970s and early 80s. In four seasons with the Cavaliers, he scored 40 or more points four times.

8. Austin Carr. One of the greatest players in the history of college basketball, Carr saw his pro career hampered by injuries. The top pick of the 1971 draft still managed to play for nine years and average 16.2 points a game. Carr was a key player off the bench on the Miracle of Richfield team in the mid-1970s.

7. Terrell Brandon. Sports Illustrated once hailed Brandon as the best point guard in the NBA. It may have been a stretch, but after playing in the shadow of Mark Price for many years, Brandon emerged in the mid 90s as one of the game's best at his position. He parlayed natural quickness with hours of working on his perimeter game to do it. How hard did he work? As a rookie, he made 1-of-23 three-pointers (a 75-footer at the end of a half). In five subsequent years, he made 260 from downtown.

6. Zydrunas Ilgauskas. He has overcome a plethora of foot surgeries to become one of the league's top centers of today. Ilgauskas does nothing spectacularly—he's nowhere near the passer Daugherty was, for instance—but when included in the offensive scheme, is good for 16 points, 10 rebounds, as well as a couple blocked shots a game.

5. Ron Harper. The most athletic shooting guard in the history of the Cavaliers teamed with Mark Price to form one of the top backcourt combinations in the early 1990's. One of the worst trades in the history of the NBA—Harper and two first-round draft picks—to the Clippers for the rights to Danny Ferry, undermined what was a championship-caliber team. Harper went on to win five NBA title rings.

4. Larry Nance. Arrived in Cleveland in 1987 and with the reputation as being a dunker, which overshadowed his other skills. As a result of assistant coach Dick Helm working hours with him, Nance became a terrific perimeter shooter who dunked when needed and blocked shots as well as any of the game's forwards.

3+2. Mark Price and Brad Daugherty. The best pick-and-roll combination in the history of the franchise must be ranked together. Price, the NBA's most accurate free throw shooter of all-time, was the league's best point guard in the early 1990s. Daugherty, the franchise's lone five-time All-Star, ranks with the game's best passing centers of all-time.

1. LeBron James. No explanation needed. In a few short years, he's done more for the franchise and the city than the next nine combined and more than any athlete in any sport in the city's history.

Livingston was standing on a scorched roadside in Megara, Greece, 60 miles north-west of Athens, in 2004, waiting to interview a Greek-American from Rocky River who was running in the Olympic torch relay, when Greek Secret Service cars pulled up and a bunch of suits started to give him the bum's rush. Bill desperately said of the runner, "He's from Cleveland and so am I. You know, Cleveland Browns?" A pause. More desperate gabble: "Ohio State football?" (said while Livingston pre-tended to throw a pass; yeah, they really follow the Big Ten in provincial Greece). Then inspiration struck. "LeBron James, Cleveland Cavaliers!" Bill cried. "Oh, I love NBA! What is LeBron like!" one of the Greek feds said excitedly. True story. The Cavs should get such honor in their own hometown. Maybe these puzzlers have some-thing to do with diminishing their appeal here.

5. The retro orange jerseys. Who the hell wants to revisit the era when former GM Harry Weltman made the team the Little Knicks? Can the ex-GM trade Charles Oakley for Keith Lee again? Those things bring back painful memories—and a desper-ate need for Visine.

4. The push to retire World B. Free's jersey. Are you kidding me? Selfish gunner and sideshow act puts a few butts in the seats when the team was a national joke and you want to hoist him up there with the greats?

3. Does loud = good? Just wondering. With the swords spouting flame, the T&A girls, the Scream Team, Loudville, the caterwauling P.A. guy, and all the other distrac-tions, it's sometimes hard to remember that, in the words of Joe Tait: "I-i-i-i-i-t's basket-ball time at The Q!"

2. Undervaluing Z. Tell me how many other guys would miss years with repeated foot injuries, come back from all that to be an All-Star, play through family tragedy dur-ing his best playoff season, then still get ripped by halfwits around town? How many guys 7-3 or taller have played in the league? How many that tall could actually play? We're pretty much talking about Yao Ming, Arvydas Sabonis, Rik Smits and Z here, and two of them are retired.

1. Back to Joe Tait. It was nice when he got a warm salute on the night he did his 3,000th game of radio play-by-play. But how come no one noticed that the "Voice of the Cavaliers" has disliked the league for years? It was really pretty obvious, after the Daugherty-Price teams all the way through the early part of the LeBron James Era. In fact, until he finally got a load of what a legit great player looks like, Tait acted like James was just another Lamond Murray. Dan Gilbert probably thought about making a change when he bought the Cavs in 2005. But Gilbert is a Detroit guy who remem-bers the backlash the Tigers suffered when they sacked Ernie Harwell and then had to bring him back. The difference is that Harwell still had a great love for his sport that shone through every word. A great, great announcer at one time, Tait has lost more than a little of that.

Note: A longtime Cleveland Press columnist, Bob August set the regional standard for grace in sports writing and acuity in perception. He omitted Napoleon Lajoie, considered by many as the best second baseman ever and for whom the Cleveland team (Naps) was named for a time, because, "He never played for a team called the Indians." August did not rate these players 1-10. So the numbers next to their names here should not to be considered rankings in relation to one another. Just as indications that, in August's esteemed estimation, they each rate as one of the Tribe's ten best ever.

10. Manny Ramirez. A close call over Albert Belle, Ramirez did not have quite Belle's power, but he had more talent, and his combination of average and power put him among the best right-fielders of his generation. Barely adequate on the bases and in the field, he set single-season franchise records for RBI (165) and slugging percentage (.592). The offensive production of the Belle-Lofton-Ramirez outfield was something we will marvel at in years to come.

9. Jim Thome. I saw my first 500-foot home run when Thome hit one that bounced to the street behind the left-center bleachers. It was measured at 511 feet, and I believed it. He hit more homers than any Indian ever. He struck out the most too. But don't overlook that he also got the most walks, giving him an outstanding on-base percentage

8. Kenny Lofton On a team of sluggers, he was a leadoff hitter the likes of which the championship teams of the past could not match. He had enough power to keep outfielders at a respectful distance, while his bunting ability kept infielders on edge. He all but obliterated the stolen base record. And while he misplayed the occasional fly ball, his speed provided enormous range. It was badly needed when playing between the defensively-challenged Manny Ramirez and Albert Belle.

7. Omar Vizquel. With casual grace, he made the spectacular look routine. He could also take it to the next level with a sleight of hand that toyed with the impossible. One season, he made only three errors. He went from an offensive liability to an outstanding No. 2 hitter.

6. Larry Doby. A major figure in baseball history for integrating the American League in 1947, he struggled in his first season and played in only a few games. Then, working with Tris Speaker, he switched to the outfield in 1948 and earned a place on the team with his speed on defense and power at the plate. He contributed a .301 average as a rookie in the 1948 title run

5. Bob Lemon. A good athlete, he didn't hit well enough to make it as a third baseman or an outfielder. The ball moved so much when he made the long throw from third that first basemen complained. The career change to pitcher was launched without a day spent in the minors. He won 20 games or more seven times and was known as a big game pitcher on the exceptional Indians staffs of the 1950s.

4. Lou Boudreau. With the nation seeking diversion after the rigors of WWII and the Indians setting attendance records in1948, the handsome "boy manager" might have been the most popular Cleveland athlete ever. He delivered the key hits and the key plays in the field, hit .355, and won the playoff game with his bat. Not big, not fast, with a below-average arm, he was sure-handed and quick with great instincts. His success as a college basketball player developed reflexes that let him, as a right-handed batter, hit with special success to right field.

3. Bob Feller. In all the seasons since 1936, no rookie pitcher has arrived in the majors with the stunning impact of the 17-year-old Iowa farm boy. Without a day in the minors, he shocked his elders with a fastball that they found, not being delivered with predictable accuracy, intimidating. He missed almost four seasons because of World War II. When an injury prematurely took the pop off his fastball, he had several more successful seasons, employing guile and a variety of pitches.

2. Earl Averill. Average-sized with a big man's power, Averill had a swing that was so unorthodox it would get a kid today tossed off a Little League team. He remains the Tribe's career leader in RBI, triples, total bases and extra-base hits.

1. Tris Speaker. He and Ty Cobb were superstars before the word was invented. Played a shallow center field and tracked balls down at a full gallop. Hit .388 in the 1988 World Series title year and batted .344 over 22 seasons.

The Ten Most Hated Baseball Players

Half of this list is composed of guys who used to play for the Indians. One of them was excused more often by Tribe fans than an unruly brat at dinner. The others didn't gain infamy here until they left (nos. 10, 7 and 1) or screwed the pooch in the clutch (3, 2). After that, their faces went up on the Post Office wall. Fickle? Who? Us?

10. Manny Ramirez. Cleveland fans' low opinion of Manny remains a puzzle. He never went back on a pledge of eternal loyalty (Jim Thome) or acted like Vlad the Impaler (Albert Belle). The louder Cleveland fans booed Ramirez, the better he hit. About the worst thing you could say about Manny is that he tried to steal first base while he was here. From second. But, hey, he thought it was a foul tip. It happens in Manny World.

9. A.J. Pierzynski. The White Sox biggest jerk outside manager Ozzie Guillen. Stepped on the back of Aaron Boone, who had dived for a ground ball, as he rounded third. His just desserts came when Boone Fosse'd him on a play at the plate. Seems to have found the appropriate place to establish his sports legacy: pro wrestling.

8. Pudge Rodriguez. Slid well out of the baseline to take out Omar Vizquel on a double play and send him to the DL with knee damage. Lost a remarkable amount of weight and power when steroid testing began, too.

7. Jim Thome. Fans don't care that you said you were going to make your home here; it only only matters where you play. You said you wanted to play out your career in Cleveland. Then you left in your prime for a lucrative free-agent deal in the National League, where you couldn't DH. "We hear ya," to paraphrase what you used to say. Just another me-first greedball.

6. Pedro Martinez. Possibly the primo weenie of his day. Threw a 95-mph fastball at Einar Diaz's head, then ran like a schoolgirl when both dugouts emptied, cowering behind hulking coach Jim Rice. Later said: "We fight as a team." Who were you fighting, oh, manos de flan (hands of pudding)? Sister Mary Assumpta?

5. Ozzie Guillen. We can suggest a whole bunch of things that could impair the respiration of the choke-signing Chicago manager. A stray wad of tobacco? Sunflower seeds gone wild? But nothing quite says it like "Eat (spit) and die!"

4. David Wells. Unlike Terry Forster, you weren't just a fat tub of goo. You were a fat tub of goo with a soul cloned from the high moral fiber of Arthur B. Modell. How did the taunting fans know about the death of your mother before the second game of the 1998 ALCS, Davey? Wasn't that pretty obscure information? We think you made the whole thing up.

3. John Rocker. It's not just that he was a dumb redneck who juiced like an orange grove, according to the Mitchell Report. (But you probably didn't require a Congressional panel to let you in on that secret once Rocker shriveled up and dipped further South than Scarlett and Rhett on the mound.) It was that this muscle-bound lunkhead with the racist streak big as the 7 Train in New York was a cheap piece of plaster who fell apart under the slightest pressure.

2. Jose Mesa. Another guy hated after he changed laundry, but beloved, despite rape charges, while he was here. It's forgotten that Mesa not only blew chunks on himself in the seventh game of the 1997 World Series, but that he gave up the season-ending home run to the Orioles' Roberto Alomar in the division series the year before. Maybe Guillen can choke Mesa, not that Jose needs any help.

1. Albert Belle. He embarrassed us when he played for the Indians, making you feel like someone rooting for Jack the Ripper. If he'd played hockey, he'd have been Jason. He cussed out Hannah Storm, tried to bean photographers, loafed on the field, beat up the clubhouse fixtures, cheated with a corked bat and generally acted like he had the reddest ass ever seen on a black man. But that was all okay. It was only after he left and ripped the city and its fans ("village idiots" he called us) that Clevelanders turned on him. He was debased, driven, and isolated by his demons all along. But it took separation and betrayal for Clevelanders to finally see Belle for who he always was and to turn cheers to boos, love to hate.

Note: The radio play-by-play man for the Browns since the team's return in 1999, Donovan has been forced to describe some difficult games for area fans. But he's also seen some good ones and feels they will soon become a regular part of Cleveland Browns seasons again.

10. Browns 33, Baltimore 30 (OT) at Baltimore, 2007. It was the first time I really thought they looked like a legitimate team. The offense was balanced. Josh Cribbs didn't have a huge game in return yardage. There had been wins before when the offense put up big numbers, like 51-45 over Cincinnati, and other wins had come when the special teams carried the Browns. But they really looked like a team in this game. I thought, 'Wow. I'm starting to think this is not a fluke. This is legit.'

9. Steelers 36, Browns 33 at Pittsburgh, 2002 wild-card playoff game. Carl Smith was the quarterbacks' coach and as nice a guy as you could find. Tim Couch had broken his leg in the final regular season game and even though Kelly Holcomb had played in that game, no one knew what to expect from him. I said to Smith, "So, what do you think? Can this guy play?" And he said: "I'm going to tell you, he's going to have a big day." Holcomb had a great game, and then (Dennis) Northcutt dropped the ball for the first down that would have won it. All the Browns had to do was take three knees to run out the clock. The Steelers were out of timeouts. But it was still a stunning performance by Holcomb and the offense for most of the day. It was just a phenomenal game to call.

8. Browns 24, Ravens 14 in Cleveland, 2001. This was Butch Davis' first season and it was so thrilling to the fans to finally beat Baltimore, to beat (Art) Modell, to beat the team that left them. For one day, it felt like the (Municipal) Stadium in the old days. They really beat Baltimore up that day.

7. Browns 21, Jacksonville 20 at Jacksonville, 2002. It never felt like they were going to win this game. Besides, how many guys hit two Hail Mary passes in a career? The fact that Couch threw it and the guy with the worst hands on the team, Quincy Morgan, caught it, made it even more incredible. It hit every part of Morgan's body before he caught it. And then there was the excruciating wait for the review before it was called a touchdown.

6. The Bottle Game: Jacksonville 15, Browns 10 in Cleveland, 2001. It was one of those times when you go from being a play-by-play man to being a newsman. There was such an emotional reaction after the completion was overruled (on the aforementioned Morgan's drop of a would-be first down pass on fourth down). The weirdest part was after we turned the broadcast over to (sideline reporter) Casey Coleman in the locker room and he had Butch Davis on. Butch was saying all the things Al Lerner and Carmen Policy didn't, that you can't throw things, someone could get hurt, and, live, on-air, here comes the referee to say: "Coach, you have to take your team back on the field. We've called New York (NFL headquarters) and they say we have to play this to completion."

5. Browns 23, Steelers 20 in Cleveland, 2001. The Browns finally won one at home. They had lost every home game the first year. Courtney Brown unleashed a pass rush out of nowhere and sacked Kent Graham and time ran out before the Steelers could kick the field goal to tie it. We found out the next day that the officials had screwed up and they should have stopped the clock to re-spot the ball after a sack.

4. Browns 16, Steelers 15 at Pittsburgh, 1999. It was just stunning to go over to Pittsburgh and beat them. They had won the opener in Cleveland, 43-0, and took great delight in beating the Browns so badly. I remember Chris Palmer didn't stop the clock, and he would have been lynched if Phil Dawson didn't make the field goal on the last play. As it was, they had to run Dawson and the field goal team onto the field to get it off in time.

3. Browns 21, Saints 16 at New Orleans, 1999. It was the first win, Halloween on Bourbon Street. Doesn't get much wilder than that. Ricky Williams fumbled all day, every time it looked like New Orleans might take a lead that would put the game away. I can close my eyes and see Couch rolling out to the right, and the play unfolding on the replay board at the end of the field at the same time. Orlando Brown got away with holding, because he just took a guy down who was chasing Couch. He threw it, and KJ (Kevin Johnson) was down there under it, and then it got tipped to him. I saw Al Lerner after the game. He had a game ball tucked under his arm and he was smiling so broadly because he finally felt like a member of the (ownership) club. I thought, 'So that's what a $535 million football looks like.'

2. Browns 24, Falcons 16 in Cleveland, 2002. William Green busted loose (for a 64-yard touchdown run) in the second half. It showed how good he could be. Remember, he had just begun to start at midseason at Cincinnati and he threw up several times during that game, possibly from the colitis he suffered from. Four or five things had to happen for the Browns to make the playoffs, but the day before our game, Kansas City had lost to Oakland out there in a monsoon, and I started to think maybe the pieces were falling into place. It was a crazy game. Couch broke his leg. The Falcons drove to the 1-yard line and Carmen Policy kept ordering the final score of the New Orleans game shown. New Orleans had to lose for Atlanta to be in regardless of the result. He wanted to make sure the Falcons knew New Orleans had lost. Then, Michael Vick had run all over the stadium getting them down there, and what do they do but run Warrick Dunn four straight times and he got stuffed. We still needed the New York Jets to win to knock the Patriots out. I was driving home, listening to it on WABC out of New York, when the Jets won. It was an amazing day.

1. Browns 20, Cowboys 17 (OT) at Canton, 1999. It was the Hall of Fame Game, in Fawcett Stadium. The Browns had returned. They were finally back. In preparing for that game, I realized I knew more about the Cowboys than the new Browns. It was my first game, and you always remember that. I know Chris Palmer coached that game like it was a playoff game. At the same time, Troy Aikman was in for five plays for Dallas. I don't think Tim Couch ever looked better. He was making all the throws to KJ. He had good footwork. The fans were so ready to see the Browns play. The future just looked so promising. Little did we know how long it would take to feel that good again.

The ground rules: No physical mistakes, so nothing about "The Fumble." No jokes about injuries, including even Kellen Winslow, Jr.'s motorcycle accident. Just these kind of things:

10. Leroy "He Snored" Hoard. The former Michigan running back was dubbed "He Scored" Hoard by the late Nev Chandler, the Voice of the Browns, when he scored nine touchdowns in the playoff season of 1994. Before that, however, Hoard was known mainly for being ripped by his college coach Bo Schembechler the day the Browns drafted him and for falling asleep during team meetings. "Not all the time," He Snored admitted, "just once or twice."

9. William Green ejected before kickoff for fighting with Joey Porter on Nov. 14, 2004. With the Browns hurting for depth at running back, Green found a way to thin their ranks further before opening kickoff. Green and Steelers linebacker Porter exchanged words during warm-ups. Then Green tried to "go Zizou" on him, head-butting Porter, albeit with less effect than the head-butt of France's Zinedine "Zizou" Zidane in the 2006 World Cup final. Porter and Green then threw wild punches, although Porter at least landed an accurate enough one to bust Green's lip. Both were ejected, or maybe "prejected" because the game hadn't started yet. The Steelers later accused Browns fullback Terrelle Smith of inciting the fight. But everyone was edgy because, in the days leading up to the game, Gerard Warren had shot off his six-gun mouth, saying . . . .

8. "Kill the head and the body will die." It didn't take much of a stretch to take Warren's words of wisdom as a threat to hurt the Steelers rookie quarterback Ben Roethlisberger. In a city that had seen running back Merrill Hoge battle post-concussion syndrome after he was forced to retire, it was considered a thuggish and stupid thing to say. Actually, people in Cleveland looked at it the same way. Especially after the Steelers won the game, 24-10.

7. Five net yards, four penalties, one punt. The Browns threatened to make ineptitude an art form with their first punt of the 2007 season. Emergency punter Paul Ernster, substituting for injured Dave Zastudil, dropped Ryan Pontbriand's perfect snap near his own goal-line and got off a 15-yard wobbler in the ensuing scrum. But wait! The net gain was only five yards. Why? Well, let the official take over: "We have four fouls on the offense. Illegal formation, offense, No. 56 (Antwan Peek). That penalty is declined. Holding, No. 90 (David McMillan), that penalty is declined. Holding, No. 35 (Jerome Harrison), that penalty will be enforced. Ten yards from the end of the kick. We had an ineligible downfield on the kick, (Who the hell knows?) that penalty is declined." Not surprisingly, the Steelers scored swiftly and were off to a 34-7 rout.

6. Why Bill Belichick (let's give him some credit) would never have drafted William Green. "Here's William with one read to make on blitz pickup. Oh, he made the wrong one," an assistant coach told Bill Livingston, while showing him some game film. When further footage revealed Green making the same mistake twice more, Livingston asked: "Is he just dumb?" Said the coach: "Yes. Very."

5. Jeff Garcia feuds with his top receiver. During Kellen Winslow Jr.'s long holdout before his rookie season, Garcia berated Winslow in the local media. Winslow threatened to kick Garcia's bald head into a place behind the "full moon," where, if well-oiled, it just might fit. After that, Garcia seldom seemed to find Winslow, even when he was wide open.

4. Oh, swell. Jeff Garcia insults his offensive line. Late to a team meeting during exhibition season in 2004, Garcia sat down and was rebuked by left tackle Ross Verba, who loudly cleared his throat and frowned. "When you've been to three Pro Bowls like I have, you can tell me what to do," responded Garcia, thus alienating the man who was his bodyguard on his blind side.

3. Take that, you inanimate object, you! What is it about the Steelers? What is it about Earnest Byner? Before a second-round playoff game against the Steelers in 1994 (Belichick's only playoff season here), Byner made a big show of stomping on a gold Steelers "Terrible Towel" at midfield. The Steelers then wiped the field with Byner and the Browns in a 29-9 win. Modell threw in the towel on Cleveland the next season.

2. Bang! Zoom! To the moon! More antics with objects that can't fight back cost the Browns again. In making (Bang!) a sack of Kansas City's Trent Green after he'd gotten rid of the ball, then (Zoom!) flinging his helmet (To the moon!) in celebration, the Browns' Dwayne Rudd became the Tiny Tim of lame-ass players. The penalty for the lid launch, added to the gain on the final play after Green got rid of the ball, set up a field goal after time had run out, allowing Kansas City to win the 2002 season opener 40-39.

1. A Moment of Bliss. In 2003, Browns offensive tackle Barry Stokes admitted after a game in New Orleans that he went piddle in the middle of a play. Stokes let loose when nature's urge struck him just before a snap. "I had to take a (bliss) and it was going to hamper me from blocking my man, so I just let 'er rip," said Stokes. "I (blissed) my pants. No big deal." Stokes claimed a mid-game tinkle is hardly a new wrinkle. "It's just like a car with a full tank of gas, it runs better when it's close to empty," he said. This practice has been a soggy little secret for years among athletes. Hockey goal-tenders are also frequent offenders. But Stokes commited his offense in the Louisiana Superdome, on a rug, leading to a "puddle in the huddle" on the next play.

Some players inspire biographies. Some warrant shrines. Some call for thoughtful retrospectives on all they contributed to their teams and communities. The only way to do justice to the bizarre and lurid career of Albert Belle is to offer up his very own edition of *The National Enquirer.*

19. BATTIN' ROUGE: TIGER STAR TURNS RED WITH RAGE OVER FAN ABUSE.

Always overshadowed by his tantrums—by what he tore down, rather than the record he built up—Belle was suspended in college from the LSU team during the 1987 Southeastern Conference baseball tournament after chasing a fan through the stands at Mississippi State. The fan, according to Belle, had been shouting racial epithets at him. This incident caused Belle to drop to the second round of the draft after teams were scared off by his temper. Atlanta told its scouts they would be fired if they drafted Belle.

18. CAPE CLOD: TANTRUM THROWER THROWN OUT OF LEAGUE

He signed with the Tribe and reported to the Cape Cod League, a noted rookie proving ground. He was sent home after arguing with umpires, fans, other player's and the Gorton's fisherman of Gloucester. (Just kidding about the fish guy.)

17. ILLEGAL ALIENATOR DEPORTED NORTH OF THE BORDER.

In winter ball, Belle was expelled from the Mexican League and asked to leave the country after throwing a catcher's mask out of the ballpark. ("Catcher's mask? We don't need no stinking catcher's mask!") It was believed to be the first time anyone had been excused from Mexico for excessive violence since The Magnificent Seven.

16. DEMOTION DEMOLITION: SINK SUNK BY PEEVED PLAYER'S OUTBURST.

In 1990, he was demoted to The Class AAA farm team in Colorado Springs. He destroyed a sink in the clubhouse there—to show it who was boss.

15. GORILLA FARTS BLOW BOOZING BELLE INTO REHAB.

After comforting himself about his demotion to the minors by downing a few too many glasses filled with a drink called a "Gorilla Fart" (which is composed of equal parts 101-proof Wild Turkey bourbon and 151-proof rum). Belle went into a 12-step program designed to treat alcoholism. He emerged cold sober, but still needed anti-berserk meds.

14. BERSERK OUTFIELDER GIVES HECKLER MORE THAN HE CAN STOMACH.

In 1991, Jeff Pillar, a heckler in the left field stands, kept shouting: "Hey, Joey. Keg party at my house after the game." Belle, who since rehab had insisted on being called "Albert" and not his old nickname "Joey," turned, threw and hit the fan more crisply in the gut with a baseball than he usually hit the cutoff man. A seven-game suspension followed.

13. FOR WHOM THE BELLE STROLLS.

Later in the 1991 season, Belle was sent back to Colorado Springs for dogging it on a ground ball he had hit to third.

12. PITCHER PUMMELLED AFTER TRYING TO KNOCK SENSE INTO BATTY BATSMAN. In 1992, he drew a three-game suspension for charging the mound when Kansas City's Neal Heaton threw two pitches close to his head.

11. BATGATE: BOTCHED BURGLARY UNCORKS SCANDAL, LEAGUE FURY. With a four-year, $13.3 million contract in his pocket in 1993 because of his slugging exploits, Belle began to really flex his temperament muscles. "He is a folk hero," gushed spinmaster GM John Hart. "We brought him up. The fans have seen him mature as a human being." Belle had indeed matured—like the aged cork in a fine bottle of champagne that is about to fly across a room on a bubbly torrent when the pressure is released. His bat was confiscated by umpires at Comiskey Park in 1994 to be checked for illegal corking. Belle's teammate Jason Grimsley crawled through the ducts in the ceiling, stole the bat, and replaced it with a another player's bat. Omar Vizquel later said in his autobiography that each and everyone of Belle's bats had enough cork inside to bottle the output of the vineyards of France in a good year. Belle's actual bat was then returned, sawed open, and found to be corked. After serving six games (reduced from 10 on appeal) of yet another suspension, Belle returned to the lineup to a five-minute standing ovation from Indians fans.

10. BELLE UNLEASHES TSUNAMI ON STORM. After a glorious 1995 season, in which he hit 50 homers with 50 doubles in a work-stoppage-shortened 144-game season, Belle launched a profanity-laced tirade at NBC's Hannah Storm in the Tribe dugout before a World Series game. At a press conference, The Buffalo News' Jerry Sullivan asked Hart: "Will he have to apologize to everyone he's dropped the F-bomb on, or just to rights-holders?"

9. DEATH RACE 1995: TORMENTED TRIBESMAN TERRORIZES TRICK-OR-TREATING TEENS. That 1995 was a busy year for Albert. After the season, he chased some teenaged trick-or-treaters who were egging his house on Halloween in his SUV, braking just short of turning them into road pizza.

8. FIELD OF NIGHTMARES. So was 96 when Belle was fined for elbowing Milwaukee infielder Fernando Vina and knocking him down after Vina tried to tag him in the base paths.

7. PHOTO FURY: BELLE SNAPS AT PICTURE SNAPPER. Earlier in the same season, he fired a baseball at Sports Illustrated photographer Tony Tomsic, who was taking pictures from the photographer's area beside the dugout as Belle played long toss with Manny Ramirez. Belle said he was fooling around, pretending to be a pitcher when, by golly, one got away from him. It was, in the words of the immortal Harry Doyle of Major League, "jusssssssssst a bit outside." After Belle delivered his remarkable alibi to former Cleveland radio talk show host Bill Needle on the air. The compliant Needle then asked him: "Do you know how much you are loved?"

6. PING KONG: PISSED PADDLER GOES APE. The Indians had a Ping Pong table in their clubhouse during the players' heyday in the mid-90s. It was a symbol of the glory days—a Xanadu in which to play in Dick Jacob's new palace, a frat boy ambience in the card games and Ping Pong battles that daily raged, everything but the royal wipers Eddie Murphy enjoyed in Coming to America. In '96, Belle gave a table tennis player, a chef from Maryland, who was annoying him a backhand swat to the face with his paddle in a Flats emporium called Julianne's. Wham! With the right hand! .

5. BONKERS BELLE PADS STATS, SUBTRACTS THERMOSTATS. Belle liked the clubhouse cold and frozen enough to gratify a penguin. He would set the thermostat at close to 60 degrees. When a teammate turned it up one day, Belle took his bat and smashed the thing apart, which showed it who was boss, too.

4. SLUGGER SURPASSES KEITH MOON'S ALL-TIME MARK FOR PROPERTY DAMAGE ON TOUR. The Indians routinely billed him $10,000 each season for damage done to the locker room on the road.

3. REPORTER UNEARTHS PRODIGAL SON OF MANSON FAMILY IN CLEVELAND. *The Plain Dealer's* Burt Graeff wandered with Livingston into the Indians' clubhouse during batting practice one day to find Belle alone. After noting the day's lineup, the reporters started walking out as Belle put a music tape in the stereo player that was always blaring and making interviewing players nearly impossible. When salsa music burst from the tape, which obviously was a Latin teammate's and not his own, Belle frowned, ejected it, put his own lovely hip-hop music on, then turned and whipped the salsa tape off the wall, kablooy-ing it a few feet above the reporters' heads.

2. THE BIRD DIDN'T JUST PITCH FOR DETROIT. Jeered by Cleveland fans chanting obscene slogans and throwing Monopoly money at him from the Homer Porch in his first return to Jacobs Field in an enemy uniform, Belle stuck his hand behind his back and made an obscene gesture to the fans, one popularly named for the nickname of Mark Fidrych.

1. BELLE'S SHAME TURNS OFF FAME VOTERS. In 2006, six years after retiring from baseball, Belle was sentenced to 90 days in prison for stalking a woman in Arizona. That year, his first of Hall of Fame eligibility, he received only 7.7 percent of the writers' votes for election to Cooperstown. He was dropped from the ballot the next season when he garnered only 19 votes in all.

A Half–Dozen Pieces of Enduring Wisdom from Satchel Paige

Leroy "Satchel" Paige established himself as one of the greatest pitchers in baseball history during his years in the Negro Leagues. The Indians signed him on what was allegedly his 42nd birthday during the heat of the 1948 pennant race. The Sporting News, the "Bible of the Game," ripped Tribe owner Bill Veeck and called the move a promotional stunt. But Paige, relying on the guile that let him remain effective long after his fastball had slowed, went on to a 6-1 record with a 2.48 ERA, two shutouts, 43 strikeouts, 22 walks and 61 base hits allowed in 72⅔ innings. Without him, the Tribe probably would not have gotten to the 1948 World Series, the last Cleveland won. In his famous "Six Rules to Keep You Young," the ageless Indians pitcher laid out what were then considered quaint, folksy maxims for living. But when re-considered in the light of recent findings, Paige and his wisdom proved to be highly-sophisticated and far ahead of their time.

6. "Avoid fried meats, which angry up the blood." An astute cardiovascular observation, decades before anyone outside the medical profession knew what "cardiovascular" or "trans fats" meant, much less how to prevent cardiovascular trouble. The Cavaliers have gone so far as to retain a chef at their practice complex so players can eat healthy foods, such as broiled fish, and avoid fried stuff.

5. "If your stomach disputes you, lie down and pacify it with cool thoughts." Plenty of rest has always been an obvious advantage for players over the long haul of a Major League Baseball season. But practicing meditation and biofeedback to mitigate health problems and manage pain came along only in the last two decades—for just about everybody but Satchel.

4. "Keep the juices flowing by jangling around loosely as you move." Usually interpreted as an endorsement of stretching and warming up. Clearly, this was a discipline ahead of its time.

3. "Go very light on the social vices. The social ramble ain't restful." If you ask a player, "What's your sign?" and he says: "Neon," that player, folks, is on the countdown clock to the minors.

2. "Avoid running at all costs." Almost all pitchers run these days, although Steve Carlton famously did not. He did okay, didn't he? Besides, you try running at 42 or whatever Methuselahan age Paige was as an MLB rookie.

1. "Don't look back. Something might be gaining on you." Be happy. Let the rooks chasing your legacy worry. The baseball version of a Zen koan.

Note: For 20 years, Maxse has covered the world's best practitioners of the Sweet Science, from Mike Tyson through Kelly Pavlik, for *The Plain Dealer*. Here, he sticks to the best the city of Cleveland has sent into the boxing ring.

10. Jackie Keough (25-15-2, 1 KO). He had a whirlwind 1947, when he won both the national Golden Gloves and AAU tournaments at 147 pounds, on his way to fighting in over 200 amateur bouts, He became a light-hitting middleweight pro who lost a title fight to champion Randy Turpin, then a long-time referee on the amateur and professional scene after he retired.

9. Jackie Wilson (62-20-6, 37 KOs). Won the 1936 Olympic bantamweight silver medal. As a pro welterweight, he defeated top fighters Cocoa Kid, Fritzie Zivic and Tommy Bell, and lost to the lengendary Sugar Ray Robinson and Jake LaMotta.

8. Carmen Barth (40-14-3, 12 KOs). He won the 1932 Olympic middleweight gold medal. As a pro, he fought Freddie Steele for the NABF middleweight title, but was stopped in the seventh round at Public Hall in February 1938.

7. Nate Brooks (10-9, 3 KOs). Brooks enjoyed a stellar amateur career, winning a gold medal in the flyweight division at the 1952 Olympics after claiming national Golden Gloves championships the previous two years. As a pro, he won the North American bantamweight title in 1954, but lost it later the same year.

6. Paul Pirrone (88-34-3, 57 KOs). This middleweight with a heavyweight punch fought over one hundred bouts from 1932 to 1939. He lost to former champs Young Corbett and Gorilla Jones, but never got a title shot.

5. Johnny Risko (78-53-7, 21 KOs). This game heavyweight fought anytime, anywhere from 1927 to 1940. Along the way, he defeated Tommy Loughran, King Levinsky, Jack Sharkey and Max Baer, after losing early in his career to Max Schmeling and Mickey Walker.

4. Lloyd Marshall (71-25-4, 36 KOs). This middleweight and light heavyweight contender from 1939 to 1951 defeated champions Joey Maxim, Ezzard Charles, Jake LaMotta and Freddie Mills, but lost to Archie Moore.

3. Joey Maxim (82-29-4, 21 KOs). The Collinwood Kid won the light heavyweight title when he beat Freddie Mills in London in January of 1950. A consummate boxer, Maxim fought all the contenders of his day. He gained his greatest victory when he became the only fighter to stop Sugar Ray Robinson, who could not come out for the 14th round because of the heat at Yankee Stadium in June 1952.

2. Johnny Kilbane (114-12-12, 25 KOs). The Irishman held the featherweight title for a record 11 years after winning a 20-round decision against Abe Attell in February of 1912. More of a boxer than a puncher, he defended his title only seven times before finally losing the belt to European champion Eugene Criqui in 1923.

1. Jimmy Bivins (86-25-1, 31 KOs). Called the "Duration Heavyweight Champion" during World War II, he fought all the contenders and defeated eventual eight world champions, but never got a title shot of his own. A controversial loss to Joe Louis in 1951 deprived him of a final chance to go for a title.

Note: Don King has come a long way since he ran a 1960s Cleveland bookmaking operation that ended with him serving almost four years in prison for killing a former employee. Within just a few years of leaving jail, King established himself as the dominant figure on the national and international sports scene by promoting a string of high-profile heavyweight fights. "Only in America!" as King, a man so patriotic his hair stands for the national anthem, will say every minute or two. And it all began here for the native Clevelander. Said King: "The first boxing event I ever promoted was an exhibition featuring Muhammad Ali at Cleveland Arena in my hometown on Monday, August 28, 1972. It was a benefit for the minority Forest City Hospital, which was in dire financial straits. It grossed $80,000—at the time the highest gross ever for a boxing exhibition in Ohio. It still lives in history as the second-largest gross ever for a boxing exhibition. No list of my favorite fights would be complete without it. It was the Alpha and the Omega for me, or, maybe the famous quote from Sir Winston Churchill captures that moment best: 'Now, this is not the end. It is not even the beginning of the end. But it is, perhaps, the end of the beginning.'"

10. Cory Spinks vs. Zab Judah, second bout, Savvis Center in St. Louis, February 5, 2005. It was the first major fight in St. Louis in 40 years, and it tore all the barriers down between rich and poor, back and white, St. Louis (Mo.) and East St. Louis (Ill.) The bout drew 22,370 fans, the second-largest crowd ever for an indoor fight in the city. Judah's TKO in the ninth round gave him the undisputed welterweight title.

9. Felix "Tito" Trinidad, Jr. vs. "Ferocious" Fernando Vargas, Mandalay Bay, Las Vegas, December 2, 2000. Vargas was 21-0 and had never been down in an amateur or pro fight. Tito knocked him down twice in the first round, was himself knocked down in the fourth, then knocked Vargas down three more times in the 12th and last round. Just an epic bout.

8. Evander Holyfield vs. Lennox Lewis, first bout, Madison Square Garden, New York, March 13, 1999. This fight was an emotional time bomb. It was the fastest sellout in the history of Madison Square Garden and the largest gate at that time. I thought Holyfield won it. But it was ruled a draw, and Lewis' people charged I fixed the judges.

7. Evander Holyfield vs. Mike Tyson, first bout, MGM Grand, Las Vegas, November 9, 1996. Every fighter has confidence and feels he's the greatest and that he will get to go places where no one else will go. Only a few go on to become champions. But even fewer capture the public's imagination and become stars. In the context of the time, no one could match Mike Tyson in terms of public appeal. But Holyfield wanted to fight him and Mike wanted to fight Holyfield, although Tyson could have made millions fighting a bunch of nobodies. Tyson had lost to Buster Douglas a few years earlier, but I will tell you Buster Douglas benefited from a long count such as had not been seen since Dempsey-Tunney. That referee could have counted to 19 before Douglas got up. Tyson recovered from the loss and reestablished himself as the most feared and famous fighter in the world. But when Mike lost to Holyfield (TKO in the 11th) in this fight, he was no longer the greatest beyond all others. Holyfield showed opponents how to beat him.

6. Julio Cesar Chavez vs. Greg Haugen, Estadio Azteca, Mexico City, February 20, 1993. This set an all-time record for the greatest attendance at a fight (136,274), topping the Dempsey-Tunney gate from Philadelphia in the 1920s. (I always had a head for numbers, you see.) Before the fight, Haugen called Chavez a "taxi driver" and said he hadn't beaten anybody but Tijuana taxi drivers that his mother could beat. After Chavez stopped him in the fifth round, Chavez asked him if he wanted to take a taxi home. Haugen said: "They must have been tough taxi drivers."

5. Larry Holmes vs. Gerry Cooney, Caesars Palace, Las Vegas, June 11, 1982. Though much of the pre-fight hype centered on the racial differences between the black American Holmes and Cooney, a white from South Africa where apartheid was still enforced, this turned out to be a great day for brotherhood and race relations. Cooney fought a good fight, landing a tremendous body shot in the fourth round. But he tired and his corner stopped it in the 13th round. Actually, Holmes and Cooney ended up becoming friends and Larry has contributed heavily to Gerry's organization (F.I.S.T.), which provides medical insurance and care for fighters after they retire.

4. Roberto Duran vs. Sugar Ray Leonard, first bout, Olympic Stadium, Montreal, Canada, June 20, 1980. This was the first time a fighter (Leonard) was guaranteed $10 million for a single bout. Nobody thought Leonard could be beaten because he had won the gold medal in the Olympics and was so fast that he threw punches in bunches. But in Roberto "Hands of Stone" Duran, Sugar Ray ran into a person with the same kind of pride. Duran won it for his native Panama and all of Latin America.

3. Larry Holmes vs. Ken Norton, Caesars Palace, Las Vegas, June 9, 1978. A classic fight, one of the great heavyweight fights ever. The 15th round alone made it one for the ages. Larry has a tremendously underestimated legacy. The fight was a split decision, but Larry won it because of his great jab. He had a piston-like jab, and he used it like a piledriver. Only the great Brown Bomber, Joe Louis, had a better one.

2. Muhammad Ali vs. Joe Frazier, third bout ("The Thrilla' in Manila"), Quezon City, Philippines, October 1, 1975. The greatest heavyweight fight ever, the "Thrilla" was a pier 6, bare-knuckle brawl. Ali said afterward it was the closest to death he ever came. Frazier was bloody, beaten, but unbowed. Eddie Futch in his corner stopped it after the 14th round. Frazier fought with superb skill and heart, with that left hook always dangerous, Frazier was always coming on, no matter how many times Ali hit him. I thought the setting in Manila tied in with all the brutal World War II battles like Corregidor, Bataan, Iwo Jima and Okinanwa that either took place in the Philippines or a short flight away.

1. Muhammad Ali vs. George Foreman ("The Rumble in the Jungle"), Kinshasa, Zaire, October 30, 1974. Ali had been away four years when he came back to the ring and the reigning champ Foreman had little reason to take the fight. If he won, he beat an old man. If he lost, he'd be on the wrong end of one of the greatest upsets ever. I sold Foreman on a campaign to shut Ali up, to rid the world of Ali's mouth. Some of Ali's people were afraid before it began that he would literally fight to the death. Absolutely nobody—Angelo Dundee, none of them—believed it when Ali started doing the Rope-a-Dope, letting Foreman pound on his arms and shoulders, letting him punch himself out. I remember Jim Brown was doing commentary with David Frost and Brown kept saying, "Ali will never last." It became almost a spiritual thing, the way he survived all those blows in such a bad situation on the ropes. And then he struck like lightning and knocked Foreman out in the eighth round. I still see Foreman going down. He didn't just fall. He circled and then went down. As soon as the fight was over, a thunderstorm hit like you have never seen. It filled the stadium with water. In the press room underneath the stadium, typewriters were floating. It was like God had shown His power and was satisfied.

Because we spend six months of the year wrapped in parkas and galoshes, Clevelanders sometimes lose sight of the fact that our city boasts some stone-cold beautiful women. As an opening argument, we offer the members of the Cavs' dance team? As further evidence, I submit the many well-endowed young ladies at The Q wearing tight T-shirts requesting a show of "Boobie" following the emergence of Cavs' guard Daniel "Boobie" Gibson in the 2007 NBA playoffs. We rest our case with this list of gorgeous local ladies who have made the boob tube and silver screen showcases for Cleveland's own Dreamgirls.

7. Sean Young, Cleveland Heights. This tall, slender brunette played the female lead in the cult classic *Blade Runner* and opposite Kevin Costner in *No Way Out*. Other notable credits include *Wall Street*, *Stripes* and *Dune*. Sean dropped off the Hollywood A-list when actor James Woods filed a lawsuit against her for allegedly harassing him after their relationship soured during the filming of *The Boost* in 1988. Young went on TV talk shows to denounce Woods and tell her side of the story. She later traveled the talk-show circuit dressed in a Catwoman suit to campaign unsuccessfully for that role in Batman Returns. Some might question her mental stability at times. But no one who has laid eyes on her can question Sean Young's physical beauty.

6. Patricia Heaton, Bay High. Before she played Debra on TV's *Everybody Loves Raymond*, Heaton won roles in such movies as *Beethoven* and *Space Jam*. The daughter of former *Plain Dealer* sportswriter Chuck Heaton and sister of the paper's "Minister of Culture" Mike Heaton, Patricia gained seven Emmy nominations for Outstanding Actress in a comedy series for her work in *Raymond*, winning twice. Her "va-va-voom" factor increased after undergoing plastic surgery before the final years of the hit sitcom's 1996-2005 run. Heaton returned to television in 2007 as Kelsey Grammar's co-anchor in the Fox sitcom *Back to You*.

5. Debra Winger, Cleveland Heights. Winger dropped out of high school to live in a kibbutz in Israel and serve in the Israeli Defense Forces. After returning to the U.S., she suffered a cerebral hemorrhage that left her blind. She vowed to move to California and become an actress if she ever regained her sight. She did and won leads in such films as *Urban Cowboy*, *An Officer and a Gentleman* (for which she gained a Best Actress Oscar nomination), *Terms of Endearment* (her second Oscar nomination) and *Shadowlands* (her third). The sight of Winger riding a mechanical bull in *Urban Cowboy* can still cinch your saddle tight.

4. Monica Potter, Cleveland Heights. Potter played Nicholas Cage's wife in *Con Air*, opposite Robin Williams in *Patch Adams* and was a regular in the first season of the television drama *Boston Legal*. Had she stuck around the show, this blonde, blue-eyed beauty would have certainly incited all kinds of inappropriate behavior from co-star William Shatner's Denny Crane.

3. Teri Garr, Magnificat.
In recent years, she's shown her bravery and commitment by becoming a spokesperson for the disease that afflicts her, multiple sclerosis. But in her younger days, this Lakewood native could really bake your beans by showing off a different side of herself. Who can forget this exchange from 1974's *Young Frankenstein*, in which Garr plays Inga, the mad scientist's comely assistant:

(Sound of giant door knockers.)
Frankenstein: What knockers!
Inga (dressed in a low-cut dress): Ohhhhh, thank you, Doctor!

2. Dorothy Dandridge, raised in Cleveland.
Dandridge dropped out of high school after moving to Los Angeles. Sexually abused as a child by her mother's lesbian partner, she rose from the struggles of her youth to become the first black actress nominated for an Oscar in a lead role for 1954's *Carmen Jones*, a modern-day remake of Bizet's opera *Carmen*. Known as "the black Marilyn Monroe," Dandridge boasted the talent and beauty to land many more glamorous roles, but was held back by the color of her skin.

1. Halle Berry, Bedford.
You expected someone else? Berry, whose first name comes from the old Cleveland department store, broke through the color barrier that held Dandridge back to become the first black to win the Best Actress Oscar when she took home the statue for 2002's *Monster's Ball*. Before going into acting, the beauty queen won the Miss Ohio USA and Miss Teen All-American pageants and took the first runner-up spot in the 1986 Miss USA contest. Berry played Dandridge in the 1999 made-for-TV movie *Introducing Dorothy Dandridge*. She broke through to the big time with her role as a recovering drug addict struggling to regain custody of her son in *Losing Isaiah*. Bullworth, in which she played an activist who brought politician Warren Beatty back to his radical roots, deserves mention as brilliant satire alongside *Dr. Strangelove* (okay, behind *Dr. Strangelove*). Halle was formerly married to one-time Indians outfielder David Justice.

Note: Classic movies provide the straight lines. The one-liners were added by Bill Livingston and our cracker-jack trivia buff, Chuck Murr, former *Plain Dealer* copy editor and all-around versatile contributor to this book. Chuck now spends his time as an Associated Press stringer and soccer aficionado in the moments when he's not settling into a seat at a multiplex near you. Chuck, taking a cue from Norma Desmond in *Sunset Boulevard*, says the movies didn't get smaller; the theaters did.

20. "Here's looking at you, kid." Not Humphrey Bogart to Ingrid Bergman in *Casablanca*, but . . . Mike Hargrove to Jaret Wright for Game 7 in the 1997 World Series.

19. "I stick my neck out for nobody." Not Bogart in *Casablanca*, but . . . Bip Roberts, begging off playing in Game 7 of the 1997 World Series with a sore throat and sniffles.

18. "Bond, James Bond." Not Sean Connery or any of his 007 successors, but . . . Bill Belichick or any of his successors as Browns head coach, explaining who it would take to make the team a winner.

17. "It's not the men in your life that counts, it's the life in your men." Not Mae West in *She Done Him Wrong*, but . . . Mark Shapiro, on what it took to get the Indians back into the World Series.

16. "I'll be back." Not Arnold Schwarzenegger in *The Terminator*, but . . . Kenny Lofton, twice.

15. "My Mama always said, 'Life was like a box of chocolates; you never know what you're gonna get.'" Not Tom Hanks in *Forrest Gump*, but . . . Dwight Clark, on his drafting philosophy.

14. "I could dance with you until the cows come home. On second thought, I'd rather dance with the cows when you come home." Not Groucho Marx to Margaret Dumont in *Duck Soup*, but . . . Cleveland fans to Art Modell after he left town.

13. "Look, Emerald City is closer and prettier than ever. Let's get outta' here!" Not Judy Garland in *The Wizard of OZ*, but . . . Art Modell in 1995.

12. "Come back, Shane!" Not Brandon DeWilde in *Shane* but . . . Browns fans after Marty Schottenheimer traded Chip Banks to move up in the draft, then selected mega-bust Mike Junkin instead of Penn State's Shane Conlan.

11. "My mind is going . . . I can feel it." Not HAL, the homicidal computer in *2001: A Space Odyssey*, but . . . Tribe GM Frank Lane, explaining his trades.

10. "Round up the usual suspects." Not Claude Rains in *Casablanca*, but . . . Butch Davis, on that dark day in 2001 when four of his Browns players were arrested in two cities in a dazzling array of law-breaking activities.

9. "I just want to wish you both good luck. We're all counting on you." Not Leslie Nielsen in *Airplane!*, but . . . Eric Wedge to C.C. Sabathia and Fausto Carmona in the 2007 playoffs.

8. "Frankly, my dear, I don't give a damn." Not Clark Gable to Vivien Leigh in *Gone With the Wind*, but . . . the Cleveland sports audience to the WNBA.

7. "If you want to call me that, smile." Not Gary Cooper in *The Virginian*, but . . . Travis Hafner, to Bill Selby, upon being nicknamed "Pronk."

6. "I want to be alone." Not Greta Garbo in *Grand Hotel*, but . . . Ted Stepien, explaining his scheme to drive off all the Cleveland fans by trashing the team so he could watch his Cavs play in privacy.

5. "Well, here's another nice mess you've gotten me into!" Not Oliver Hardy to Stan Laurel, many times, but . . . pitching coach Carl Willis, upon visiting Joe Borowski on the mound, too many times to count.

4. "Fasten your seat belts, it's going to be a bumpy night." Not Bette Davis in *All About Eve*, but . . . Indians fans watching Ernie Camacho, Jose Mesa, Bob Wickman or Joe Borowski coming in from the bullpen to try to close a game.

3. Not "Luca Brazzi sleeps with the fishes" from *The Godfather*, but . . . 25,000 tons of debris from Cleveland Municipal Stadium, which now form an artificial reef for fishes to sleep inside at the bottom of Lake Erie.

2. "What we've got here is (pause) failure to communicate." Not Strother Martin or Paul Newman (who added an "a" before "failure" when he said it) in *Cool Hand Luke*, but . . . Sam Rutigliano to Brian Sipe after Red Right 88.

1. "Made it, Ma! Top of the world!" Not James Cagney in *White Heat*, but . . . still waiting.

The 20 Best Tribe Nicknames

Baseball has inspired the most nicknames because it's been around far longer than the other sports. Also, because, what else are you going to do while waiting for Rafael Betacourt to throw the ball already?

20. Johnny "Patcheye" Gill.

19. Bristol "The Human Eyeball" Lord.

18. Guy "Alabama Blossom" Morton.

17. Leon Joseph "Bip" Roberts.

16. Mike "The Human Rain Delay" Hargrove.

15. Bernie "Barnyard" Henderson.

14. Tom "The Gray Flamingo" Brennan.

13. Leroy "Satchel" Paige.

12. Leon "Daddy Wags" Wagner.

11. "Sudden" Sam McDowell.

10. George "Eaglebeak" Beck.

9. Charles "Piano Legs" Hickman.

8. Bob "Rapid Robert" Feller.

7. Covelli Loyce "Coco" Crisp.

6. George "Snuffy" Stirnweiss.

5. Tris "The Gray Eagle" Speaker.

4. Harry "Deerfoot" Bay.

3. "Shoeless" Joe Jackson.

2. Jim "Mudcat" Grant.

1. Travis "Pronk" Hafner.

The Ten Best Cavs Nicknames

Nobody really calls LeBron James "King James" outside of a marketing meeting. And Damon Jones' billing as "The World's Great Shooter" stinks of false advertising. We want better.

10. Robert "Tractor" Traylor.

9. William "Smush" Parker.

8. Alfred "Butch" Beard.

7. Bubby "Bingo" Smith.

6. Daniel "Boobie" Gibson.

5. Anderson "Wild Thing" Varejao.

4. Wayne "Tree" Rollins.

3. John "Hot Rod" Williams.

2. Vernel "Bimbo" Coles.

1. Clarence "Foots" Walker.

The Ten Best Browns Nicknames

The last time the Browns were consistently good, back in the 1980s, their nicknames were depressingly monogrammatical: E.B. for Earnest Byner, B.K. for Bernie Kosar. We yearn for better stuff. The best we get is K2 for Kellen Winslow Jr. We love it because, playing off both his lineage and the world's second-tallest mountain, it's there. So are these.

10. "The Wizard" Ozzie Newsome.

9. Ray "Rabbit" Renfro.

8. Eddie "Bullet Head" Johnson.

7. Joe "Turkey" Jones.

6. Dick "Bam-Bam" Ambrose.

5. Dub "Special Delivery" Jones.

4. Walter "Flea" Roberts.

3. "Automatic" Otto Graham.

2. Dante "Glue Fingers" Lavelli.

1. Lou "The Toe" Groza.

Note: What times they were! Five playoff berths in a row, four division championships, three heartbreakers against John Elway and Denver and one, big love affair between a gangly kid and a scorned city that swept us all away. They were good times for Bernie, too, and he shares his fondest memories from his days with the Browns.

5. First training camp, Lakeland Community College, 1985. Nowadays,

they can only get 2,000 fans out to Berea at camp. But Lakeland had a lot more space. There would be 8,000 fans there. This was before all the rules about security and we would run out with fans gathered on both sides of us. They would be cheering so loud. I was a rookie, and I always stopped and signed every autograph they asked for, without charging. It was such a great atmosphere, a college atmosphere. It was when the Dawgs thing was just getting started. It was before everyone began to love himself. I roomed with [Gary] Danielson, which was all a rookie quarterback could ask for. I think that's why that team did so well and why those players bonded so strongly. It was just a very special time.

4. Denver 29, Browns 14, Cleveland Stadium, November 7, 1993. It was

my last play with the Browns. I drew it up in the dirt in the huddle. Steve Atwater and Dennis Smith were really aggressive safeties. I told Michael Jackson to run a square-in, and that they would jump it when I pump-faked, then for him to go long. We hit it for a touchdown, but (Bill) Belichick just went nuts, screaming at me that I was insubordinate. He fired me the next day.

3. Browns 34, Cincinnati 3, Riverfront Stadium, December 14, 1986.

The winner would take the division. Everybody always had scripted plays to start games. They were always so conservative. Get a feel for the game. Don't make mistakes. I wanted to come out firing. (Offensive coordinator) Lindy Infante and I almost came to blows in the locker room. I hadn't played in that many big games yet, so I wanted to show everyone on the team I was ready to go. If you're a big, slow quarterback, you have to have other things. I had the thing Patton said in the movie about Napoleon: Audacity, always audacity. I figured if we hit it, it would send a big message that we were going to kick their asses. If we missed it, it still meant we weren't afraid. I hit Langhorne deep and he got right down to the goal line.

2. Browns 27, Pittsburgh 24, Three Rivers Stadium, October 12, 1986.

That was the year we broke the Three Rivers jinx. It was huge to me, growing up in Youngstown, halfway between Pittsburgh and Cleveland. We had the lead late, less than a touchdown, and the calls were all first down, second down, third down, run, run, play-action pass. I was supposed to throw it into the flat where it was safe. It was always run-run-pass with us. I butted heads with the coaches about it all the time. I'd almost gotten Earnest Byner killed with a pass in the flat before that. So I said, "The hell with that," and I was going to fake it in the flat and hit Reggie Langhorne down the sideline on either the bomb or the fade. I hit him for a 40-, 50-yard play and they (Pittsburgh fans) cried into their Terrible Towels.

1. Browns 23, Jets 20 (double OT), Cleveland Stadium, January 3, 1987. It was my first playoff game at the old Stadium and the first home playoff game for the Browns since Red Right 88. We were down 10 (with 4:54 left in the fourth quarter) and I had thrown two picks, one in the end zone. Gary Danielson (backup quarterback) was in my ear, telling me to stay positive and to just take it one drive at a time. We got into overtime and everybody was so positive, even after (Mark) Moseley missed a short field goal. The Jets were deflated. They thought they had it and we had Big Mo (momentum) on our side. (Author's Note: Kosar completed 33 of 64 passes for 489 yards in that epic struggle.)

David Glasier has covered CSU basketball since 1984 for The Lake County News-Herald. He and Livingston differed on some choices here. Both, however, deny the usual perception that the CSU basketball program only mattered when Kevin Mackey was its coach from 1983-90). Two of our top five choices played for Ray Dieringer before Mackey even arrived. To give Mackey his due, the 13,610-seat Wolstein Center was only built after he hit Euclid Ave., talking fast and playing faster. Mackey was the first coach—even before Rick Pitino at Kentucky—to use the full-court press all game. His great 1986 Sweet 16 team had the second worst defensive field goal percentage in the nation among NCAA Tournament teams, but the Vikings turned opponents over so often for easy baskets that it hardly mattered. With former Kent State and Rutgers coach Gary Waters taking the Vikings to the NIT in 2008, there is hope now that the great players might come again to Cleveland State.

Sixth Man: Weldon Kytle (1961-65). He won a close call over Eric Mudd, the center on the Sweet 16 team. Kytle ranks seventh at CSU in career points with 1,408, third in scoring average at 18.8 per game, first in career rebounds with 1,241 and tops in rebound average at 16.5 per. Despite his impressive individual stats, he's held back from the starting five because CSU's record during his time there was an unimpressive 35—40. We go with Kytle because he bridges the gap between the Fenn College and Cleveland State eras. He was a co-op student through his four years in college. During the winter semester, which included the lion's share of basketball season, Kytle worked full-time at a Cleveland factory. After long days on his feet as a machinist, he'd go to practices or games and still managed to earn his degree in four years.

5. Clinton Smith (1984-86). When Mackey lured him back home after an unhappy season at Ohio State, he told Smith: "Don't let anyone take away your game." No one did. Some of us still see Smith's 25-footer bouncing off the back of the rim at the final buzzer in the Vikings' one-point Sweet 16 loss to David Robinson's Navy team. Better to remember his overall contribution and athleticism, which made Mackey's Run 'n' Stun go.

4. Darren Tillis (1978-82). Thin but tough at 6-11, Tillis rates as the best power forward in CSU history. He combined with Franklin Edwards to give CSU a nice one-two punch. Stepped up his senior season after Edwards left as the team's main man, before following Edwards to the NBA as the first-round pick of the Celtics.

3. Clinton Ransey (1983-87). Polished on offense and underrated on defense, Ransey was the little brother of Kelvin Ransey, an Ohio State standout. He seemed to hit every big shot in the signature game of the Kevin Mackey era, the first-round NCAA tourney upset of Indiana. Against the Hoosiers, Ransey had 27 points, 5 rebounds and 3 steals. He proved to be an integral part of Mackey's first recruiting class, along with Eric Mudd, Shawn Hood and Ed Bryant.

2. Ken "Mouse" McFadden (1985–89). He was never a real pro prospect because of his lack of NBA size and quickness. But the "Mouse" had the survivor instinct of cartoon Jerry always slipping the jaws of Tom. An archetypal Kevin Mackey recruit who did not play high school basketball or graduate from high school, McFadden established himself as the star of New York's cutthroat AAU leagues, then earned a GED (Chris Rock's Good Enough Degree). He went on to become the most charismatic and highest-profile player in CSU history. Decent from the outside and great on dribble penetration, the Mouse roared his way to national prominence and played a big part in putting the CSU program on the map.

1. Franklin Edwards (1977–81). A prolific offensive player, Edwards could score on jump shots or by slashing to the hoop. He had a nice NBA career as a bench player with the Philadelphia 76ers, hitting a buzzer-beater to nip the New York Knicks in a playoff game during the Sixers' 1982-83 championship run. But even if he'd never made a single shot in the pros, Edwards would still easily rank as the best player in CSU history.

Cleveland began serving as annual hosts for the MAC's season-ending basketball tournament in 2000. The arrangement has worked out great for everyone involved. Holding their single-elimination showdown in a big-league NBA arena in a major city stuck a big feather in the cap of the mid-major league. Cleveland proved a natural fit for the event, with strong, local alumni bases for all six Ohio MAC schools. The league's headquarters sit on Public Square in Cleveland, and its hoops heart beats here too. The MAC tourney made previous stops at such places as gloomy Sea Gate Center in Toledo, Detroit, Rockford, Ill, and—here's a bad idea, let's go to Big Ten country—Columbus and Ann Arbor. The 2002 championship game between Kent State and Bowling Green drew over 14,000 to the Cavs' arena, about 10k more than they averaged at those other locations.

The tourney has benefited Clevelanders, as well, providing an annual showcase for basketball the way it oughta' be played—with players diving on the floor for loose balls and generally competing like there is no tomorrow. Because with their league usually limited to just one entrant into the NCAA Tournament later in the month, there really is no tomorrow for losers in the MAC's mini-March Madness. There is, however, plenty of enthusiasm from cheerleaders, pep bands, students, alumni, and fans, plus the overriding sense that you are watching a brand of basketball and unbridled, community spirit that you assumed had died out decades ago. All that offered a nice contrast and a brief, welcome respite during the slothful, selfish, pre-LeBron Cavs era of Ricky Davis, Darius Miles and Lamond Murray.

Then there's the surprisingly high caliber of players. Though usually overlooked by the NBA scouts and draft pundits, the MAC has produced one NBA All-Time Top 50 Team member (Nate Thurmond, Bowling Green) and one ring-bearer to Michael Jordan (Ron Harper, Miami of Ohio) as well as such recent first-round NBA draft picks as Antonio Daniels (Bowling Green), Bonzie Wells (Ball State) and Chris Kaman (Central Michigan). We picked our top five MAC players from the tourney's Cleveland years of 2000-2007. Their ranking is based on how they played throughout the season, although none of them had bad tournaments either. Kent State's Andrew Mitchell was our most reluctant cut. "Drew" would make a fine sixth man for our team, but we only go five-deep.

5. Trevor Huffman, Kent State, G.
A two-time MAC tournament MVP, Huffman admitted the second should have been a team award. What a year it was for Huffman and KSU, with 30 victories, 18 of them in a row, a 17-1 MAC record and an edgy victory in the quarterfinals over a very talented Marshall team with Tamar Slay and J.R. VanHoose. Horizon League favorite Butler had lost at Cleveland State in the league tourney's q-finals the week before and would miss the NCAA Tournament, which ratcheted the pressure even higher on the Golden Flashes. Andrew Mitchell hit the big shot in the Marshall game. But the edge on the All-Cleveland Team goes to Huffman for his continual arc of improvement, from a too-small, too-slow kid out of a wind-swept town near the Mackinac Bridge, a player ignored by Michigan and Michigan State, to the man who made Kent State champs.

4. Keith McLeod, Bowling Green, G. He took MAC Player of the Year in 2001-02, despite it being Kent State's great season, McLeod transformed into a pure thoroughbred when the game was on the line. His three-pointer from the corner, fading away, on the fly, saved the Falcons against Akron in 2002.

3. Lonnie Jones, Ball State, C. His inside dominance in 2000 was awesome to watch. But his story line was even better. An asthmatic, Jones was treated periodically during tournament games for the affliction. Had the tourney not been held in a well-equipped NBA arena, BSU officials later said that Jones would not have been able to keep playing. He did, leaving the guys trying to guard him sucking wind.

2. Antonio Gates, Kent State, F. A terrific athlete, he went on to become (sorry, K2) THE model of the pass-catching tight end in the NFL with San Diego. Before that, the junior college transfer formed the final piece to the puzzle in Kent's astonishing 2002 run to the NCAA Tournament's Elite Eight. Quick enough to blow by the big guys, big enough to overpower the quick guys in the post, able to handle and run the floor well, Gates was the MAC's Charles Barkley. Too bad he was playing on a bad leg in the finals against a loaded Central team his senior year.

1. Chris Kaman, Central Michigan, C. The seven-footer was so impressive in college that he climbed all the way up to the sixth pick in the 2003 NBA draft. He was Lonnie Jones, the tall shot-blocker who keyed Ball State's title run in the tournament's Cleveland debut, with offensive game, too. Nearly ambidextrous around the rim, Kaman was such a weapon that even the second-best player of the Cleveland era was blown away by him in 2002.

Note: The former Browns defensive end owns Bubba's Q in the Cleveland suburb of Avon (the place is easy to find—just follow your nose down Route 83). The man is passionate about his product, with his ribs racking up awards about as regularly as he sacked quarterbacks during his playing days. A native of the southeast, Bubba grew up feasting on Carolina mustard-based sauce. Baker, who has taken courses from Texas A&M in meat preparation, toured the legendary Central Texas barbecue joint circuit, with good friend Earl Campbell, to gain more insights into his art. The man knows his 'cue.

9. Don't cheat on the meat. Get a quality piece of meat, whether it's baby backs, spareribs, whatever.

8. Pre season. It's too late to season the meat after it's cooked. You've seared it and closed the pores. Put your dry rub and spices on before you start.

7. Choose the right method. You have two choices: grilling or barbecuing. Grilling is done at high temperature, 400 degrees Fahrenheit, to cook the meat quickly and sear the juices in. Barbecue is done at a lower temperature. Low and slow is my motto.

6. Choose the right chips. If you have wood chips, be careful what kind you use. Hickory and mesquite have a very strong flavor that not everyone likes. I tell people to use indigenous wood. What is Ohio chock full of? Apple trees! So use applewood.

5. Don't boil ribs. If your mama ever made soup, you might remember how the stock looked, all the stuff floating in the water after she boiled the meat. With ribs, that's flavor you're boiling out. You can wrap the ribs in foil and bake them at 300 degrees for three hours, then grill them quickly the next day. If you try to barbecue them then, you will dry them out.

4. Sauce is a condiment. Don't make the meat swim in sauce. Only baste it with sauce the last 5 minutes. Every commercial barbecue sauce out there has some sugar in it. Under heat, what does sugar do? It carmelizes. So you have burned sugar on your good piece of meat,

3. Be passionate about it. Don't just try to make a good meal. I tell my staff, the enemy of great is good. I'm not satisfied with good barbecue.

2. Use the fat. Take the fat you cut off pulled-pork sandwiches and add it to the grill before cooking ribs. The smoking fat gives the ribs even more flavor.

1. Pace yourself. You can't eat barbecue every day. If you did, you'd be on Oprah Winfrey as the fattest man in America.

Cleveland's Top Ten Sports Bars

We sent out our trusted spy, bartender extraordinaire Jake Thomas, to eat, drink and gauge his merriment at local sports bars on the night of a Browns' exhibition game. (Hey, it's tough duty, but someone had to do it.) We limited their range to places near downtown, figuring fans would need nearby refuge or a place to celebrate after attending home games. Or even before attending them.

10. Cleats, 27200 Detroit Road, Westlake. The wing is the thing, and its glorification here might be the best anywhere outside Buffalo. Sports fans know chicken wings are a separate, nutritious food group anyway. But when you can choose from American, Cajun, Cambodian, Caribbean. Brazilian, Asian . . . Stop! We have to mop the sauce off sometime.

9. BW3's, 1313 Old River Road, Cleveland. Chow down on wings and enjoy what's left of The Flats while not wandering too far from Browns Stadium.

8. Panini's, 840 Huron, Cleveland. Atmosphere, atmosphere, sandwiches!

7. Harry Buffalo, 2129 E. Fourth Street, Cleveland. Multi-level bar and restaurant located in the middle of the city's sports action and all the loyal fans.

6. Champs Americana, 5989 Canal Road, Valley View. A casual family place you can bring the kids to. Enjoy the big screams!

5. Don Shula's, 6200 Quarry Lane, Independence. A higher-end sports bar where you can get a steak instead of a burger and a martini instead of a beer.

4. Dave & Buster's, 25735 First Street, Westlake. The national chain offers a roomy atmosphere, large portions of food and lots of gaming options to kill time before going to a sporting event.

3. Thirsty Parrot, 812 Huron, Cleveland. This indoor/outdoor patio restaurant is just a LeBron trey from The Q or a dinger from The Jake. And they know how to cook up a good meal.

2. Harpo's Sports Café, 5777 Smith Road, Brookpark. Eight big screens. 82 television sets, over 100 beers, good food, easy to get to. The only things missing: better Cleveland teams to root for.

1. The Winking Lizard, 811 Huron Road East, Cleveland. This is the ultimate downtown Cleveland sports bar. A lot of great food, 100 different beers to choose from and a TV set everywhere you look.

Party Names: Six Guys You'd Want to Party With

The Beeeeeeeeer Guy (as in the leather-lunged Indians baseball vendor who cries "The Beeeeeeeeer guy's here!") would never have ventured far from these gentlemen.

6. William Lush, Indians, 1904

5. Jamie Brewington, Indians, 2000

4. Jim Brewer, Cavs 1973-79

3. Ron Brewer, Cavs, 1981-86

2. Carlos Boozer, Cavs, 2002-04

1. Ken Swilling, Browns, 1992

This Bud's for You: 13 Area Sports Guys Nicknamed "Bud" or "Buddy"

We've had enough good "Buddies" in Cleveland sports to re-start the CB radio fad. So many "Buds," so few championships flowering.

13. Ray "Buddy" Baker. A cup-of-coffee first baseman with the Indians in the 60s.

12. Leavitt Leo "Bud" Daley. Spent three years with the Tribe in the 50s, during which time he proved more of a "buddy" to opponents, posting a 3-9 record.

11. Harold "Bud" Kurtz. A middle reliever in the 1960s for Cleveland, in the mode of Cliff Bartosh. He lasted less than a year in the Majors.

10. Clarence "Bud" Podbielan. Joined the Tribe at the end of a career that was as curiously long as it was unsuccessful. The right-handed pitcher went 25-42 (.373) over the course of a decade, including a 1-6 record with Cleveland just before retiring in 1959, much to the dismay of opposing batters.

9. Karl Adam "Bud" Anderson, The righty went 4-10 in the '80s with Indians, who apparently had yet to learn their lesson about signing pitchers nicknamed "Bud."

8. Richard Lee "Buddy" Booker. An Einar Diaz type, Booker came up through the Indians' farm system, but was dealt to the White Sox in '68.

7. Wilson "Bud" Schwenk. The young quarterback joined the AAFC Browns after a three-year layoff following his outstanding 1942 rookie season with the NFL's Chicago Cardinals. But with Otto Graham ahead of him on the depth chart, Schwenk only saw enough playing time to complete 15 passes. He left for Baltimore the following season.

6. Charles "Buddy" Bradford. This Indians outfielder from the late '60s had good tools, but he fanned too much. He went on to play for the Reds, Cardinals and White Sox.

5. Charles Budd "Buddy" Schultz. A superstar high school lefty at Shaw High School in the 1960s, Schultz set an NCAA record at Miami (of Ohio) by whiffing 26 batters in a nine-inning game (think about that for a minute). Schultz pitched his way into the Majors and posted the third-lowest E.R.A. in the National League in 1977 with the Cardinals. He retired a couple seasons later after only five years in the majors. In today's game, he would be Alan Embree and play forever.

4. Warren "Buddy" Rosar. Played from 1930-51 in the bigs with the Tribe, Yanks, Philly and Bosox. The slick fielding catcher played error-free in 1946 and led the AL in assists. He appeared in five All-Star games.

75

3. Leon H. "Bud" Carson. The Browns' head coach after Marty and before "Mumbles," Carson established himself early in his career as one of the league's leading defensive gurus. He helped build the Steelers' dominating Iron Curtain defense of the early '70s as a defensive coordinator in Pittsuburgh. He took the same position with the Rams for a few seasons, helping them reach the '77 Super Bowl, where they lost to his old team the Steelers. He worked for the Chiefs, Colts and Jets before taking over as Browns head coach in 1989. He guided the team to a division title, then yet another AFC title game loss to the Broncos. The team went to hell the next season and Bud went to Philadelphia.

2. Harry Ralston "Bud" Black. Not the one who played for Detroit in the 50s. But the lefty pitcher who had a couple of stints with the Indians in the late 80s and early 90s during his 15-year playing career, before becoming a manager in San Diego last season.

1. David Gus "Buddy" Bell. The Pittsburgh native established himself in the '70s as the Indians third baseman nonpareil (except maybe, for one season, Matt Williams). Bell went on to play for the Rangers, Reds and Astros, before retiring and becoming a decidedly less-successful manager.

Note: Michael Reghi served as the Cleveland Cavaliers television play-by-play announcer from 1994–2006. He coined "Flight 23, cleared for landing!" for LeBron James' dunks and "D.J. gonna lift and lace that triple" for Damon Jones' three-pointers, while also enlivening the Cavs' less exciting plays and games. Reghi, who also worked as play-by-play man for the Baltimore Orioles from 1997–2003, lists his favorite Cavs' games and moments as experienced from behind the microphone.

10. Reward from the Reign Man! April 27, 1998, first round of Eastern Conference playoffs. Shawn Kemp came up with 31 points and 13 rebounds at Gund Arena as the Cavaliers fought off elimination with an 86-77 win over Indiana in Game 3 of the best-of-five series. Kemp's 17-foot, face-up jumper clinched it with less than a minute to play. Calling the game with my partner for six seasons, the incomparable Matty Guokas, made the moment a professional delight, as it would be the Cavaliers' last playoff win until the young man from Akron showed up five years later to save a franchise, and more importantly, a city!

9. Damon dooms D.C! May 5, 2006, first round of Eastern Conference playoffs. After sitting on the bench for the first 52 minutes and 46 seconds of Game 6, Damon Jones, the self-proclaimed "best shooter in the world," sticks a 14-foot baseline jumper with :05 seconds left to win it for the Cavaliers. It sent the franchise into the second round of the playoffs for the first time since 1993. Jones, much maligned through the regular season, redeemed himself, while etching his name into Cavaliers' playoff lore.

8. Boozer a Beast! January 17 and January 20, 2004. In a two-game stretch, the young strong man from Duke, who averaged a double-double in his second year in a Cavaliers uniform, went for 64 points and 38 rebounds on 66% shooting from the field in a pair of wins over Utah and Seattle. He had 32 points and 18 rebounds at Utah, and 32 more points and 20 rebounds three nights later at home against Seattle. I vividly remember proclaiming on the air that Boozer was not only a perfect complement to LeBron, but also an integral ingredient to the resurgence of the franchise. Ahhhh...not so much, as it all would play out in the summer of 2004.

7. NBA All-Star Game in Cleveland. February 9, 1997. What's not for a hoop junkie to salivate over when the 50 Greatest Ever show up at Gund Arena! Oscar, Dr. J, West, Bird, Magic, Michael, 'Nique and Zeke and the rest of the finest ever to grace the courts! And all on display in Cleveland! The fans appreciation of what stood before them that cold and wintry Sunday evening was a sight to behold!

6. Ping Pong Heaven! May 22, 2003. The day that turned the fortunes of the Cleveland sporting scene forever! The Cavaliers won the NBA's Draft Lottery to earn the right to select LeBron James. I was sitting in the television booth in Angels Stadium in Anaheim, California, preparing for my call of an Orioles-Angels game. My fist pumped the air at the great fortune of the long-suffering Cleveland sports fans!

5. The Debut! October 29, 2003. No "prep-to-pro" in the history of the game had a coming-out party like this! LeBron James dazzled in his highly anticipated NBA debut with 25 points, 6 rebounds and 9 assists on a variety of superb offensive moves. Included were four tough mid-range jumpers that made me realize his potential for greatness has no boundary!

4. 'Bron & D-Wade play Bird & 'Nique! April 1, 2006. No April Fooling! Fourth quarter explosiveness as the Cavaliers beat Miami. Bron goes for 47 with 12 rebounds and 9 assists, Wade for 44. Yet it was their fourth-quarter "I can top that" performance that made it special! Both of the young megatalents were incredible! It closely resembled the Bird-Jordan and Bird-Dominique shootouts of years gone by.

3. Going for 51! January 21, 2006. LeBron takes over in the second half on a Saturday night in Salt Lake City with one of his first Jordan like efforts! He scored 32 of his 51 points in the second half to beat the Jazz 108-90. He did it despite dealing with flu-like symptoms before the game and the fallout from the altercation his mother experienced the night before in Akron with the police.

2. Setting new Standards! March 20, 2006. 'Bron goes wild in Toronto. A 56–point, career-high effort in front of the Canadian fans. He went 18-for-36 from the floor with six treys! Ironically, it would be the final game of the Paul Silas regime. The Cavs' coach was fired the next morning after benching starting point guard Jeff McInnis in the Raptors game.

1. Center Stage—and then some! May 3, 2006, Game 5 of the first round of the Eastern Conference playoffs. With the series tied 2-2, James flexed his flair for playoff dramatics. An amazing fourth-quarter run by Washington sent the game into OT, where the Cavs found themselves down by one with time running out. Lebron tiptoed baseline to finish at the rim, topping off a 45-point effort to beat the Wizards with less than a second left. Given the enormity of the moment, I believed it to be the finest virtuoso performance of his young career.

We don't know. Maybe it's the height. Maybe the brain gets starved of oxygen up there in the rare air.. Anyway, the Cavs have had their share of guys (and one self-styled royal personage) who put up the intellectual equivalent of an air ball in incidents on- and off-the-court.

12. Gordon Gund for pioneering a new brand of frivolous lawsuit. After firing Mike Fratello, who led injury-ravaged Cavs teams to the playoffs four times in his six seasons, the Cavs owner sued his former coach, arguing that he did not have to pay Fratello the rest of his $3 million salary because he took a job as a commentator on TNT. The stated reason was that Fratello "could not devote his full time to his basketball duties." Well, he could not do that because you relieved him of those duties! Remember Catch-22, the Joseph Heller novel? Catch-22 was a bureaucratic device that kept the flyers flying in the novel during World War II. You had to be crazy to get out of bombing missions, but you weren't crazy to want to get out of bombing missions. So either way, you had to keep flying. Bill Livingston called the lawsuit's logic "Catch 39 Percent" because a 30-52 record (.390 winning percentage) was what the Cavs did under Randy Wittman and John Lucas, Fratello's successors.

11. David Wesley gets rejected down under. Roaring in on the fast break against Dallas in 2007, Wesley watched his layup anemically bump off the rubber padding around the bottom of the backboard. He did not trip, he did not let the ball slip out of his hands and he was not rushing the shot because of a possible block. He did, however, look like a man who was so far over the hill that he'd dipped into a valley. "They might as well bring out the podium (for his retirement speech) now," said the *News-Herald's* Bob Finnan.

10. Jiri Welsch goes on a bender. In LeBron James' rookie year during a game in Indianapolis, Jiri Welsch squared up and let' er fly from the corner on a 3-pointer. His shot seemed to curve, like a well-struck draw in golf, then landed in the paint, two feet wide of the basket. As James arrived at the bench during the ensuing timeout, he stared at Welsch with an 'Excuse me, but are you with us?' look and said: "What the hell was that?"

9. Jerome Lane for shooting 25 percent from the foul lane in 1993.

8. Larry Hughes sings "C'mon, Get Happy." In the first meeting of the Cavs and the Bulls since the blockbuster trade between the teams, Hughes shot 23 times to score 20 points in a nine-point loss to the Cavs. Then he said of his Cleveland experience: "We had 50-plus wins, made the Finals and I learned from it. I was unhappy. I wasn't myself. I'd rather enjoy the game than all that." He also received $4 million in team-oriented bonuses while suffering through his Cavs years because the team won 50 games in spite of him twice. We're not sure Hughes was the most overrated loser ever to play for the Cavs because Shawn Kemp might have retired that trophy. But he's in the discussion.

7. Ricky Davis mentors LeBron. It was James' first public appearance in a competitive NBA environment for the exhibition opener of his rookie season at The Palace outside Detroit. On the Cavs' first possession, "Wrong Rim" Ricky Davis took an inbounds pass and jacked up a wild jump shot with 22 seconds left on the shot clock. Welcome to the NBA, kid.

6. Drew Gooden goes pubic in public. At the Palace in 2006, Gooden unveiled his new hairstyle—a completely shaven head, except for a Phil Jackson-like goatee peeking out from below the back of his headband, leading a Detroit heckler to hail him with: "Hey, Vagina Head!"

5. LeBron James tips his hat to the enemy. James showed up at Jacobs Field for the opener of the 2007 division playoff series wearing a New York Yankees cap. James can root for whomever he pleases. Clearly. But if he felt that way—despite the fact that Grady Sizemore, C.C. Sabathia and other Indians cheered themselves hoarse from the Tribe's suite at The Q during the Cavs run earlier that year to The Finals—he should have worn a Cavaliers cap. James inspired further headscratching from the Cleveland faithful when he began marketing a shoe (in New York only) in Yankee pinstripes.

4. Pollard just says, "Yes." When TV cameras caught seldom-used Scot Pollard sitting idly on the bench during the 2006-07 season, he smiled brightly and said: "Hey, kids. Do drugs." He later apologized from the tip of his Mohawk to the soles of his feet, 83 inches, in all, of pure contrition.

3. Kempton shows it's sometimes better to keep your mouth shut. Asked by an interviewer if he could do anything unusual that people didn't know about, Tim Kempton revealed that he could put a whole Burger King Whopper in his mouth at once. (To be fair, Kempton gets miffed every time Livingston describes him as a big galoot with flame-broiled crumbs littering his jersey because the molar-to-molar mouthful was digested for charity.)

2. Davis puts up a triple-dummy. In a 2003 game against Utah, "Wrong Rim" Ricky Davis deliberately clanged a shot off the Jazz's basket so he could grab his own rebound and secure a triple-double for the game.

1. Lebron shows that speed kills . . . brain cells. Rushing to the airport with his girlfriend to catch a flight to Las Vegas to celebrate his 23rd birthday in the wee hours of December 30, 2007, LeBron James was stopped for speeding. The cops clocked him traveling at 101 mph in his Mercedes Benz, the one with the understated, personalized "King of Ak" (for Akron) license plates. James observed that going 101 mph wasn't so bad since his car's speedometer went up to 200. (Hey, at least when Wilt hit 100, it was on the basketball court.) A Medina County judge fined James only $259, including court costs. Happy New Year, Your Heavy (But Chic and Nike-Shod) Footedness.

Note: Dwyer worked for 36 years as a reporter for *The Plain Dealer*. He started following high school sports religiously in 1957, when he was seven. Back in those days, you could get into West Tech Field, near his house, for a quarter if you were a kid, then pick up nickel popcorn and dime pop inside. In the autumn, with the money he made delivering *The Plain Dealer* and *The Cleveland Press*, Dwyer would buy tickets to the Friday night game, the Saturday matinee encounter and, after rushing home to check in with his mom and dad, return for the Saturday night game. In the years since, he has seen hundreds of fine players take the field for St. Ignatius. And more than a few great ones. How many great football players has St. Ignatius produced? Just check out the guys who only merited honorable mentions.

Honorable Mentions: wideout Anthony Gonzalez (Ohio State star and NFL first-rounder), defensive lineman Chris Hovan (Boston College star and NFL first-rounder), and LeCharles Bentley (Ohio State star and NFL Pro Bowler).

10. Lenny Brickman, triple-threat quarterback. Impact years were 1923, '24 and '25. Brickman led the Golden Tornado (as Ignatius was known in the Roaring '20s) to the city's Catholic and Scholastic championships in 1925. He garnered first-team All-Scholastic honors from *The Plain Dealer* and the *Cleveland News*, which described Brickman as the best player in the city and "the local scholastic Red Grange." Brickman returned to his alma mater as head coach in the late 1930s.

9. Oliver Luck, quarterback. Impact years were 1975–77. "Ollie" helped the Wildcats win city championships in 1976 and 77, gaining All-Scholastic honors. He had a successful career at West Virginia, leading the Mountaineers to a 26-6 victory over the Florida Gators in the 1981 Peach Bowl. Drafted by the Houston Oilers in the second round of the 1982 NFL, Luck played in the NFL through 1986.

8. Roger Andrachik, running back/kicker. Impact years were 1971, '72 and '73. After the 1973 season, Andrachik was honored with an all-state selection, the MVP of the West Senate and the Cleveland Touchdown Club's Lou Groza Award as the area's top all-around player.

7. Jim Grace, two-way back. Impact years were 1962, '63 and '64. This All-West Senate and All-Scholastic performer was an exceptional runner and receiver. He led the Wildcats' 1964 Hall of Fame team with 22 touchdowns (11 running and 11 receiving). That season, he scored three-or-more TDs in five games, including the 48-6 victory over Benedictine in the Charity Game.

6. Eric Haddad, running back. Impact years were 1991, '92 and '93. As *The Plain Dealer* columnist Bill Livingston wrote, "Haddad could cut on a snowflake." The powerful and graceful Haddad is arguably the most prolific running back in Wildcats history, as he still holds the Jesuit school's records for most rushing yards in a season (1,906 in 1993), most touchdowns in a season (38 in 1993) and most points in a game (36 in 1993). He also threw for two TDs as a tailback, including the game-winner to Mike Sako in the 1991 state-championship showdown with Centerville. Haddad earned

All-Ohio, All-American and *Plain Dealer* and AP Northeast District Offensive Player of the Year honors.

5. Scott Mutryn, quarterback. Impact years were 1992 and '93. An athlete who thrived on the big-game atmosphere, Mutryn helped the Wildcats to consecutive unde-feated seasons, back-to-back state crowns and a national championship ('93). A Parade All-American and an All-Ohio honoree, Mutryn tallied 42 touchdown passes, over 3,700 yards passing and nine rushing TDs in his two seasons as a starter.

4. Tom Forrestal, quarterback. Impact years were 1952 and '53. Forrestal became the first Ignatius player to be named to the country's All-American High School Team ('53). He also garnered All-State, All-West Senate, All-Scholastic and All-Catholic honors. He went on to enjoy an outstanding college career at the Naval Academy.

3. Trent Zenkewicz, two-way lineman. Impact years were 1988–90. One of the most dominant defensive lineman in Ohio high school football history, Zenkewicz was a two-time All-Ohio, All-Scholastic and All-District honoree who led the Wildcats to a 39-game winning streak. Despite being double- and triple-teamed on every play his senior season, Zenkewicz racked up 60 solo tackles, 42 assists and 22 sacks. Following the 1990 season, he garnered Parade All-American, Gatorade Player of the Year in Ohio and the AP Division I Ohio Lineman of the Year honors. He also finished second in the balloting for Ohio's Mr. Football Award, the highest ever placement for an interior lineman. Zenkewicz had an All-Big Ten career at Michigan.

2. Joe Pickens, quarterback. Impact years were 1988 and '89. The humble, yet fiercely competitive Pickens was the field general who began the march of the great-est run of success in the history of Ohio high school football—nine Division I state cham-pionships, including a record five-in-a-row (1991-95). In 1988, Pickens shattered Brian Dowling's single-season record for passing yardage by throwing for 2,178 yards while guiding St. Ignatius to a 14-0 record and their first state crown in what was then the OHSAA playoffs. The next fall, he helped engineer a 13-0, state-championship and national-championship season. A Parade All-American and a two-time All-Ohio, All-Scholastic and All-Northeast Lakes District selection, Pickens was lauded by coach Chuck Kyle as "the greatest football player ever to walk the halls of St. Ignatius."

1. Brian Dowling, quarterback/safety/punt returner. Impact years 1962, '63 and '64. Dowling's athletic accomplishments at St. Ignatius and Yale gained him mythical stature. He even provided the inspiration for a famous comic strip character— the football-helmet-wearing "B.D." in Gary Trudeau's nationally-syndicated Doonesbury. A three-time All-Scholastic and a member of virtually every "All" team his senior year, he passed for 2,602 yards and 39 touchdowns during his two seasons as the Wildcats' starting quarterback, notching 22 TD tosses in their undefeated, city-championship season of 1964. Dowling also played as the team's punter for two sea-sons, averaging 37 yards a kick. What is often forgotten is that Dowling was also one of the premier safeties in Ohio. A three-year mainstay at safety, he helped St. Ignatius to 29 victories in 30 games by racking up more than 30 interceptions, including what is still an Ohio single-season record of 16 picks in 1964. Described by the late Wildcats coaching legend John Wirtz as "by far the best football player I ever coached," Dowling also excelled in basketball, baseball and tennis while attending St. Ignatius.

Top 12 St. Edward High School Football Players :: "Deep Snap"

Note: The desire to continue attending St. Ed's high school class reunions without being berated by guys he left off this list led our man about Lakewood to author this under the cloak of anonymity. Trust us, the guy knows where the Eagles nest is feathered. "Snap" is so deep, we left him undercover after his initial submission. Eddie Dwyer pitched in with some additional commentary. The players are ranked in no particular order.

12. Alex Boone, Class of 2005. Our Mr. Ed says Boone, who went on to become a left tackle at OSU, underachieved his senior season in high school. Still, Boone finished in the top five in the voting for "Mr. Football" honors, a rarity for a lineman.

11. DeJuan Groce, DB, 1998. Groce was a *Plain Dealer* All-County selection and an AP All-District honoree as a two-way back and kick returner. After a solid college career at Nebraska, he was drafted by the Rams in the fourth round and has played with three NFL teams.

10. Bobby Adams, QB, 1994. Guided a St. Ed's team that pushed eventual national champions St. Ignatius to the limit before going down in triple-overtime, 35-34, in what many consider Cleveland's finest-ever prep football game. After being named best QB in *The Plain Dealer*'s seven-county coverage area his senior season, Adams played at Baldwin-Wallace, although Illinois had offered him a scholarship.

9. Tom Coughlin, QB/RB/TE, 1962. Probably the Eagles' first big-name player, Tom gained Catholic High School Player of the Year honors. He went on to become a three-year starter in college at Miami (Fla) back when you could only play three seasons in college.

8. Tom Cousineau, LB, 1975. One might think he's overrated here because of what he went on to accomplish in college and as a professional. But not anyone who saw him play in high school. Cousineau was a unanimous All-State and All-Scholastic selection his senior year at St. Ed's. After an intense recruiting battle between Woody Hayes, Bo Schembechler and Joe Paterno, Cousineau followed Woody to Columbus and became St. Ed's first alum to go on to claim All-American honors in college, a distinction he earned twice. In 1978, he broke the Buckeye record for tackles in one season with 211 and for one game with 29. The following year, Cousineau became the #1 overall pick in the NFL draft.

7. Paul Girgash, LB, 1979. After an All-State and All-Scholastic high-school career, Girgash went on to become a three-year starter and captain for the Michigan Wolverines. A bit undersized, he was one of the most passionate and hard-nosed players of his generation, both in high school and college.

6. Kevin Graven, RB/DB, 1981. Graven garnered All-State and All-Scholastic honors as a two-way mainstay in high school. He still holds the record for the longest touchdown run from scrimmage in the storied St. Edward-St. Ignatius rivalry. He galloped 86 yards for a score with 1:04 left as the Eagles defeated the Wildcats, 11-0, on

October 11, 1980. The 1980 "Holy War" was played in old Municipal Stadium as part of a doubleheader. (The other game saw Benedictine and Holy Name play to a 7-7 tie.) On a cold, rainy night, Graven navigated his way through the muddy Municipal Stadium field for 151 yards on 19 carries. He furthered his education and football career at Arizona State, where he twice earned Pac 10 Player-of-the-Week honors.

5. Kevin O'Keefe, OG, 1985. Kevin was and is an inspiration, as well as a dominating blocker. Despite playing with Hodgkin's Disease his senior season, he established himself as one of Ed's all-time best and won a scholarship to Michigan State. Health problems related to the disease cut short his Spartan career. Kevin still lives in his boyhood home.

4. Dan Andrews, RB, 1986. Danny was part of the legendary Andrews football family on Detroit Avenue in Lakewood, a clan that also featured his three brothers and started with his dad, Bob, Sr. A versatile back who could run, catch and throw, Danny remains one of the leading rushers in Eagles history. He earned All-Scholastic, and All-State honors his senior season.

3. Chris Williams, RB, 1987. In November of 1986, Chris put on one of the greatest offensive displays in the history of the OHSAA playoffs, racking up over 600 yards rushing in leading the Eagles to regional victories over Midpark and Berea. He finished the postseason with more than 1,000 yards rushing and was over 2,000 for the entire season. His efforts helped St. Edward advance to the 1986 Division I state championship game at Ohio Stadium in Columbus, where they lost to Fairfield, 21-20. Chris was a unanimous *Plain Dealer* All-Scholastic selection and earned District Player of the Year and All-State honors.

2. Rodney Bailey, DE. 1996. Rodney was the best player on the field in St. Ed's 12-9 overtime victory over St. Igntaius in 1996. He sped through the wind and sleet to make tackles from sideline-to-sideline in Lakewood Stadium. Bailey's fierce pass rush led to a blocked punt and a second-quarter safety, and he also blocked a field-goal attempt in the second quarter. For his efforts, Bailey won Player of the Week from *The Plain Dealer* and later claimed the paper's Defensive Player of the Year award, as well as All-State honors.

1. Shaun Carney, QB, 2003. How good was Shaun Carney? He started at quarterback for St. Ed's in front of future Heisman winner Troy Smith in both his sophomore and junior seasons, causing Smith to transfer to Glenville during the winter of the 2000-01 school year. An unmatched leader and as gritty a signal-caller as a coach could hope for, Carney led the Eagles to playoff appearances in 2001 and 2002. An All-State and All-District honoree, he was named *The Plain Dealer*'s "Best of the Best" quarterback in 2002. Carney went on to the Air Force Academy, where he started as a freshman (the first Air Force QB to do so) in the Falcons' wishbone offense. In his final game, Carney ran for over 100 yards and two touchdowns while throwing for another as Air Force. Carney had the Falcons ahead of favored Cal late in the third quarter of the Armed Forces Bowl when he tore up his knee on a goal-line play. How tough was Shaun Carney? He refused to be taken off on the motorized cart and instead walked, proudly, to the sideline, with the assistance of two teammates.

The Indians' play-by-play man doesn't go "waaaay back" in the manner of his home run call. But he reaches the warning track for sure. "Hammy" has been behind the mic calling Indians games since 1990, serving seven years as Herb Score's sidekick and the last 11 as the "Voice of the Tribe." He injects the quick-paced excitement of college basketball, his second love, into the big moments in the slower tempo of a baseball game. The four-time Ohio Broadcaster of the Year winner has become a Cleveland institution and offers a list of his most memorable games broadcasting for another local institution—the Indians.

10. Indians 9, Toronto 8, 1995. Paul Sorrento's walk-off homer in the ninth won it after the Indians had fallen behind, 8-0 to Yankees starter David Cone. At that time, David Cone was as good as you could get. That game was the first of that season's many walk-off homers by the Indians to cap incredible comebacks. It typified what 1995 would be all about.

9. The first game at Jacobs Field, 1994, Indians 4, Mariners 3 (11 innings). President Bill Clinton threw out the first pitch, but only after (Tribe Vice President) Bob DiBiasio advised him to warm up wearing a jacket because of the cold weather. Clinton, in the indoor batting cages, had been warming up in his shirtsleeves. Bobby told him, "It's going to be different in a jacket. You better get used to it." Wayne Kirby was the unlikely guy who got the winning hit. What I remember most was former Indians great Bob Feller pacing around the corridor outside the press box. He had pitched the only Opening Day no-hitter in history and he didn't want Marines' starter Randy Johnson to no-hit us.

8. Game 5, 1997 AL Division Series, Indians 4, Yankees 3. I grew up in Wisconsin, but it wasn't hard to see how much it meant to the people of Cleveland after years and years of losing to New York. The Yankees were the defending World Series champions, and the reaction to winning that series from them was so powerful that I think it was equated to winning the World Series. I think people just thought the Indians were going to beat Baltimore after that, no matter how improbable that looked, too. And the Indians did it at home. Not too many teams lately have won anything big at home.

7. Game 2, 1997 ALCS, Indians 5, Orioles 4. Marquis Grissom had the flu and was in danger of being dehydrated. He was hooked up to IVs in the trainer's room, then came out and hit the three-run homer off Armando Benitez that completely changed that series.

6. Game 7, 1997 World Series, Marlins 3, Indians 2 (11 innings). "Game 7" is the most magical term there is for a broadcaster. Game 7 of the World Series is what you're in it to do. It was such an emotional game and an extra-innings game, too. Tony Fernandez was the goat with the error in the 11th, but he was also the only reason the club ever scored with a two-run single. Grover (manager Mike Hargrove) gave the ball to Jaret Wright instead of Charlie Nagy because he thought Wright was better at that time, which was a very gutsy decision. Sandy Alomar, Jr. had his greatest year and then went in standing up at the plate in the eighth, when that run could have meant so much. Except for Jose Mesa and the ending, it was everything I thought it would be.

5. Game 6, 1997 World Series, Indians 4, Marlins 1. Omar Vizquel made the greatest play in World Series history that's not talked about, with his diving stop in the hole with runners on second and third in the sixth and then threw Charles Johnson out for the third out. Chad Ogea won his second game of the Series and Chad went 2-for-3 with a double, driving in two runs off Kevin Brown. It was just great entertainment.

4. Game 6, 1997 ALCS, Indians 1, Orioles 0 (11 innings). There was the "wheel" play in the seventh inning on Robbie Alomar's bunt, and Matt Williams got the lead runner at third. There was the fact that Mike Mussina was virtually unhittable (1 hit in 81/3 innings) and Charlie Nagy was in trouble every inning (7 hits, 9 innings) and always worked out of it. That said so much about Charlie. But what I remember most is how much it meant to Herb Score. He was always so laid back, but he got out of his chair as he was calling Tony Fernandez's home run.

3. Game 1, 1995 AL Division Series, Indians 4, Boston 3 (12 innings). People forget that John Valentin had homered for Boston in the top of the 11th and that Albert Belle tied it in the bottom half before Tony Pena won it in the 12th. I've always wondered how it would have worked out if the Indians had lost that game. It would have changed the entire dynamic of their first postseason series since 1954.

2. Game 6, 1995 ALCS , Indians 4, Mariners 1. It won the first pennant since 1954 so it was enormous to the people in Cleveland. I will always remember Kenny Lofton coming around to score from second base. To this day, I couldn't tell you if it was a passed ball or a wild pitch. The game was over when Lofton scored (for a 3-1 lead). I remember being so happy for Herb. I don't think anyone alive had seen more bad baseball than Herb Score.

1. Season opener, 1990, ppd, snow. Nothing ever tops your first game in the big leagues—and this was my first regular season game as a big league announcer. Or it was supposed to be. I had just gotten to Cleveland and we were living in a condo downtown. It was really cold, and you could see chunks of ice bobbing in the lake. My son Nick was five months old, and you know how that goes. He cried all night, which meant neither my wife Wendy nor I got any sleep. We get to the old stadium and, here it is, my debut in the bigs. And a blizzard moves in off the lake and wipes out the game in the fourth inning. Wendy said to me as we left, "We aren't going to have another night like that, are we?"

Five Things Other Than Rain That Stopped Indians' Games

Talk about plagues! We've had swarms of gnats. We've had locusts (the Yankees, who used the Indians as a farm team for years). We've had drunks. On the bright side, we haven't seen the Cuyahoga's waters turn to blood. But on several occasions, Cleveland sporting events have turned into sneak previews of the apocalypse with outbreaks of strange phenomena, leading to delays, cancellations and forfeitures.

5. Snow. The entire home-opening series against Seattle in 2007 was snowed out. Over two feet of the stuff fell during the first week of April. The "home" opener migrated to Milwaukee's Miller Park, a stadium with a retractable roof. The Indians were also the "home" team in a make-up game in Seattle later that season.

4. Fog. As noted elsewhere in this book, Mel Hall could have at least tried to "cowboy up" when sent out to center field as a guinea pig to shag flies in the thick fog for a 1986 game against the Red Sox. Mel's pronounced instinct of self-preservation led him almost to adopt the fetal position on the outfield grass as the unseen ball hurtled his way. It also led to an early end of the game with Boston winning and to Dennis "Oil Can" Boyd's famous 'putting a ballpark on an ocean' comment.

3. Midges. The little flying insects have caused temporary halts in a number of early-summer baseball games. But for Cleveland, they decided to return in early autumn as well. On October 4, 2007, fooled by a freakish hot spell into thinking June was bustin' out all over, the midge hordes invaded the Jake, drawn by the lights of the park and the sweat of the players. In particular, they unnerved Yankee reliever Joba Chamberlain. Driven "buggy," Chamberlain threw two wild pitches, allowing the Indians to force extra innings in the division series playoff game and win 2-1 in 11 innings. New York writers whined that play should have been stopped due to the midges. But Fausto Carmona pitched nine strong innings for Cleveland, unfazed by the bugs. When you grew up in the Dominican Republic, as Carmona did, you have seen worse th ings flying through the air at you.

2(a). "Midgets." *Akron Beacon Journal* sportswriter Sheldon Ocker was infamously victimized by his paper's copy editing desk in the 90s when he wrote, "Swarms of midges invaded Jacobs Field last night and temporarily halted play." The paper's copy editor changed it to—wait for it—"swarms of midgets"! Veteran press boxers risked rupture of internal organs by trying not to laugh out loud the next day when Ocker berated the editor responsible by screaming: "Now why in hell would you think midgets invaded Jacobs Field." But we digress, the real second choice is . . .

2. Mike Hargrove. We'll never pass up a shot to have fun with the "Human Rain Delay," Dudley Michael Hargrove (with his stalling and fussing tactics every time he stepped into, and out of, the batter's box) added more minutes to Indians' games over the years than pitching changes. Hargrove spawned a number of spiritual descendants, including Manny Ramirez, who habitually straps and re-straps his batting gloves, and Albert Belle, who sacrificed the back line of the batter's box to the deity of delay by carefully erasing it, again and again, with a pawing foot. Remember, there's no clock in baseball. It's part of its charm.

1. Drunks. An ill-fated Stroh's promotion drew a crowd of over 25,000 (during a season when the Indians averaged fewer than 8,000) to the old stadium for Ten-Cent Beer Night on June 4, 1974 and a game against the Texas Rangers. Ten ounces of beer for 10 cents. It turned out to be the going price for civic dignity. As the game in Cleveland wore on, the crowd got more unruly. A large woman jumped into the Indians' on-deck circle in the second inning and flashed her breasts. In the fourth, a naked man slid into second base as Texas' Tom Grieve circled the bags with his second homer of the game. In the fifth, a father-son duo ran to the infield and mooned the crowd. A steady stream of interlopers menaced the Rangers' Jeff Burroughs in right field. In the ninth, after the Indians rallied to tie the score at 5-5, fans pelted the field with rocks, batteries, and anything else that came to hand. Rangers first baseman Mike Hargrove (yes, that guy) was almost hit by a thrown jug of Thunderbird wine. Eventually, someone ran out and stole Burroughs' glove. Burroughs chased the drunk back into the stands. Then fans stormed the field, needing only pitchforks and burning torches to complete the scene. Out charged frequently deranged Texas manager Billy Martin, holding a bat and leading his team on a mission to right field to rescue Burroughs. Hargrove swore he saw the bat later and it was broken. Asked about the crowd, umpire Nestor Chylak who stopped the game in the ninth and awarded a forfeit win to Texas, said: "I never saw anything like that except in a zoo."

Cleveland teams have enough trouble winning when they are healthy. And when they are winning and on the brink of glory, their key players have a knack for suffering devastating injuries. Here's an unlucky thirteen, plus one, of the worst.

14. Zeus takes a thunderbolt to the face. In 1999, hulking Orlando "Zeus" Brown, a seven-year NFL veteran at offensive tackle for the Browns, was accidentally struck in the right eye by the tip of a penalty flag, weighted with BBs, thrown by referee Jeff Triplett. Known as "Zeus" for his 6-foot-7, 365-pound, blot-out-the-sun size, an enraged Brown shoved Triplett to the turf and was suspended for the remainder of the season. Brown, whose father Claude lost his sight because of glaucoma, remained in both physical and emotional pain from the bizarre accident. Still, the national media lapdogs for the NFL, harping on a Sports Illustrated item in which Brown was called "the dirtiest player in the NFL," vilified him. Nothing much happened to Triplett, although Brown, who suffered serious damage to his eye and had to spend four years of his prime rehabbing, received a reported $25 million settlement from the NFL. Zeus kept himself in shape and finally was able to return to the NFL. His revival would have been a sight for sore eyes, except the team he signed with was the Baltimore Ravens.

13. LeCharles Bentley's 2004 knee injury. The Cleveland native won Sports Illustrated's 2002 NFL Offensive Rookie of the Year award as a guard playing with the New Orleans Saints, along with a spot in the Pro Bowl. The versatile St. Ignatius High grad earned a second Pro Bowl berth after switching to center for the Saints in 2004. Then he came to the Browns. The sputtering franchise wanted to rebuild their offensive line around free agent Bentley—a hope that lasted only until summer training camp's first 11-on-11 drill when Bentley snapped his patellar tendon. Four knee operations and two seasons of rehab later, the Ohio State grad who seemed on his way to Canton still hasn't found his way back onto the field. The hardworking Bentley may yet play, but it's hard to imagine him approaching the high level he competed at before the injury.

12. John Smiley's 1997 broken arm. Warming up is designed to help pitchers avoid injury. But shortly after putting on an Indians uniform, lefty hurler John Smiley somehow suffered a broken arm while warming up for his first start since being traded from the Reds. The Indians hoped the two-time All Star would help solidify their starting rotation for another run at the World Series. But Smiley never pitched again.

11. Mark Carreon's 1996 leg injury. It seemed innocuous enough when the Indians' starting first baseman fouled a ball off his shin during the '96 season. But the resulting injury knocked Carreon out of the division series vs. the Orioles and forced manager Mike Hargrove to play Jeff Kent out of position at first base. Kent couldn't handle a short-hopped throw from Sandy Alomar, Jr. on a potential double-play ball in the division series, allowing the go-ahead run to score from second base and Baltimore to break open a tie game with a three-run, eighth-inning rally. The O's closed out the game to take a 2-0 series lead over the soon-to-be-excused 1996 Indians.

10. Mark Price's 1990 torn ACL. The Cavs undermined their status as title contenders by trading Ron Harper for Danny Ferry in 1989. But then their hopes of even being a playoff contender ended early the following season when Price stepped on the cylinder that made different advertising signs revolve into view at courtside in Atlanta and ripped up his knee. The Cavs finished the season 33-49. The night Wayne Embry traded Harper, he called Bill Livingston and former Cavs beat man for *The Plain Dealer* Burt Graeff over to a table at the University Club where the deal was announced. Everyone ordered drinks. Embry drained his Absolut vodka on the rocks in one gulp, then shivered, like a bear climbing out of an icy stream. Neither reporter was around Embry the night Price got hurt, but I'd put the chances of Embry draining an adult beverage or two in response as an "Absolut certainty."

9. Pete Rose making road pizza of Ray Fosse in 1970. The media shills who failed to notice all the cracks in the Pete Rose myth tried to spin this as just a great example of Charlie Hustle's drive. Actually, Rose began to lose his balance as he neared home plate and the head-long, full-speed, blindside crash into Fosse was as much a result of nearly falling on his deceitful mug as it was of reclaiming the "hardball" ethos of the past. The collision separated Fosse's shoulder and effectively ended his run as one of the best catchers in baseball. Fosse gained some revenge years later when Rose was sentenced to five months for tax evasion in a federal penitentiary in Marion, Illinois—Ray Fosse's hometown.

8. Larry Hughes' 2007 left foot sprain. The delicate, would-be sidekick to LeBron James was always injury-prone. But Hughes won the respect of his Cavs teammates, fans and reporters by gutting it out with a torn plantar fascia in his left foot in the upset of Detroit in the Eastern Conference Finals in 2007. He actually did a good job covering Detroit's Chauncey Billups, an outside bomber and former Finals MVP whose ability to post up was negated by Hughes' strength. It was unfair to ask a hobbled Hughes to then try to guard the Spurs' Tony Parker, one of the quickest point guards in the league, in The Finals, especially given the development of teammate Boobie Gibson. But that's exactly what coach Mike Brown did. Which is one reason why few people think Mike Brown is an elite coach. Hughes lasted part of two games in the Finals, then went to the bench because the only other option was the glue factory.

7. Brad Daugherty's 1994 back injury. He came to the team at the age of 21 as the first overall pick in the 1986 NBA draft, looking like he would be a force in the paint until the turn of the century. But in Cleveland appearances are often deceiving. Surgery failed to alleviate the pain from two herniated disks that were pressing on the lower back nerves of the best all-around center the Cavs ever put on the floor. The five-time All Star's most serious basketball after that might have been during a cameo appearance along with several teammates in the mercifully forgotten Whoopi Goldberg movie Eddie.

6. Joe Charboneau's 1980 back injury. The ultimate one-year wonder, Charboneau claimed AL Rookie of the Year honors in 1980 with 23 homers and 87 RBI. He also established himself as one of the game's leading flakes by opening beer bottles with his eye socket, drinking the beer through a straw inserted in his nose and eating cigarettes. But his play and poetic last name inspired great hope and even song. "Who's the newest guy in town? Go Joe Charboneau! Turns the ballpark upside down. Go Joe Charboneau! Who's the one to keep our hopes alive? Straight from seventh to the pennant drive. Raise your glass, let out a cheer for Cleveland's Rookie of the Year!" Those were the lyrics Indians fans sang for one hopeful season. There was no second verse to Charboneau's career, though.

5. Bernie Kosar's shoulder injury in 1988. Chiefs' linebacker Derek Thomas' sack on a blitz eventually turned Kosar from a Browns legend leading them toward the Super Bowl into just another quarterback. It was a clean, but vicious blindside hit as Kosar was throwing. Eventually veteran QB Don Strock was signed and managed to coax the Browns into the playoffs, where they lost, 24-23 in the wild-card game to Houston. Kosar would have returned to the lineup the next week, had they won. Bernie made it back for the next season, his only good one after the injury.

4. Zydrunas Ilgauskas' broken foot in 2000. Z had already missed almost 300 games due to foot problems since coming to the Cavs in 1996. But this was the injury that almost forced the Lethal Lithuanian into retirement. After a procedure that included breaking the heel bone to lower the angle of Z's foot, he returned, clanking with surgical screws like Frankenstein's monster with the neck bolts. But against the odds and past history, he regained his form and has remained relatively healthy since, providing the Cavs with one of the league's most reliable low-post scorers and rebounders. LeBron James justifiably gets the credit for the Cavs' recent renaissance. But it is worth noting that the first player he hugged when the Cavs overcame the Pistons in the 2007 Eastern Conference Finals was Z.

3. Herb Score's broken face in 1957. A left-handed starter with a nasty fastball, the Indians' Score might have become the American League's Sandy Koufax. But Gil McDougald's line drive changed that. Score, who led the AL in strikeouts his first two seasons, finished his pitching motion with his eyes rolling upward, making it difficult for him to pick up the ball off the bat. So he never knew what hit him when the Yankees' McDougald lined a fastball back at the mound on May 7th of 1957. Score missed the rest of the season due to numerous broken bones in his face and blurred vision. He tried to return the following year with an adjusted pitching motion. But he was never the same.

2. Jim Chones' 1976 broken foot. The day before the NBA's Eastern Conference Finals began, Cavs' center Chones came down on a teammate's foot in practice and was done. Nate Thurmond had to play too many minutes and couldn't hold up against an aggressive Boston front line composed of Dave Cowens, Paul Silas and Don Nelson. With Chones, the Cavs probably would have brought a title home to Cleveland that season. We're still waiting.

1. Ray Chapman killed by pitch in 1920. The sidearm offering from Yankees starter Carl Mays crushed Chapman's skull and ended his life the next day when the Indians starting shortstop died in the hospital after failing to regain consciousness. It should have also ended the Indians' drive for their first pennant. But Joe Sewell took over at shortstop for Chapman and became a Hall of Famer. With the late-season suspension of the "Black Sox" who had conspired to throw the previous year's World Series, the Tribe rallied to win the pennant and the World Series. Still, the season's enduring memory was of the 29-year-old Chapman laying unconscious at home plate. Like Dale Earnhardt, Sr.'s violent demise at the Daytona 500 eight decades later, Chapman's shocking death led to many rules revisions, including the removal of balls from play after they become dirty or misshapen. He remains the only MLB player to have died due to an injury suffered during a game.

Colorful guys brimming with talent for outrageous quotes and antics always attract the interests of the fans and the media. Unfortunately, their palettes often fade to beige and their vocabularies diminish to "uh" and "oops" once they get on the court or playing field. Here are some of Cleveland's feckless flakes, listed, not by rank of eccentricity or interview intrigue, just in an order as random as their thought processes.

8. Jody Gerut. The former Tribe outfielder discussed who Argus (a mythical monster with 100 eyes) was in a memorable conversation with Bill.

7. Edgar Jones. The story goes that he showed up at UNLV, even though his scholarship was to Nevada-Reno. A man can get his gambling towns confused, so it's just fortunate that the University of Nevada didn't have a branch campus in Monte Carlo. The on-court highlight of Jones' brief career as a Cavalier forward was tying for fifth in the NBA's 1984 slam-dunk contest, during which he may have made more baskets than during the rest of his two years with the Cavs. Off the court, he established himself as the go-to guy in the interview room, offering such quotes as "I'm not talking anymore. That's it. No more words. It's over. Wanna know the deal? Mum is the word here. My game talks and conversation walks. It's just that I'm basically a quiet guy who keeps to himself. I don't like to talk. Mum's the word," said Jones, in the most garrulous vow of silence since Bugs Bunny was warned to "shuddup shutting up." Then there was his immortal: "A man has to know his limitations, and I don't have any."

6. "Touchdown Tommy" Vardell. Hailed as "the next Kevin Mack," he scored five TDs in four inconsequential seasons, defying the raves heaped upon him in college by Sports Illustrated's Doug Looney. Movie-star handsome and well-spoken, this Stanford grad might have been the prototype, albeit at a different position, for Brady Quinn. Time will tell.

5. Casey Candaele. The Tribe utility player was known for sitting on a dining tray and sliding down the aisle of the Tribe's jet as it climbed during takeoffs. He also occasionally took batting practice naked, although not with the Indians. He said just the possibility of foul tips tended to concentrate the mind wonderfully. As an Astro, he tried to cash in on the memorabilia craze by announcing that he was selling used sunflower seeds, personally chewed and ejected by future Hall of Famer Craig Biggio.

4. Jeremy Sowers. Tribe pitcher and former political science major from Vanderbilt tossed references to Aristotle, John Locke or a Founding Father or two into his conversation as often as he tossed distressingly fat pitches to opposing batters.

3. Earthwind Moreland, Browns DB. Lasted only the 2001 season. One supposes he lacked fire.

2. The immortal Dave Bresnahan. On Aug. 28, 1987, Bresnahan morphed from a light-hitting, low-minor league catcher with the Indians' Williamsport, Pa. farm team into a legend as "Mr. Potato Head." With a Reading Phillie perched on third base, Bresnahan called time, saying his catcher's mitt was broken. He returned from the dugout with a peeled potato of almost exactly the same size as the baseball hidden in the mitt. After the next pitch, he fired the potato into left field, ostensibly attempting to pick off the runner, who then ran toward home, only to be tagged out by Bresnahan, who had diabolically kept the real baseball hidden in his mitt. Pulled from the game by his manager, Bresnahan, a distant relative of Hall of Fame catcher Roger Bresnahan, was soon cut by the Indians. Tribe bosses harrumphed and said Bresnahan wasn't supposed to make a mockery of the game, they could do that just fine by themselves. (Just kidding about everything following the last comma, although it was true.)

1. Joe Charboneau. He went 3-for-3 in his first major league game with the Indians, including a homer in his first at-bat. He went on to hit .289 with 23 homers and claim Rookie of the Year honors for the strike-shortened 1980 season. Then during spring training the following year, Charboneau suffered a serious back injury while making a head-first slide, and never fully recovered. But while "Super Joe" could actually play more than a little bit on the field, he still got more attention horsing around in the clubhouse. He dyed his hair strange colors years before anyone had heard of Dennis Rodman. He could open beer bottles with his eye socket and then slurp the suds up with a straw through his nose. He claimed that he had fixed his broken nose with a set of pliers and performed his own dental work with same set of "yank' ems." He also reportedly was stabbed in the side by an autograph seeker with a ballpoint pen, then removed the writing implement and gave the person his John Hancock, presumably signed in blood. How much of this was true, as opposed to fables attached to the "Super Joe" myth? Enough that his release by the Indians before the 1984 season made a whole city want to snort a beer in salute.

Note: If he hadn't grown to 6-11 and could have fit into a roll cage after squeezing through a car window, Big Brad might have turned into the next Dale Earnhardt. Daugherty even wore No. 43 throughout his NBA career in tribute to "The King." No, not LeBron James. This is good ol' boy royalty he was talking about—NASCAR legend Richard Petty. Fortunately for us, the Black Mountain, North Carolina native chose NBA night games over "Talladega Nights." But the lifelong NASCAR fan always kept in touch with the sport. And fortunately for us again, Daugherty has shared his insights and vast knowledge of the sport through this list of NASCAR'S best drivers.

5. Tony Stewart. This guy reminds me a lot of A.J. Foyt. He can be ornery. He is a great driver, but he also has a lot of energy, a lot of piss and vinegar, and that is what makes him who he is. When Tony races, he's not out there to make friends or even to find a drafting partner. He's just out there to win.

4. Cale Yarborough. I loved watching him drive. He was a little guy, no neck, sitting in one of those big old cars with no power steering, bouncing around in that seat. But he was competitive as all get-out. He was the one who had a fistfight with Donnie Allison in the first-ever, nationally-televised NASCAR race (in 1979), introducing the rest of America to the culture of the Southeast.

3. Jeff Gordon. He's moving into position to be the greatest of all-time. Now, the NASCAR record of 200 wins will never be eclipsed, even by Gordon. But the sport has changed so much since Richard Petty's day. Gordon's ability in a race car is just remarkable. The only thing that keeps him from being as good as Dale Earnhardt, Sr. was Earnhardt's ability to win in a bad race car. People said Jeff Gordon was just a creation of his crew chief (Ray Evernham), but they were wrong. If you give Gordon a chance, he'll drive the wheels off that car to win.

2. Richard Petty. Everything he achieved in the sport speaks for itself. As in: 200 WINS! But "The King" did so much more for the sport. There was his demeanor, his interaction with the fans, the way he represented the sport. Earnhardt, Sr. was the best I ever saw, but Richard Petty was the sport's Arnold Palmer. He was loved by everyone and popularized NASCAR.

1. Dale Earnhardt, Sr. An iconic figure in the sport, "The Intimidator" boasted unbelievable ability in a race car. Nowadays, the cars are so dialed in that if they're not set up right, drivers don't seem to be able to overcome it. Ninety percent of the time they are dialed in. Dale Earnhardt was the first guy I ever saw who could take a bad car and get it up to the top five. And if Earnhardt got into the top five, the other drivers knew they were going to have to drive like hell to keep him from winning. Dale was coming after them.

Note: Elton Alexander probably drinks Valvoline instead of orange juice in the morning. The longtime *Plain Dealer* auto race writer and car expert has covered every Cleveland Indy car race at the Burke Lakefront Airport since they began under the title of Budweiser Cleveland 500 back in 1982. The race's usually top-notch field, along with its unusual track conditions (the site was designed to land airplanes on, not race cars), have led to a number of thrilling events over the years.

5. 2003. In the first (and, to date, only) night race in Cleveland, rookie Sebastien Bourdais overcame late-race contact with another driver that sent him into the marbles and cut his tires to make a last-lap trophy dash and win under the lights.

4. 1993. Paul Tracy was the easy winner, but nobody noticed. Fans focused on a race-long, back-and-forth battle for second place between two former Formula One champions, Nigel Mansel and Emerson Fittipaldi. "Emmo" won out with Mansell finishing third.

3. 1985. Mario Andretti had the dominant car all race, building a 36-second advantage over the field, when his engine blew four laps from the checkered flag, paving the way for Al Unser, Jr. to snatch the victory.

2. 1983. The second Grand Prix of Cleveland proved to be the last run at 500 kilometers as the oppressive, 100+ degrees heat on the track forced drivers to abandon their cars in the middle of the race. Tony Bettenhausen was knocked unconscious by heat exhaustion and Kevin Cogan (for Desiree Wilson) became the last relief driver ever in an open wheel race. Al Unser, Sr. won.

1. 1988. Three former Indy 500 winners, Mario Andretti, Bobby Rahal and Danny Sullivan, battled nose-to-tail, side-by-side for the final ten laps before Andretti emerged the winner by .91 of a second.

Note: Jim Tressel has established himself as one of the greatest coaches in Ohio history in any sport. Beginning as an assistant at the University of Akron, the University of Miami (of Ohio) and Ohio State, he took his first head-coaching job in 1985 at Youngstown State, where he went on to win four Division I-AA national football championships. Since becoming head coach at Ohio State in 2001, Tressel has guided the Buckeyes to four Big Ten titles, three national title games and an undisputed national championship. He has won over 80 percent of his games and, most importantly, racked up a 6-1 record vs. that school up north. A native of Mentor, Ohio, Tressel grew up in Berea rooting for the Browns and has remained a lifelong fan. Until Romeo Crennel got the Browns turned around in the 2007 season and Tressel lost the opportunity to buy his way out of his Ohio State contract after Florida shocked the heavily-favored Buckeyes in the BCS Championship Game earlier that year, it seemed possible that Tressel might actually become the Browns coach. Paul Brown, who made the same career move, has always been one of his idols. Tressel has gained plenty of more idols and favorites in his years as a Browns fan.

6. Ernie Kellerman, safety. He was a very good safety for the Browns. I got to know him when I was at Miami of Ohio. He was a college quarterback at Miami and he handled our alumni recruiting. I really got to know him when he helped us recruit players. He, like all these guys, has been a big success in many facets of life.

5. Jim Houston, defensive end. He is one of those solid, solid guys in life. He was probably a little unsung on those great Browns' defenses of the 60s. There wasn't as much analysis and replay and things like that then. But he was tough when he took the field. Let me tell you, he is a patriot. Many mornings, I wake up and he has forwarded something inspirational to me.

4. Paul Warfield, wide receiver. I remember him more with the Browns than as a Buckeye. He was just so graceful running those post patterns. He was so humble as a person, yet was this unbelievable athlete. Paul is as graceful a gentleman as he was a player.

3. Dick Schafrath. He succeeded Groza, who became a kicker only, at left tackle and stayed there for 12 straight years, including the 1964 championship season. Just a great Buckeye, and that includes his Cleveland Browns days and when he was a state senator. His roots run so deep in Ohio that he came back and got his Ohio State degree two summers ago. Some of our players would talk to him after they were in the same class with him. What sticks with me is how he said that even though he had been a senator and a member of an NFL championship team, the day he stood in that Horseshoe to get his degree in front of his seven children and 18 grandchildren was the best day he ever had.

2. Jim Brown, running back. Paul Brown and Art Modell made sure that local coaches and their families could get tickets to games. We couldn't go until the final games of the season because my dad's season hadn't ended. I remember watching Jim Brown run in that old Stadium. I idolized him. He was just the ultimate warrior. What's interesting is how much he revered his teammates. But more than football, Jimmy always had had a deep concern for mankind. He has done tremendous good working with gangs.

1. Lou Groza, kicker, offensive tackle. To me, he was always "Mr. Groza." His son Jeff and I were in the same class in high school. He had a great sense of humor, but he was very serious about his craft. I used to hold for him when he practiced kicking, and they didn't use a tee, you just placed it on the grass. So it had to be perfect. He had that big, square-toed shoe because he was a straight-ahead kicker. You know how they say the ball sounds different coming off a great hitter's bat in baseball? It was like that when Lou Groza kicked a football, like an explosion.

The Ohio State coach grew up in Berea, where he would watch the annual Ohio State-Michigan showdown with his father, Lee, a national championship coach at Baldwin-Wallace College. It was the only game he could watch with his father, who was occupied with his own coaching tasks on Saturdays until B-W's season was over. The names Tressel chose for this list appear in no particular order. We have numbered them this way solely for convenience.

3. Rex Kern, quarterback. He was simply my idol. I thought if you could be like him, you had everything you would need. He was a great ball-handler as a quarterback, but it went beyond that. Kern was a leader, a winner. I felt that way even before I met him. After meeting him, I fully realized what a special guy he is. (Author's note: Tressel wore a Number 10 Kern jersey as a kid.)

2. Jack Tatum, defensive back. We named the "Hit of the Week" the "Jack Tatum Hit of the Week Award" when my staff and I came to Ohio State. Every time Jack talks to the players, you can see them, gripping onto every word he says. They've seen the film clips. He's famous to them. Also, he just has great spirit, even through all his health issues. When he lost a leg, it was not going to keep him down. Shortly after he got his prosthetic one, he was at practice. He wanted everyone to see that he could overcome that.

1. Archie Griffin, running back. He was playing in Columbus when I was playing at Baldwin-Wallace. He wasn't just a great football player, he was a guy who truly was selfless. Archie was always deferring to his teammates. He lobbied for Corny Greene to be Big Ten Player of the Year in 1975—the year that Archie won the Heisman!

This list shouldn't have been that hard, but you know how it usually goes with things that shouldn't be that hard. Tough final cuts included: Mike Brown, the only coach to reach the NBA Finals with the Cavaliers, but one who doomed them to be swept aside by the Spurs with his Hoops 101 offense; Sam Rutigliano, who, just as he always claimed, really was good for Cleveland, but who also lost his biggest playoff game—at home; Mike Fratello, who won a lot of games with subpar Cavs teams, but who showed no shame about winning some of them 66-62, and we can't forgive that because pro basketball is supposed to be entertainment, too.

But it's no shame to be left off this list when you consider that its topped by the guy who invented the modern form of the game on which the country obsesses. Still, he may not even be familiar to some younger football fans because it's been a long time since he was sending in plays from the sidelines via messenger guards. How long? His Cleveland Browns ranked as the most dominant team in pro football—for years. And, no, those years did not have B.C.s attached to them.

10. Eric Wedge, Indians (2003-). Okay, maybe the farm system bailed Wedge out in 2007. And he is guilty of running off a fine young player (Brandon Phillips). And of being asleep at the switch with his situational relievers. And shouldn't they just call Wichita State "Casey Blake U." if Wedge insists on playing his fellow alum as much as he does? Still, the Indians had only a pittance to spend compared to the payroll of the Yankees and Red Sox, and they took down the former and almost whipped the latter. Sabathia and Carmona helped, but through WedgeSpeak he hypnotized the team into a state of intense focus. He got them to ramp it up, think in terms of situations, envison best case scenarios, go through the process, take command and . . . quick, somebody snap their fingers, he's got me, too.

9. Marty Schottenheimer, Browns (1984-88). He was corny. He was sentimental. He couldn't win the big one. But he could get you to it. Browns games haven't had nearly the gleam and importance since Marty left.

8. Bill Fitch, Cavs (1970-79). He endured a lot of rebuilding projects, coached a lot of great players, won a lot of games (944) and lost a lot more (1,106). Fitch was Old School, and modern players often need a primer course in Remedial Professionalism. You miss him when the team fails to execute some fundamental. Like when no Cavs player retaliated on Rasheed Wallace for busting Z's head open a couple of years ago, leaving Z to knock Wallace down himself in the rematch a few days later. Cavs analyst Austin Carr grumpily noted: "Fitch would have fined everyone of us."

7. Lenny Wilkens, Cavs (1986-93). We didn't like the excuses either, but if it hadn't been for overreacting owner Gordon Gund (the Ron Harper trade), Mark Price's groin pull late in the 1989 season, and that Jordan fellow, Lenny's Cavs would have hung a championship banner or two.

6. Al Lopez, Indians (1951-56). He had great pitching with the Big Four, and he finished second five times to the Yankees at their dynastic best. 111-and-43 ought to be what we remember him for, not "The Catch" and Dusty Rhodes.

5. Blanton Collier, Browns (1963-70). No, he wasn't "my best coach," as self-serving Art Modell maintained. But he was probably his second-best, behind the first coach Modell fired. Collier won with players he inherited. He also inherited an idiot owner looking over his shoulder. Like Mike Brown with LeBron, he knew how to amicably co-exist with the game's reigning superstar (Jim Brown). Under Paul Brown, Collier's predecessor, player relations barely mattered—the coach always had the last word. Collier gave the players a bigger say and they responded. And how can you not score Collier pretty high in the ranks of Cleveland coaches? He was the last one to bring home the bacon.

4. Tris Speaker, Indians (1919-26). He kept the 1920 Indians together after shortstop Ray Chapman was beanballed to death during the season and while game-fixing allegations regarding their rivals, the Chicago White Sox, from the previous World Series threatened to turn the pennant race into an orgy of sensationalism. He also had to manage a new ballgame with the lively ball, all while playing a pretty fair center field.

3. Mike Hargrove, Indians (1991-99). Too high? Consider that he never had the great pitching that made Lopez before him and Joe Torre (concurrent with him) look like geniuses. He also had to control the egos of a very volatile clubhouse, led by a Vesuvius with legs named Albert Belle. A whip and a chair was the only way to handle some of those guys, but Hargrove still tamed and herded them into two World Series. His second World Series team in 1997 might have been the least-talented of any from 1994 until the end of Hargrove's tenure, and yet they came the closest of any to breaking the spell.

2. Lou Boudreau, Indians (1942-50). With everything on the line in the 1948 playoffs and Fenway's Green Monster looking to gobble up routine fly balls to left and spit them out as doubles and home runs, he went with lefty Gene Bearden, a rookie knuckleballer pitching on one-day's rest. He stacked his lineup with righties to face Red Sox righthander Denny Galehouse. He put outfielder Allie Clark at first for the first four innings in the game. All those moves risked turning Lou Boudreau into a laughingstock. But they worked and got the Indians to the World Series, which they went on to win without a single "W" from Bob Feller. And the 31-year-old player-manger did it all while performing well enough in the field to claim the league's MVP award—a year after Tribe owner Bill Veeck tried to trade him.

1. Paul Brown, Browns (1946-62). Brown simply invented pro football as we now know it. Film study, IQ tests, facemasks, plays shuttled in from the sidelines by substitutes on every down, meticulously-timed practices—his inventions, one and all. So was racial integration. Only a 4-5 playoff mark in the NFL portion of his Browns coaching career mars his extraordinary record: 111-44-5 and three NFL titles; a preposterous 52-4-3 and four titles in as many years in the All-America Football Conference, Along the way, Brown mentored Chuck Noll, Bill Walsh, Don Shula, Weeb Ewbank, Sid Gillman, Ara Parseghian and Collier. After accomplishing all that, Art Modell showed him the door. But considering how the franchise lost its way shortly thereafter and is still wandering around the wilderness 40+ years later, being fired only increased Paul Brown's stature.

A Baker's Dozen Cleveland Coaches Who Became Famous Elsewhere

We don't just grow geniuses to guide our own teams to glory, we export them to the rest of the sports world. You'll find Super Bowl winners, coaches who broke Ohio State's heart and the biggest winner in pro football history in this list of the ones that got away from Cleveland. And those are just the football ones.

13. Norb Hecker. The Berea native made a game-saving tackle for the Los Angeles Rams in their 1951 NFL championship game win over the Browns. One of the great players in Baldwin-Wallace history, Hecker also was the first president of the NFL Players Association. As a coach, he served as an assistant to Vince Lombardi when the Packers were making "dynasty" the new catch word in football circles. He later assisted Bill Walsh with the San Francisco dynasty in the 1980s. After contributing to eight championship teams as a player or coach, Hecker began his only NFL head-coaching job inauspiciously in Atlanta when his kicker whiffed the opening kickoff in the exhibition opener. It ended badly too, as he compiled a 4-26-1 record. But his achievements as an assistant coach still earned him a spot on this list.

12. Flip Saunders. The Cuyahoga Falls native shepherded Kevin Garnett to superstardom in Minnesota, but never has advanced past the conference finals. Ironically, he took the Detroit job, and spurned the Cavaliers, because he thought it was the shortcut to the top. Braaack! Wrong answer! Allowing LeBron James to score 25 straight points in the pivotal fifth game of the 2007 conference finals and to score the winning basket without double-teaming him is a brain cramp Saunders will spend a long time shaking out.

11. Frank Solich. The day before the 1994 Orange Bowl (the one in which Nebraska should have beaten Bobby Bowden's first national championship Florida State team), Solich was almost quivering, like a tuning fork at a high pitch, The Holy Name legend and Nebraska assistant under Tom Osborne was ready to run out on the field himself to hit somebody with little tomahawks on his helmet. When Solich finally got his chance as the head man at his alma mater a few years later, he won three out of every four games for the Cornhuskers and played for and lost a national championship game. But that just wasn't enough for Steve Pederson, the mule-headed Athletic Director. Citing the need for a "change in direction," he fired Solich. Personnel change meant Bill Callahan. Directional change meant lopsided defeats and the end of Nebraska as a national power. It all led to the eventual firing of the man who fired Solich. In making Ohio University a winner for the first time since 1968 in his current job, Solich has showed everyone just how bad a decision Pederson made.

10. Les Miles. The Elyria native and two-year Michigan letterman was one of the hot names on the possible list of Lloyd Carr successors at his alma mater. He was known for winning his big game and spoiling Oklahoma's season when he was at Okie State, but his team quit on him against Ohio State in the 2004 Alamo Bowl when word leaked out that Miles' bags were packed for LSU. When Justin Zwick, on one leg, carves you up, folks, you have quit. At LSU, he lost the 2005 SEC Championship game big as a big favorite. Even with two losses, both in triple overtime, his 2007 team reached the

BCS Championship Game and, cheered on by a crazed Cajun crowd in the Louisiana Superdome, defeated Ohio State for the national title. We should be thankful Michigan athletic director Bill Martin couldn't figure out how to use his Blackberry in time to hire Miles.

9. Don James. The Massillon native coached Kent State to its only Mid-American Conference football championship, then won a half-share of a national championship at Washington. At Kent, he coached future Pro Football Hall of Famer Jack Lambert and also a kid from West Virginia who became pretty famous...

8. . . . and that kid was: Nick Saban. College football's equivalent of a traveling salesman, the young Saban took the Toledo head coaching job; left that after about five minutes to be one of Bill Belichick's assistants with the Browns; left that to go to Michigan State and spoil the 1998 national title dreams of Ohio State (who had a stronger team by far that season than their 2002 national champion club); left that the following year for LSU, where he won the more-recognized national championship award—the one that gives the crystal football to the winning team (USC won the writers' poll that season); left that for the Miami Dolphins; and left that to try to be the new Bear at Alabama. The "Nicktator" is flighty, but he can coach.

7. Don McCafferty. An 11-year assistant at Kent State, he played for Paul Brown at Ohio State. In 1970, he succeeded Don Shula as head coach of the Baltimore Colts, leading them to the NFL title. McCafferty remains the only first-year coach to win a Super Bowl. His easy-going personality relaxed the players after Shula's intensity, but he had his own core of toughness. When megalomaniacal Colts GM Joe Thomas ordered him to bench the great John Unitas, McCafferty refused and was fired with his dignity intact.

6. Jerry Tarkanian. "Tark the Shark" swam out of Euclid and has fond memories of Euclid Beach. The NCAA does not look upon him so fondly. He coached at three schools— Long Beach State, UNLV (where he won a national championship) and Fresno State. All went on probation for rules violations committed during Tarkanian's tenures. But he did win a lot of games at each stop and establish top programs at schools most hoops fans probably didn't even know fielded Division I teams. When he was not nervously chewing on a towel on the bench, Tark authored one of the great lines ever about the NCAA's protection of fat cats and its scapegoating of have-nots. "The NCAA," said Tark, "was so mad at Kentucky that they gave Cleveland State two more years' (probation)."

5. John Heisman. It tells you how distinguished the class is that the man for whom the top award in college football is named can't crack the top three. He invented the pulling guard tactic, championed the forward pass and won at Akron, Clemson, Auburn and George Tech—where Heisman ran off a 32-game unbeaten streak. His Rambling Wrecks once beat poor Cumberland College by a record 222-0, setting the precedent for stat-padding in routs that won the award named after him for too many ordinary players in the decades to come. Still, a win only counts as one win, regardless of the final score. And Heisman racked up 185 Ws during an era when college teams played less than ten games per season.

4. Bo Schembechler. The Barberton native learned at the feet of the best, Woody Hayes, then used his knowledge of how Woody worked to spring the biggest upset in the history of college football's greatest rivalry in 1969. The 24-12 Michigan victory over Ohio State in Ann Arbor ignited the 10-Year War—a decade of brutal Wolverines-Buckeyes end-of-regular-season showdowns that almost always had national title implications and always determined the Big Ten title. The day before Woody died in 1987, he traveled through the snow to Dayton to tell an audience how highly he esteemed Bo.

3. Jim Tressel. The Berea-born, Baldwin-Wallace-bred son of legendary B-W coach Lee Tressel is possibly the best coach Ohio State has ever had. Woody could stock-pile players to keep them away from Bo, not to mention all the Purdues and Northwesterns cluttering his schedule. Tressel coaches in the era of 85 scholarships and Appalachian State-over-Michigan upsets lurking around every corner. Was Craig Krenzel in the top 20 quarterbacks nationally in 2002? The top 30? Could anyone else have gotten a 14-0 season out of him? A four-time national champion at Youngstown State before getting his big break, Tressel beats the teams he's supposed to beat and many of those he's not.

2. Chuck Noll. The Benedictine grad served as a messenger guard for Paul Brown back before the Browns forgot how to win championships, Noll did not forget, going on to win four Super Bowls as head coach of the hated Steelers. He strategically shifted from power running to a bombs-away offense when the rules were changed to encourage passing. He did it all mostly with one cast of characters, or he would be No. 1.

1. Don Shula. Who else but The Jaw from John Carroll and Painesville could be No. 1, though? "Shoes" ranks as the winningest coach in NFL history with 328 victories and a mind-boggling .679 winning percentage. And he did it across 33 years with a lot of different players while adjusting to, or leading the way in, a half-dozen revolutions in playing styles. Shula did it with Larry Csonka's legs, then did it some more with Dan Marino's arm. He did it so adeptly in so many different ways that, in Bum Phillips' words, "he could take his'n and beat your'n and take your'n and beat his'n." An NFL icon, Shula began his head coaching career with Baltimore, losing the Super Bowl to the Jets in 1967, and ended it in Miami in 1995, still struggling, after many years of close-but-no-cigar futility with Marino, to win The Big One. But he won two Big Ones in-between and a whole mess of others.

Top Ten Reasons Why the "Genius" Label Didn't Stick to Bill Belichick in Cleveland

Was it that he hadn't figured out yet how to use a video camera? Probably not, because after the Partiots' Spygate scandal broke veteran Belichick aide Ernie Adams hinted, "You oughta see what we did in Cleveland." Actually, we Clevelanders know enough about what Mr. Bill did and didn't do in Cleveland. Still, we have accepted that despite his sorry tenure here, Bill Belichick will end up winning more Super Bowls than any other head coach. He may even claim more NFL titles than he won regular season games in his final, dismal 5-11 Browns campaign. We're Clevelanders. This stuff happens to us. And seeing a coach who failed miserably with the Browns marching toward Canton in a Patriots sweater doesn't hurt as much as watching Art Modell celebrating his Super Bowl triumph a few seasons after he hijacked our franchise to Baltimore. But the fiction that the Cleveland media got Belichick fired (Modell wasn't about to take the un-mediagenic Mr. Bill to the new market in Baltimore) or that we hid Belichick's genius under a bushel of dog bones has to be dispelled once and for all. Bill Belichick failed here because he was a young, first-time head coach who was finding his way under an impulsive, under-financed owner and lifelong Cleveland non-Super Bowl qualifier, Art Modell. And because over the course of five seasons from 1991-'95, he lost a lot more often than he won while committing a series of often bizarre blunders that undermined the idea that he was competent, much less an imminent coaching legend and genius. Here are some of the top reasons nobody ever used "Bill Belichick" and "Mensa" in the same sentence during his time in Cleveland.

10. Speaking skills? The head coach serves as the face and, more importantly, the voice of a football franchise. Belichick had two speaking modes: controlled mumble and profane outburst. The latter was nothing new for most reporters, who are not delicate souls. But it had no place on television, where it occasionally cropped up. Belichick also proved tone deaf when others tried to speak to him. Near Christmas one season, Belichick grimly manned the mic for his weekly radio show to discuss an upcoming game against the Houston Oilers. "Before I ask my question," said a caller, brightly, "I'd like to wish Bill and his staff 'Merry Christmas.'" This did not compute. The caller wasn't asking Belichick about getting pressure on Warren Moon or the drawbacks of the run-and-shoot in the rushing game or the worn turf at the Astrodome. He was just reaching out, one human heart attempting to speak to another. Belichick responded with thirty seconds of dead air, during which you could almost here hundreds of listeners screaming, "Wish him 'Merry Christmas' back, you twit!"

9. The gratuitous degradation of Kevin Mack. After two years as coach, Belichick proved as cruel and unusual toward his veteran stars in the prelude to the 1993 season as he would be during it in his clash with Bernie Kosar. Mack had retired before the season began, then un-retired. An unhappy Belichick put him on the practice squad, then watched Mack run roughshod over his young defensive line candidates. "Get him out of there before he hurts somebody!" Mumbles screamed, we think. In the final game of the year, Belichick kept Mack stapled to the bench, defying the home crowd chants of "We want Mack!"

8. Hah! I scoff at your stinking presents! After Belichick's then-wife Debbie gave birth to a son, two Browns beat reporters handed Belichick nicely wrapped presents for the kid, whose main function in life seemed to be screaming through press conferences at the back of the room. Months later, the two boxes, still unopened, were spotted stuffed under Belichick's desk.

7. Mr. Empathy. After Bernie Kosar broke his ankle in a Monday night loss to Miami in 1992, it came out that one of his offensive linemen, John Rienstra, a past steroid abuser, had suffered a panic attack before the game. The rest of the season, an aide put Rienstra through an exhaustive and public pre-game workout. Explained Belichick: "We just lost Bernie Kosar with a broken ankle on national television and now the whole nation knows we had a f***ing nut case blocking for him."

6. The purge of Reggie Langhorne. In a 1991 contract dispute, Langhorne reluctantly reported after the Browns began taking money off the table. He was fined $50 a pound when he reported two pounds over his prescribed weight of 202, then was fined $50 per pound any time he went over 202 during the season. Two pounds is no big deal, of course, but the weight issue allowed Belichick to turn Langhorne into his whipping boy. Langhorne started the season as the fourth receiver, then was dropped to the scout team. (Next stop, tackling dummy?) When Langhorne asked to be traded and it leaked into the papers, Belichick suspended him without pay for a game. As Langhorne left for free agency in Indianapolis at the end of the year, Richard Mann, then the Browns receivers coach advised him: "The Man don't like you. Don't come back." Over the next two seasons with the Colts, Langhorne caught 150 passes—62 more than the Browns leading wide receiver Michael Jackson managed over the same period.

5. With their first pick of the 1995 draft, the Cleveland Browns select Craig Powell, linebacker, Ohio State.
"He can run," said Belichick.
"He's not ready," said OSU coach John Cooper.
Cooper was right.

4. Three points, three TDs, who can keep track? Down 21 points in San Diego during the 1995 regular season, Belichick chose to kick a field goal on the last play of the game.

3. Adios, three amigos. After the 1991 season, Belichick chased off or cut the team's three top wide receivers—Webster Slaughter, Brian Brennan and Langhorne. They were the "triplets" who made Bernie Kosar's offense go and had combined for 134 catches the previous season. In response, *The Plain Dealer* ran a rare signed editorial by Op-Ed Page Editor Brent Larkin that began: "Do the Browns know what they're doing?" Kosar didn't think so. "He (Belichick) said I wasn't productive," Kosar recalled, "but he got rid of all the guys who made me productive."

2. He cut Bernie Kosar. Oh, he was right, in his limited way. All he could go by was what he saw, and what he saw was an "immobile quarterback with diminished skills" (that was Art Modell's assessment of Kosar at the dismissal press conference, by the way, as composed by PR toady Kevin Byrne, not Belichick's). But he had no idea how deep a negative impact that the curt gesture would make on the community. Belichick also had no concept of how unready Kosar's backup was to take over. Which begs the question: did Belichick make Tom Brady in New England, or was it the other way around?

1. He replaced Bernie Kosar with Todd Philcox. Everyone forgets that Vinny Testaverde wasn't healthy and on the injured reserve list at the time of Kosar's dismissal. In stepped the least adequate Todd since the Bill Murray character of that name was hanging out with Mrs. Loopner and Lisa on Saturday Night Live in the late 1970s. In a humiliating 22-5 loss in his first game in Seattle, Philcox fumbled on his first play (and watched the Seahawks return it for a TD), threw two interceptions and fumbled again. A Browns team that started 1993 with a record of 5-2 finished it 2-7. Chris Mortensen, NFL TV apologist, said: "Belichick's people skills let him down."

Butch Davis didn't have much luck during his 2001-04 run as the Browns head coach. Who else had a quarterback break his leg on a sneak? But the former University of Miami coach popped a few caps into his own foot, as well. Davis didn't display much ability to judge talent or character. The self-styled Generalissimo wasn't much for organizational politics, either, preferring the head nodding of young lackeys to the sage advice of elder statesman. Candor was also in short supply during the Davis era as facts seldom derailed his optimistic assessments. This list's name comes from Davis' ridiculously sunny take on QB Kelly Holcomb's 2002 broken leg, which he described as "a teeny-tiny crack in a non-weight-bearing bone."

10. Blaming Lal Heneghan. Davis conceived of himself as the franchise's Generalissimo after the 2002 team got into the playoffs. Power-hungry from the start and looking to erase all vestiges of the past, Davis revamped the whole team and basically started anew in a puzzling offseason. When the Browns he built flopped, it was somehow all the fault of team VP and resident salary-cap expert Lal Heneghan. Heneghan was respected around the NFL. Davis soon became a joke in his own locker room.

9. Scaring off Ron Wolf. Given the chance to use former Packers general manager Ron Wolf as a personnel consultant—and perhaps to dissuade Davis from, oh, using a fifth-round draft choice on a long snapper (a skill, we guess, you just can't teach)—Davis chose to insult Wolf by neglect. Wolf, who had built the Packers into Super Bowl champions, left the Browns to sink under the cumulative dead weight added to the roster by Davis and his right-hand nitwit Pete Garcia.

8. Taking Quincy Morgan. Davis drafted Morgan in the second round of the 2001 draft, only to find that Morgan had more drops in him than a vat of Visine and coughed it up often enough to guest star in a Hall Brothers commercial on the occasions he managed to hang on to a pass. But Davis kept playing him. The play we remember, no matter how hard we try to forget: the Browns were desperately rallying against Jacksonville late in the 2001 season on the Day of 10,000 Bottles when Morgan snagged a fourth-down whistler from Tim Couch just past the first-down sticks. Then, with the clock still ticking along in the last minute and his team still down, 15-10, the self-aggrandizing knucklehead Morgan decided it was time to celebrate. He took a few moments to dramatically signal "first down" by thrusting his arm toward the Jaguar goalline, still nine yards away. In the meantime, the replay review revealed that Morgan had actually dropped the ball. Had Morgan not held up the game with his showboatintg, the replay official would not have had time to review the play before the next snap. As it was: game, set, match, season, rolling barrage of plastic.

7. Loving Luke McCown. If Davis recruited you, successfully or not during his time as head coach at the U. of Miami; or if he coached against you there; or if you once caught a plane anywhere in Florida, well, then he loved you. McCown was the designated cannon fodder for the Hurricaines pass rush when the QB was at Louisiana Tech and Davis was capo at Thug U. But he apparently played well enough to impress the impressionable Davis, if not Browns fans, or anyone else, for that matter. Embattled Terry Robiskie, the interim coach after Davis bailed from Cleveland in 2004, let

McCown lead the Browns offense for most of a cold afternoon in Buffalo. Cleveland gained a total of 19 yards. One-nine. Or less than the distance from home plate to the pitcher's mound.

6. Bringing in Jeff Garcia. Acquired because he was not Tim Couch, Garcia generated headlines off the field when his Playboy Playmate girlfriend and future wife, Carmella DeCesare, cat-fought another stone-cold fox, Kristen Hine, over him. (How does this happen? Does Terrell Owens, who intimated Garcia was "gay" in San Francisco, know about this?) Then Garcia flexed his team leadership skills by dissing his offensive line and feuding with tight end Kellen Winslow Jr. before the first-round pick was even on the roster. On the field, Garcia generally just made bad throws and poor decisions and quickly made himself into an impacted hemorrhoid. "I'd have cut that quarterback," Robiskie said.

5. Cutting Kevin Johnson. He was Chris Palmer's guy, not Butch's. So Davis cut him, claiming it was not a "knee-jerk reaction," while mournfully noting that his staff of Larry, Curly and Moe had not been able "to get him to accept the expectations we have of how the wide receiver position should be played." KJ, who liked to say he was "just like 7-Eleven, open all night" had been the team's leading receiver each of the first four seasons after the Browns returned to Cleveland, two of them under Davis. So for once, Davis was right: cutting Johnson was more of a "jerk" than a "knee-jerk" reaction.

4. Bringing Thug U. player behavior with him to Cleveland. Browns teammates Mike Sellers and Lamar Chapman decided to celebrate their bye week in 2001 by getting high and getting arrested on November 19 in Cleveland. Facing felony cocaine possession charges, Sellers, the team's starting fullback, pled guilty to a DUI and was cut. Chapman, a cornerback who was on the injured list at the time, was suspended.

3. The bye week of living dangerously. In the wee hours after the Sellers/Chapman 2001 bust in Cleveland, teammate Gerard Warren became a guest of the city of Pittsburgh. Warren, "one of the nicest guys they ever arrested," according to Carmen Policy, the best spinner this side of a tarantula, had an unregistered firearm in his car, a sure sign of a "nice guy." Fellow passenger and Browns teammate O.J. Santiago was nailed for disorderly conduct and marijuana possession, Percy Blue, a mystery figure with a Damon Runyon name, occupied Warren's back seat. Blue was rolling a marijuana blunt at the time police happened by. When Policy claimed at the subsequent press conference that Warren did not know Blue, the *Akron Beacon Journal*'s Pat McManamon interrupted The Little Mob Lawyer's Story Hour to yelp, "What, he was just some guy?"

2. Drafting William Green. The Browns used their first pick in the 2002 draft on Boston College running back Green (in part to make up for passing on LaDanian Tomlinson the previous year for the ludicrous "Pocket Change," er, excuse us, "Big Money" Gerard Warren). Davis and his brain trust chose to overlook that Green suffered from chronic colitis and had a history of getting caught smoking chronic before BC's biggest games. Carmen Policy, spinning so much by this point you half-expected his head to do a 360 during press conferences like Linda Blair's in *The Exorcist*, explained that, other than the colitis and cannabis addiction, Green was the healthiest running back in the draft. Halfway through his second season, a 9-1-1 caller reported Green for weaving his car from curb to curb. He was charged with DUI and marijuana possession. Then a month later, along came the stabbing incident with his girlfriend, followed by his Ripleysque explanation ('see, I tripped on the stairs and accidentally gave myself the shiv in the back'), cementing his status as a figure of ridicule. Then, just to make sure we knew it was okay to laugh, Green got himself expelled from a game with the Steelers for fighting with Pittsburgh's Joey Porter during pre-game warm-ups. After that, he might as well have stood around, rocking back and forth on oversized clown shoes.

1. Jeremiah Pharms. Sure, he spent a few years in prison for pistol-whipping and shooting a drug dealer. This is because Pharms, who never played a down for the Browns despite being drafted in the fifth round by them in 2001, kept getting stumped by the same question Ricky Williams flunked so many times with New Orleans and other teams: Do I take the NFL millions or another bong hit? Pharms, a linebacker at the University of Washington, purchased one-eighth ounce of marijuana from a Seattle dealer, left, then returned three hours later with an accomplice, masked and armed. In a scuffle to steal the dealer's quarter-pound of grass, the intruders pistol-whipped and then shot him. A bloody fingerprint on the getaway car proved to be that of Pharms. But even before the robbery, the Pharms-acological one proved to be one whacked-out guy. He had a pit bull tattoo. He would glare at opposing players and then-as proof of derangement, one supposes-urinate in his pants, which would steadily darken and begin to stink. Pharms' alarming personality problems eluded the Browns' character detectives, including team security chief Lew Merletti, the former head of the Secret Service, which made you wonder how the U.S. managed not to lose a president or two on his watch. On the bright side, Merletti ensured that no outraged Browns fan got close enough to take a pot-shot at Davis or Policy. By the time Butch slipped out of town, there were probably more than a few trying.

Cleveland has mastered the art of the painful, unjust loss so thoroughly, we suffer them in the literary and music worlds as well as in sports. It would be too painful to remember them all at once. So here are just the ones that hurt the most.

10. The 1999 AL Division Series (aka, "The Last Pitcher Show"). The next time Mike Hargrove decides to use starters on short rest with a 2-0 series lead when one more win takes the series, somebody tell him to call Trivisonno and defend drunken Vice Presidents with shotguns instead.

9. "The Holcomb Bowl." Dennis Northcutt drops the ball with a run-out-the-clock first down in hand. Browns waste a bazillion point lead, lose to Steelers in playoffs. Doesn't get any worse that that . . . wait, actually, it does.

8. James Frey's *A Million Little Pieces* turns out to be a million little lies. Oprah disses him after first championing the Cleveland-born "memoir" writer. In the literary and pop culture world, that's the equivalent of getting trashed by Brit and K-Fed.

7. Scott Savol gets bounced from American Idol.

6. Vic Wertz/Dusty Rhodes. Wertz's 475-foot bomb disappears into Willie Mays' glove while Rhodes' 250-foot home run ("a Chinese homer," as they called it in those ethnically-disparaging days) wins the first game of the 1954 World Series. Second baseman Bobby Avila pounded the wall with his fist, Rhodes hit such a cheap-jack pop up.

5. "The Shot." It was only a first-round series, but the soon-to-be Eastern Conference champions Pistons cheered in their locker room while watching it. They wanted to play Michael Jordan, not the Cavs. (Be careful what you wish for.)

4. "The Fumble." Shouldn't be rated this high. There was over a minute to play when Byner oopsied the ball. So even if he held on and the Browns had tied the score, Elway would have just taken the infernal Broncos down for a field goal.

3. Red Right 88. To appreciate the full agony of this, you have to remember the civic context in which it happened. Cleveland in 1980: bankruptcy, near-recall of the Boy Mayor, Stepien owned the Cavs, Gabe and Phil ran the Tribe, the Browns hadn't been in the playoffs since 1972. It still hurts. But it really hurt then.

2. "The Drive." The Browns are the biggest team in town, but, lest we forget, they never made the Super Bowl. This was their closest approach. But 98 yards and 5 minutes-or-so of what became that old black magic from John Elway later, they were in overtime. Then Rich Karlis' field goal miss (yes, "miss"; look at the tape) gets called "good" and its over.

1. Game 7, 1997 World Series. Jose Mesa shakes off Sandy Alomar, Jr. (himself a dishonorable mention for not sliding at the plate in the top of the ninth) time and time again with a 2-1 lead in the bottom of the ninth, deciding to throw a wimpball instead of his heater. Indians become first team in MLB history to blow a ninth-inning, seventh-game lead in the World Series. Charlie Nagy took the loss in the 11th, but Mesa took the blame. No doubt about it. And no, it didn't make anyone feel a whole lot better when Mariano Rivera spat the bit against Arizona four years later in the ninth. That just meant that another city (Phoenix, of all places) got to celebrate a championship before Cleveland did.

Bill admits a prejudice here. He met Drew Carey before the Cleveland comedian's 1991 breakthrough appearance on *The Tonight Show*, when an impressed Johnny Carson unexpectedly invited Carey over to sit next to the desk to chat after Drew's hilarious monologue. Not only is Drew falling down funny, he has an infectious laugh that shows he enjoys his own and others' stuff. The ability to chuckle in the face of disaster is important when you're a Clevelander. If the biggest laughs really are formed by the deepest pains, it would explain why our city has produced so many great comedians. Or maybe these people are just exceptionally funny and bright and happen to be ours. Anyway, as No. 1 on our list might say, "Thanks for the memory."

12. John Henton, Shaw HS. He appeared as a semi-regular on the TV show *The Hughleys* and starred with Queen Latifah in *Living Single*, a sitcom about unmarried friends in a Brooklyn brownstone. *Single* did well enough, lasting from 1993-98 and generating plenty of laughs. But much of its thunder and potential audience was commandeered in 1994 when NBC "debuted" *Friends*, a sitcom with a suspiciously similar premise and more People magazine friendly cast.

11. Pat McCormick, Rocky River. Pat stole scenes as Big Enos Burdette, the man who wanted to run Coors out of Texas, in Smokey and the Bandit. The 6-4, 250-pound McCormick also wrote some spectacular lines for Johnny Carson on *The Tonight Show*, including, "Due to today's earthquake, the 'God is Dead' rally is postponed."

10. Steve Harvey, Glenville. Playing the vice principal and music teacher on the eponymous *Steve Harvey Show*, he coped with pupils Romeo and Bullethead, and faked his way through music and drama classes because of school budget cutbacks.

9. Martin Mull, North Ridgeville. He made his first splash as Garth Gimble in the 1970s soap opera spoof *Mary Hartman, Mary Hartman*, then starred as the host of the Hartman spin-off *Fernwood 2Nite*, the hilarious send-up of Midwestern late-night local programming that was decades ahead of its time.

8. Fred Willard, Shaker Heights. Willard established himself as a great dim-witted wit playing Mull's clueless sidekick Jerry Hubbard on *Fernwood 2Nite*. He went on to play Brad Garrett's father-in-law, an intolerant fundamentalist, in *Everybody Loves Raymond*. Willard established himself as a regular in Christopher Guest's troupe in a series of popular films satirizing various American subcultures, including *Best of Show* and *Waiting for Guffman*. He was particularly funny in *A Mighty Wind*, Guest's take on *60s folkie* scene decades after the fact, as the smarmy Mike LaFontaine, the former star of the fictitious (and no doubt execrable) *Wha' Happened*?. Willard currently appears as Marsh the sports guy in *Back to You*, starring Kelsey Grammar and fellow area native Patricia Heaton.

7. Don Novello, Lorain. He bought the clerical collar, floppy hat and cape that made him famous as Father Guido Sarducci on *Saturday Night Live* for $7.50, total, at a St. Vincent de Paul thrift store. With his cigarette holder and thick Italian accent, Novello convinced millions of American viewers he really was as a Vatican priest and Pope groupie. But he didn't fool Vatican City's Swiss Guards, who nabbed Novello, in character at St. Peter's Basilica in Rome, a few years after a priest impersonator tried to smash Michelangelo's Pieta statue with a hammer.

6. Molly Shannon, Shaker Heights. The armpit-sniffing, neurotic Catholic schoolgirl Mary Katherine Gallagher; her spot-on impersonations of Monica Lewinsky (with John Goodman, in drag, as girlfriend Linda Tripp); as well as Liz Taylor, Courtney Love and Bjork—this local redhead's *SNL* work shows her versatility and comic talent. She made make you laugh just by walking down the street (but not swinging her arms), while driving Elaine crazy on *Seinfeld*.

5. Arsenio Hall, Warrensville Heights. Told in junior high school to give up his dream because a black man would never host a network talk show, he persevered, broke through racial barriers and finally reached his goal with *The Arsenio Hall Show*. Debuting in 1989, the show went on to win a couple Emmys and host numerous iconic moments. Bill Clinton chose Hall's show as a forum to reach out to young voters by playing the saxophone. Hall sat in to do a quarter of play-by-play with Joe Tait when the Cavs were in L.A. to face the Lakers, leading to repartee like:
Hall: "The Cavs throw it inside to a gentleman with whom I am not familiar.
Tait: "That's Hot Rod Williams, Arsenio."

4. Drew Carey, Rhodes. No one showed the world how great this city could be more than the bespectacled native of Old Brooklyn with a crew cut. He originated the commendable idea that a Cleveland joke is a joke only Clevelanders understand, and the hell with everybody else. Debuting in 1995, *The Drew Carey Show* ran on ABC for a decade. It lives on in our memories, not to mention reruns that keep us in touch with the Winfred-Louder store gang: Drew, the assistant manager of personnel; his archenemy Mimi of the odd attire; Lewis Michelangelo Kiniski, secret genius; Oswald Lee Harvey (betcha didn't know his full name); Nigel Algernon Wick, Drew's supervisor; Kate, always looking gorgeous, even at the Warsaw; Drew's cross-dressing brother, etc. Cleveland rocks. Guffaws, too.

3. Tim Conway, Willoughby. He at first turned down the role that made him famous—Ensign Parker on the hit 1960s ABC sitcom *McHale's Navy*—because he wanted to stay with Channel 8 in Cleveland. His boss forced him to go. Conway achieved his greatest and most lasting fame in the 1970s on *The Carol Burnett Show*, where his improvisations often caused fellow cast members to break up live on camera. His one-man cast of characters included Dwayne, the white-haired ancient, shuffling through tasks he was decades too creaky to complete, and the would-be Swedish office tyrant Mr. Tudball with an accent that would stump anyone outside Stockholm. His battle with a fly that was disturbing his sleep, accompanied only by the sound of the fly's buzzing, was pure comic genius reminiscent of Red Skelton's brilliant pantomimes.

2. Patricia Heaton, Bay Village. On *Everybody Loves Raymond*, she cut uncomfortably close to the bones of many sportswriters and other middle-aged Lost Boys whose not-so-secret truth was that they had chosen a Peter Pan existence. Heaton's Debra Barone character offered Donna Reed with a bite, Harriet Nelson away from the 50s fantasy and lots of laughs.

1. Bob Hope, born in England, raised in Cleveland. Maybe the funniest sportsman ever, Hope was a golfer who went on to found the Bob Hope Desert Classic, a boxer (under the alias Packy East), a comedian who introduced the Associated Press College Football All-America team for years as part of his Christmas show and a part-owner, at one point, of the Indians. He had fun with himself in the latter role, getting beaned by a foul ball as guest star in a memorable episode of *I Love Lucy*. He risked his life many times to entertain American troops in hot spots around the world and seemed so impervious to danger that he even outlived his prematurely released obituary by six years. Hope died at the age of 100, a decade after singing his theme song, "Thanks for the Memory" during the last Indians game at the old Stadium. He said: "No matter how much I travel or how far I go, Cleveland is with me. So I've never left home. I was raised on the sidewalks of Cleveland, but then my father found a house . . . .When I walk through my old neighborhood, I always have a lump in my throat. That's the only safe place to carry your money."

Top Ten Lame Things Done by Indians' Personnel

Baseball always produced more flakes than a two-day-old croissant on a windy afternoon on the *Champs-Elysee*. We've certainly seen our share float through Cleveland. More than our share, really.

10. Sugar Bear en fuego? Enraged by manager Frank Robinson, who was good at that, Larvell "Sugar Bear" Blanks, a utility infielder with the Indians from 1976-78, tore off his uniform, threw it into a trash barrel and set it on fire.

9. Ocean's 9? During a home game against the Red Sox in 1986, a pocket of fog moved in (no doubt "on little cats' feet") from Lake Erie and blanketed the old Stadium in an eerie, cottony cloud. Umpires sent Tribe outfielder Mel Hall out to test if he could see well enough through the mist to shag some flies. Yeah, it was like being assigned food taster for an unpopular medieval king. But did Mel have to duck and cover up the first time he lost sight of the ball, like a frightened child in the 1950s during a drill to survive that pesky A-bomb? Especially considering that the Red Sox were ahead and the game had already lasted long enough to be official if the umps called it. Hall's courageous display did indeed convince the umps to end the game and award it to the Sox. Afterwards, Sox pitcher and geography specialist Dennis "Oil Can" Boyd observed: "This is what happens when you put a ballpark on an ocean."

8. The Cork Consortium. Former Cleveland pitcher Steve Farr claimed the Indians had a woodworking shop at the old Stadium where enough cork to send a New Year in with a champagne bang was inserted in Wahoo war clubs. Cork, of course, is used to lighten the mass of a bat and create a swifter swing, though that's illegal in baseball. It is also effective as a muffler, leading to the common phrase "Put a cork in it." Which is something you might say to a person about to embarrass himself, his former employer and teammates by yapping about an alleged illegal corking operation.

7. The Dirty Cork Socker. When the White Sox had Albert Belle's bat impounded in 1993 over suspicions it was corked, they set off a series of events more comical than Trot Nixon trying to pretend that acting like a Stooge in a pie fight was instrumental to the Indians' 2007 success. Enter pitcher Jason Grimsley, surreptitiously, after crawling through the heating ducts in the ceiling and into the umpires' room. Out went Belle's bat. In came a Paul Sorrento model bat, an unsatisfactory yet necessary substitution. Because, as Omar Vizquel wrote years later in his autobiography, all of Albert's bats were laden with enough cork to stump Letterman on "Will It Float?"

6. Follow the leader? During Dave Garcia's tenure as the Indians' manager in the 1980s, he called a meeting and decried the lack of leaders on the team. First baseman Mike Hargrove, who had earlier in the evening led the team off the field after only the second out of an inning, wondered: "What does he mean no leaders? I led them to the dugout."

5. Alex Cole takes an early lead in cluelessness. With Brian McCrae on second base and one out in the first inning of a 1991 game at the old Stadium, Alex Cole gloved a fly ball by George Brett. He then put his head down, jogged toward the infield and rolled the ball toward the mound, blissfully unaware that the inning wasn't over yet. Or of his infielders waving their arms and screaming "No!" Or of the Kansas City third-base coach windmilling his arms, urging McRae home from second on what became a two-base sacrifice fly. Cole's act of oblivion will likely stand the test of time because it can only be bested by someone losing track after the very first out of a game. The Tribe manager, by this time none other than Mike Hargrove, said: "If I'd have had a rifle, I'd have shot him."

4. The Not-So-Great Wall. It stood 415 feet from the plate in 1992 and was shaped like one of the figures that always puzzled you as a kid in geometry class (a trapezoid, maybe?), Tribe management designed it for Alex Cole to send gap shots rolling and rolling to the land of triples and help the Indians win more games. The Tribe went 30-52 at home in front of the wall and 57-and-a-club-record-105 overall that season. Cole hit .206 in 41 games before being traded.

3. Spygate, the Original. Bob Lemon and Bob Feller used a high-powered telescope to steal signs from opposing catchers through holes in the outfield wall scoreboard at the old Stadium in 1948. After getting the word from Lemon or Feller, members of the Bossard family, the team's scorekeepers, signaled what kind of pitch was coming to Indians batters by extending their elbows through an open window they used to change numbers on the manual scoreboard. "It won us a half-dozen games," said Feller.

2. Oedipus Vex. Alex Cole was a Greek tragic hero. The first manager who had to deal with the talented but tragically flawed Cole was John McNamara. After the bespectacled Cole, center fielder of tomorrow for the Tribe, was picked off first with the bases loaded in Toronto by Tom Henke on his fifth attempt, thereby becoming the final out in a 1-0 loss, "Mount Mac" was close to eruption. He chased the Canadian writers out of his office and told traveling secretary Mike Seghi to close the door before he and the Cleveland writers resumed talking. Running his fingers wildly through his thinning white hair, his Irish face flushed as red as sunset over Galway Bay, McNamara said: "That four-eyed motherfucker is killing me!"

1. Speak-ing of scandals . . . . Tris Speaker retired as the Indians' manager in 1926 before he quit as a player, shortly after former major leaguer Dutch Leonard accused Speaker and Ty Cobb of fixing a game earlier that season. Leonard later refused to testify at a hearing, possibly fearing recriminations. With the Black Sox still a recent memory and with two of the game's biggest stars possibly facing indictment, Commissioner Kenesaw Mountain Landis let each know it was time to move on. Players were indentured servants then, bound to their teams, if the teams so chose, for life. Suddenly, Cobb and Speaker were free agents. Amazing coincidence, huh? Speaker ended his career with the Senators, Cobb with the Philadelphia A's.

What, you expected ten? There just weren't that many tough outs for right-handed pitcher Bob Feller during his 1936-56 career with the Indians. Even the greats of his era had trouble handling his 100+ mph fastball. For instance, you'll notice Ted Williams, considered by many as the greatest hitter in baseball history and a contemporary of Feller, didn't make the list. "Ted Williams was a .241 hitter against me," explained Feller. "Bullet Bob" never lacked confidence, and for good reason. Debuting in the bigs at the age of 17, Feller struck out 17 in one game during his first season and would go on to K over 2500 batters before he was done. He notched a 24-win season before his 21st birthday on his way to 266 career victories. Feller also tossed three no-hitters and 12 one-hitters, appeared in eight All-Star games and led the AL in wins six times. He accomplished all that despite sacrificing three-and-a-half years during the prime of his career to World War II. Even though Feller's father was dying of brain cancer and, as the sole support of his family, he could have received a draft deferment, he enlisted in the U.S. Navy the day after the attack on Pearl Harbor. "I have made a lot of mistakes in my life. Joining the Navy was not one of them," he says. Bob Feller gained entry into the Hall of Fame on the first ballot in his first year of eligibility, 1962.

9. Joe DiMaggio, Yankees. Joe liked the ball away from him. He couldn't hit it on his hands. I had some good luck against him his last two years when he was slowing down. Joe couldn't hit sinkerballers like Mel Harder, either. Unfortunately, my sinker wasn't worth a damn.

8. Cecil Travis, Senators. He had a .329 lifetime average until he went to war, got his feet frozen in the Battle of the Bulge, then played two years after it when he couldn't do much. He was a good shortstop, too. Probably belongs in the Hall of Fame.

7. Stan Spence, Red Sox and Senators. One of the few power hitters who did well against me.

6. Johnny Pesky, Red Sox and Tigers . Had the perfect name. A little bloop-hitter who could spray the ball.

5. Roy Cullenbine, Tigers and St. Louis Browns. A good low-ball, fastball hitter. If I knew the reason he hit me so good, I would've gotten him out.

4. Nellie Fox, Philadelphia A's, White Sox and Astros. He had almost a bottle bat and he choked up on it. He could hit to any part of the park and was very difficult to strike out with a man on third and less than two out.

3. Taffy Wright, Senators, White Sox and Philadelphia A's. He had a little, small strike zone. He would spray the ball all over the ballpark.

2. Rip Radcliff, White Sox, St. Louis Browns and Tigers. He was another low-ball hitter and a very good fastball hitter. Of course, I knew that. But it didn't help.

1. Tommy Henrich, Yankees. He was a great clutch hitter. They called him 'Old Reliable' for a reason. I don't know what his batting average was against me, but he was one of the left-hand hitters who really gave me problems.

Note: While growing up, Egan, a longtime outdoor writer for *The Plain Dealer*, watched his father help build the Cleveland Barons teams of the 1940s and 50s as publicity chief. *The Plain Dealer's* Feran, a big hockey fan, was watching, too. So were a lot of other Clevelanders. The old Barons were so good for so long, they were considered the seventh-best team in hockey (after the six NHL teams of the time) and attracted a lot of top talent to their roster. The city's other hockey franchises weren't around nearly as long, but still showcased some good players. We tried to factor that in, and included players from the short-lived NHL Barons, the Jacks and the beloved Crusaders.

Honorable Mentions: Tommy "Red" Williams (a defensive "octopus" who was a five-time AHL All-Star and three-time Calder Cup champion in 1951, 1953 and 1954), Les Binkley (a good goalie in the mid-60s for the Barons), Jack Gordon (a fondly-remembered player/coach from 1952-62), Paul Shmyr (a team leader and one of the WHA's top defensemen in four seasons with the C's), Dave Michayluk (a Lumberjack who had his really big seasons in Muskegon), Fred "Bun" Cook (former Ranger and Bruin who merits mention for his work behind the bench as Barons coach from 1943-56, guiding them to seven first-place finishes in the regular season and five Calder Cup championships during that time and becoming the winningest coach in AHL history), "Big, Bad" John Ferguson (a Barons enforcer from 1960-63, who went on to beat up the baddest guys in the NHL with the Montreal Canadiens), Emile "The Cat" Francis (a goalie who didn't let many pucks past him from 1953-55).

10. Dennis Maruk. A budding superstar, this prolific scorer and team leader played two seasons with the short-lived NHL Barons from 1976-78.

9. Gerry Cheevers. Famed for his trademark stitch-patterned mask and exciting play, "Cheesy" was a daring, aggressive goaltender and three-time WHA All-Star for the Crusaders from 1972-76.

8. Bill Needham. The Hall of Fame defenseman became the all-time team leader in games played with the Barons in 15 seasons from 1956-71. As head coach, Needham led the Crusaders to second place in their first WHA season.

7. Tommy Burlington. "One Eye" has been called "the Wayne Gretzky of his day" and the greatest North American player never to play in the NHL, which barred him because he was blind in one eye from a childhood accident. An All-Star in four seasons with the Barons (1942-45), he set an AHL-record 24-game scoring streak, twice led the team in scoring, and led them to two first-place finishes and a Calder Cup.

6. Cal Stearns. An outstanding stick handler and scorer, Stearns was considered the best penalty-killer in the AHL in his 12 seasons with the Barons from 1951-63. Stearns played center, wing and defense on three Calder Cup teams.

5. Bobby Carse. The two-time, first-team AHL All-Star was considered one of the greatest players on a dominant Barons team, despite a career interrupted by service in the Canadian army in World War II, when he was shot in the shoulder and held more than six months as a German prisoner. In retirement he developed the Parma youth hockey program.

4. Johnny Bower. Regarded by some as the best player ever to skate in Cleveland, "Panther Man" established himself as a top netminder from 1945-53 with the Barons. The AHL career-leader in shutouts, Bower, who was originally signed by the New York Rangers, claimed he passed up chances to play in the NHL and stayed with the Barons because he liked Cleveland so much. But according to insiders, Bower had been exiled from the NHL after his wife insulted the New York Rangers GM for not giving her husband enough money. Bower eventually left for the NHL, only to return to the Barons a few years later for the 1957-58 season. He then played for the Toronto Maple Leafs for 12 years and eventually gained entry into the Hockey Hall of Fame,

3. Jock Callender. The heart of the IHL Cleveland Lumberjacks for seven seasons from 1993-2000, he became the league's all-time leading scorer. Callender played in four All-Star games and was named director of Cleveland's AHL Lake Erie Monsters for their inaugural 2007 season.

2. Les Cunningham. This five-time All-Star and three-time Calder Cup champion averaged better than a point per game in ten years with the Barons. He retired in 1948 as the AHL's career leader in points. He was so good, the league named their MVP award after him.

1. Fred Glover. Simply the foremost hockey player in Cleveland history. Two-fisted No. 9 played for the original AHL Barons—considered at least the seventh-best team in the world at the time behind the six NHL clubs—from 1953-68, coached them from 1962-68 and led them to four Calder Cup Championships. He retired as the AHL's career leader in games played, goals, assists, points and penalty minutes. He led the league in scoring twice and won its Les Cunningham Award as Most Valuable Player three times.

Bill's Five Crummy Things About the NHL

Bill owns a Toronto Maple Leafs jersey, bought during a baseball playoffs trip at the Hockey Hall of Fame. He loves how maple syrup is a point of civic pride there. Then again, what do hockey people talk about? Dentistry? How cold it was when they were growing up in Flin Flon or Medicine Hat? The good old days, when people cared?

5. Gretzky sucks as a coach, compared to as a player, doesn't he? Well, I guess just about every coach sucks compared to Gretzky as a player. So how about: Gretzky sucks as a coach compared to Kelly Buchberger as a player.

4. The Stanley Cup champions from 2005-07 were based in Tampa, Raleigh, and Anaheim.

3. When Nashville has a team in hockey and Quebec doesn't, something has gone bad in the creme brulee, mon ami.

2. Versus. If I can't get it on TNT, TBS or ESPN, it doesn't exist.

1. They did away with the infraction for a two-line pass. (And you thought I didn't care.)

My Top Five Memories of the 2004 Athens Olympics
:: Tim Mack

Note: In 2004, Tim Mack became Cuyahoga County's fourth athlete to win an individual track-and-field Olympic gold medal. Mack's unlikely triumph became the subject of Bill Livingston's book *Above and Beyond — Tim Mack, the Pole Vault, and the Quest for Olympic Gold.* Competing in his first Olympics at nearly 32 years of age, the St. Ignatius grad from Westlake savored every part of the experience, even filling the specimen jar.

5. In the drug-testing room. After winning the gold medal, I was sitting in the testing area, firing back water and Gatorade, because that's what you have to do. My manager, Mark Block, kept getting calls on his cell phone from meet promoters. He kept saying to me, "Mack, Mack. Things are changing. Things are changing fast." I felt the same calm then that I had felt before the competition. But that's when I realized that when you get to a certain level, the whole world is looking at you. I thought, "Wow! So this is what happens after you win the gold medal."

4. On the victory podium. I had so many flashbacks as I walked out there. Then to have Sergey Bubka present me with my medal! He was always my idol. I looked at the American flag when the national anthem began, and it was like parts of my past were flying by at 100 miles an hour. Situations, pieces of memories about things I had done, about my family. I wanted the anthem to be ten minutes long. I wanted to stay up there forever.

3. Walking through the tunnel before the pole vault finals. I had done visualization exercises so often that I already felt in my bones what it would be like. Walking through the tunnel toward the field, the security people would look at you and just nod. The volunteers in the tunnel would stand back and watch you go by. It was like walking out for a gladiator battle. And *Gladiator* is one of my favorite movies. When I got out into the stadium, I felt it was sort of the calm before the storm. I watched all these other athletes looking around, sort of overwhelmed by the noise and by how many people were there. And I felt a source of strength because I knew that distraction was taking energy away from them, but not from me.

2. Going to the stadium for qualifying. I was sitting on the bus by myself and I felt very calm. My whole idea was to conserve and excite: stay calm until I was on the runway, waste no energy and then let it all out on the runway. Usually, I feel little body aches right before competing. But I was just completely focused on my jumping cues, on hitting the takeoff mark and working my arms. My body felt like it was floating. I was so incredibly ready.

1. Family and friends. Beyond any doubt, having so many family members and friends and former teammates come to Athens is my top memory. The day before qualifying, I told them, "I love you guys and I'm glad you're here, but right now, I have to close off and go kind of into my shell." I didn't want to have to waste any energy by then. I told them that we'd have a big party afterward. And, when I won, we did.

Top Five Reasons the Summer Olympics Beat the Slush Off the Winter Ones

Bill has been to two editions of the Winter Games. Calgary was Fort Worth with funny money. Norway was ruddy-cheeked Vikings with miner's hats on, heading off to cross-country ski in the darkness, which fell at about four in the afternoon in Lillehammer. It looked like more fun than by-pass surgery, anyway. In the immortal words of his Texas pal David Casstevens, "If biathlon is a sport, so is armed robbery of a 7-Eleven in Duluth."

5. No ice or snow.

4. Not everything is a half-ass, made-for-TV sport, like hotdog skiing—and the ones that are (women's gymnastics) are not locks for medals by the USA.

3. No shootouts to decide basketball ties, as in hockey.

2. The men's 100 meters in track, the only event anywhere that creates the buzz that used to attend a big heavyweight title fight.

1. No French judge to put the fix in.

For a taste of Cleveland, you have to start with Bertman's Ball Park Mustard, slathered on a bratwurst, Polish sausage or even a humble hotdog. It's almost indistinguishable from Stadium Mustard, served, among other places, at the Horseshoe for Buckeye football games. We won't go into the legal issues that led to the break-up of the original company. We like the Ball Park over the Stadium just a squirt more. Any self-respecting sausage is honored to be in the company of either. After you've downed one (or two or three) of those, try a tour of these places:

10. West Side Market Café. This European-style market already rates as a Cleveland ethnic cuisine classic. It's just the place for that elusive goat dish or the perfect fig. The restaurant inside does good work, morning and night, although the waitress who looks like Mimi from *The Drew Carey Show* is usually on in the morning. Try the pork chop.

9. Bearden's. Since 1948, the Rocky River eatery has been serving glorious burgers, wrapped in paper like at the drive-in, and home-made onion rings that treat the bulb better than anything bloomin' at Outback.

8. Mama Jo's Pies, Lorain. Available at some area restaurants and Heinen's stores, these pies boast a crust so upper it hardly seems possible that it comes from humble flour. Chocolate ice box is our favorite, but they're all good. Some swear by the German chocolate-pecan, but you need to order it a day or two in advance.

7. Barberton fried chicken. Available at the birthplace of yardbird deification, Belgrade Gardens, as well as Hopocan Gardens and White House Chicken in Barberton and at Milich's Village Inn in nearby Norton. It's fresh, never frozen chicken, dusted only with salt and pepper. The secret to its greatness lies in the breading, which might give manna from give heaven a run for best bakery product from a celestial kitchen. It's cooked in lard, lending it a uniform, deep-brown color. The four-piece serving is plenty.

6. Weber's custard, Fairview Park. The demanding sweet tooth's harbinger of spring, Weber's opens around Opening Day and closes around the end of the World Series. Go for the Higbee's malt, if you're a newbie. And examine the wall full of pictures of famous people, all of whom swear by Weber's.

5. Honey Hut ice cream. When former St. Edward star Mike Rupp scored the goal that became the Stanley Cup winner for the New Jersey Devils against Anaheim in Game 7 of the 2003 Finals, he spent part of his day with Lord Stanley's Mug at the Parma Honey Hut. There, it was filled with 20 scoops of ice cream, doused with hot fudge and topped with clouds of whipped cream. The battered old trophy never had it so good. Their honey pecan on a hot day at Huntington Beach in Bay Village, eaten while sitting on the bench behind the stand, with its stunning view of downtown to the east, is one of the sweet pleasures of northeastern Ohio life.

4. Swensons drive-in, Seven Hills, Akron and Akron suburbs. An Akron tradition that has now expanded to Cuyahoga County, Swensons might not enjoy the national rep of Fatburger, the West Coast chain that has invaded the area. But the Galley Boy (two patties, cheese, special sauce, all on a buttered bun) will make you swear this is the best thing from Akron since LeBron James. The sweet taste to the burgers comes, reportedly, from the generous dusting of brown sugar the patties receive before cooking.

3. Slyman's, Cleveland. Silky corned beef, the best in a corned beef town, piled high on chewy rye. It's hard to top their breakfast of two eggs over easy, home fries and a fragrant mound of corned beef.

2. Sokolowski's University Inn, Cleveland. Oh, where to start? What comfort food! Stuffed cabbage the size of a small football, pierogies that are little pillows of bliss, soft drinks in intriguing flavors bottled just for the cafeteria-style restaurant, chicken paprikash that is as fowl a celebration as the Barberton fired version. Don't be put off by the long line. It goes almost as quickly as you can clean your plate.

1. Midway Oh Boy, Elyria. As if little jukeboxes on each table and another Big Boy version (with "Cleveland White Sauce")on your plate weren't enough, the strawberry shortcake is a staggering exercise in decadence. It says summer as much as firecrackers on the Fourth and the Yankees coming to town for a big series. Real shortcake, flavor-burst berries, a colossal mound of vanilla ice cream, and, finally, whipped cream, all served in a bowl big enough for two or more.

My Top Ten Best Area Hot Dogs in Cleveland
:: "Iron Chef" Michael Symon

Note: Now for a real foodie and his ranking of the area's franks. The hotdog practically ranks as a separate food group to sports fans. The first time that the Indians hosted a dollar dog night, they ran out of franks. That hasn't happened again. Michael Symon won a grueling reality show marathon to become The Food Network's newest "Iron Chef." Symon prepped for national prominence by wowing local foodies as owner and executive chef at Cleveland restaurants Lola and Lolita. A big fan of all Cleveland teams, the St. Edward High School grad invented a gourmet version of trash talk during a December 2007 game featuring the NBA's leading scorers LeBron James and the Lakers' Kobe Bryant. During a timeout, Symon appeared on the Quicken Loans Arena Jumbotron in a filmed skit, pounding a piece of Kobe beef with a mallet. But when Kobe isn't in town, Symon would just as soon grab a hot dog from one of these local eateries. Symon says (sorry, can't resist the pun): "What in the world is better than encased meats? I love of good hotdog whether it be on a golf course, at a bar or watching a ballgame."

Honorable Mentions: Any dog at Tony Packo's in Toledo, hot dogs at Hot Dougs in Chicago (maybe the best dogs on the planet), a Polish Boy with carmelized onions from most street vendors in Cleveland, the dogs at Fowlers Mill in Chesterland.

10. Pine Hills Golf Club, Hinckley. They used to soak them in the dreaded hot dog water. But the kitchen finally bought a griddle to cook them, which changes everything.

9. Progressive Field, Cleveland. Always get it with Ball Park Mustard. Not my favorite, but how can you keep it off this list?

8. Elryia Country Club, Elyria. They use great Chicago red hots and top them with red pepper relish.

7. Fahrenheit, Tremont. Try their Kobe Dog at happy hour. It's more like a "haute" dog, but, man, is it ever tasty!

6. Hot Dog Diner, Cleveland. This new kid on the block makes a mean Chicago-style dog with the works. Just ask for the Windy City Jumbo.

5. HoHot Dog Heaven, Amherst. Although I have only been there twice, it is tough to beat their cheddar and chili dog.

4. Steve's Lunch, Near West Side, Cleveland. With cheese and coleslaw, Cleveland's oldest hotdog hut fills those three in the morning cravings.

3. Springvale Golf Club, North Olmsted. This place ranks as the king of golf course hotdogs. I'll play there just to get a dog with Stadium Mustard and onions at the turn!

2. Hot Sauce Williams, Cleveland. Get the Polish Boy with barbecue sauce and coleslaw. I'll grab one of these a week. The perfect-sized dog with the perfect mix of spice and slaw.

1. Lakewood Country Club, Westlake. A hot dog wrapped in bacon and salami, stuffed with cheese then fried—are you kidding me? This thing alone is worth the club dues and the cost of the extra Lipitor.

The Indians have hosted the All-Star Game more often than any other MLB franchise, providing the stage for the Midsummer Classic in 1935, 1954, 1963, 1981 and 1997. (Hmmm...the Tribe went on to win the pennant in two of those five seasons,'54 and '97; so maybe the stardust lingers?). The Cavaliers rolled out the red carpet for the NBA All-Stars in 1981 and 1997. (Though in the heart of darkness that was the Ted Stepien era, the league took over the '81 game to spare itself the embarrassment of letting the Cavs' owner try to recast the festivities in his own, deranged image). The 1997 game formed the centerpiece of the league's glorious 50th Anniversary celebration, replete with a ceremony for its just-named 50 Greatest NBA Players of all time. Every one of them was on hand, except Pete Maravich, who had passed away in 1988. These All-Star games were supposed to be nothing but exhibitions. But if you had the foresight to buy this book, then you can probably appreciate the profound, new insights these games provided for thinking fans like us.

5. Jim Bouton was right. In the famous last line from his memoir *Ball Four*, the veteran big league pitcher told how he had spent his life gripping a baseball before realizing it was the other way around all along. Three of the MLB All-Star Games (1935, 1954, 1981) that the Indians hosted drew the largest crowds in the Midsummer Classic's history. The all-time attendance mark of 72,086 in 1981 came after a 50-day labor stoppage and months of growing fan discontent over the troubled state of baseball. But we showed up in record numbers anyway. Such is the game's hold on us.

4. Inspiration flows strongest from the beyond the grave. The week his beloved grandmother died in 1997, the Indians' Sandy Alomar, Jr. hit a two-run, tie-breaking homer off Shawn Estes in the bottom of the seventh at Jacobs Field, giving the AL a 3-1 victory. Sandy had helped carry his grandmother to her grave. She helped carry him to the All-Star MVP award and a career season.

3. Rivalries are forever. The real stars of the 1997 NBA All-Star Game (at what was then called Gund Arena) were the 50 members of the NBA's 50th Anniversary All-Time Team. Wilt Chamberlain drew the biggest crowd in the interview room. He also had the best line in his never-ending battle to upstage his rival center Bill Russell of the Celtics. When former Philadelphia teammate Billy Cunningham paid a waitress for soda pop and popcorn for himself and fellow honorees Chamberlain and Hal Greer, Wilt quipped: "Now, Billy, did you tip the young lady? Or did you pull a Bill Russell?"

2. Jeff Van Gundy was right. A few days before the 1997 NBA All-Star game, Van Gundy, then the Knicks' coach, complained that Michael Jordan ingratiated himself with opponents (read: Charles Barkley), then exploited the friendship to lull them into a false sense of camaraderie on the court before beating them mercilessly. With 41 seconds left in the first half of an East victory in 1997, Jordan began chatting amiably with the West's Mitch Richmond at mid-court as Grant Hill of the East shot the second of two free throws. Like a bolt of lightning that had been in for a lube job, Jordan burst away from Richmond, leaped over the unsuspecting West rebounders and ferociously dunked Hill's miss with two hands. As the crowd erupted in roars, Jordan skipped and laughed while running downcourt past Richmond. Got 'em again.

1. The circle will be unbroken. The halftime ceremony for the 50 Greatest Players was the highlight of the 1997 NBA game. It began with Jordan stepping on a riser as his name was called. Then the line of players, literally stepping up, weaved the length of the court and back again on the long risers as each name was announced. The last called was George Mikan, the oldest of the 50 greatest and the first NBA superstar. Unobtrusively, Bill Russell, standing on the last riser above the ailing Mikan, bent his arm and let Mikan pull himself up. Although Mikan is gone now, the memory of how he created the role of superstar, as well as that of how Russell played the role of the perfect teammate to the end, will never fade.

A Major League baseball dugout holds more guys who believe in the voodoo and the hoodoo than your average Haitian village. And while they probably lead the way in the sports world, baseballers aren't the only players carting around a personal religion's worth of rituals, beliefs, icons and taboos. Some are just more fanatical about it than others. And strange. Like our list leader, who can really bring the mojo.

15. Mike Hargrove. Clearly, some dugout seats can bestow runs in bunches while others give them up as reluctantly as C.C. and Carmona in 2007. Or so believes former Indians skipper Mike Hargrove. When things are going poorly on the field while he sits at one end of the dugout, Hargrove migrates to the other. Or moves to the middle. Or goes back to whatever part of the dugout he'd sat in the last time the Indians scored, like a wildcatter in his native Texas peering down a dried-up hole that had previously gushered oil.

14. Derrick Chievous. Despite a Cavs career recalled mainly for his habit of being the last one on the practice floor and the first off, Chievous did nonetheless leave us some lasting memories about Band-Aids. Seems he could not bear to play without several of them affixed to his body. When it came to stopping the bleeding from the points hemorrhage that occurred with the Cavs disastrous 1989 trade of Ron Harper, Chievous proved nothing more than his good-luck charm.

13. The 1995 Indians. Life imitates art. Indians players rigged up a replica of Jo Buu, the grass-haired voodoo god (think of him as a Chia pet with dark spiritual undertones) worshipped by Pedro Cerrano (Dennis Haysbert) in Major League. Alas, the god began balding, a development attributed to the damage inflicted on the Jacobs Field outfield grass during a Jimmy Buffet concert staged there just before the playoffs. When things got dicey in the postseason, Jo Buu was "sacrificed" in the bullpen.

12. Chico Salmon. Known as "Super Sub" with the Indians, Chico was terrified of ghosts. He refused to sleep in any room without the lights on.

11. Albert Belle. An Indians video crew employee known as Joe Vid would run around Belle before games in a circle, clicking Albert's bats together. Think of it as a wine connoisseur sniffing the cork on a dusty old bottle of fine vintage.

10. Bud Black. No haircuts on the day he pitched. It was a firm rule, devised after Black, like a post-Delilah Samson, got knocked around following a clip job.

9. Joe Carter. A former catcher who was part Native American, Mark Salas owned a beaded headband with knitted fabric in the middle. Carter insisted that he had to rub his bats against it before games.

8. Bob Feller. Always carried a lucky buckeye in his pocket during playoff games.

7. John Cooper. Given Cleveland's absorption with Ohio State football, mention must be made of John Cooper's abrupt switch in good luck charms. One day, while being interviewed by former *Plain Dealer* reporter Bruce Hooley, Cooper pulled a small statuette of a pig from his pocket and began making eerie sounds that were supposed to mimic horror movie sound effects.

"What's the deal with the pig?" asked Hooley, ad-libbing one of the most remarkable questions in the history of journalism.
"It's a lucky pig," replied Cooper.
"I thought you carried a buckeye," said Hooley.
"Carry my pig," said Cooper, settling the issue.

6. Bill Fitch. With the Cavaliers 0-and-15 in their inaugural 1970-71 season, head coach Bill Fitch and assistant coach Jim Lessig were walking the streets of Portland before the Cavs met fellow expansion team, the Trail Blazers. In the window of a curio shop, Fitch spotted a skull with a rat attached to it. It wasn't a real skull or a real rat, but the Cavs were just barely a real team. The object so summarized the Cavs' season to that point, Fitch figured it had to change their luck. Fitch bought it for $8 and placed the grisly purchase beneath his courtside chair for the game that night. Several Cavs players touched it for good luck. The Blazers' Shaler Halimon threw a towel over it to darken its mojo. And, lo, the Cavs beat Portland. Cavs win! Cavs win! For the first time ever! Fitch continued to lug the lucky skull cum rat to games. The Cavs lost their next 12. If, in the words of Haley Joel Osment, Fitch saw dead people, it wasn't beneath his seat, but on the court, wearing wine-and-gold uniforms.

5. Ernie Camacho. Reasoning that baseball is a game of threes, the reliever tied three knots in each shoestring, wore three pairs of socks on each foot, and would don three undershirts in cold weather. Not a lot of it helped when Camacho went one-for-ten in save situations with a 9.22 ERA for the Tribe in 1987. His only save came when Joe Carter threw out Cal Ripken, Jr., of all people, trying to stretch a long single into a double.

4. Willie Tasby. Don't baseball spikes seem just the thing to attract lightning? They did to Tasby, who played in the late 1950s and early 60s for Tribe, BoSox and Orioles. Worried that a lightning bolt was destined to slash down from a storm cloud and strike his footwear, with dark clouds gathering, the outfielder played in his socks one day. After lightning hit the area around shortstop during a rain delay in Baltimore, Tasby refused to return to the field.

3. Kevin Rhomberg. Former *Plain Dealer* reporter Bob Dolgan detailed this bundle of neuroses disguised as a professional baseball player. Whenever anyone touched him, Rhomberg had to touch him back. Tribe teammate Rick Sutcliffe once touched Rhomberg's toe while he was sitting in a clubhouse toilet stall. After emerging, Rhomberg went around and touched everyone in the clubhouse, since he had no idea who had initiated the contact. While playing winter ball Venezuela, Rhomberg once set his alarm and arose at 3:30 a.m. He then knocked on the door of a White Sox player, who had gotten away with a touch the previous day, and touched him back when he sleepily opened the door. If Rhomberg could not physically touch someone back, he tracked down his address and sent a note that read: "This counts as a touch." Rhomberg, who only made it through 41 games in the Majors and never found a position in the field he was comfortable playing, still found the time in that brief span to establish a number of his other mystic pet peeves: he would not make right turns (because you always turn left in baseball). He thought unseen "little people" helped station him in the exact right spot in the field. There's more, a lot of it. Basically, Rhomberg performed every superstitious ritual on the books but clapping his hands to dispel evil spirits. But he probably didn't clap because that would have counted as a touch.

2. Omar Vizquel. When a new glove under his own name led to a clutch of errors in 2003, Vizquel needed some leather he trusted. That happened to be a model used by second baseman Zach Sorensen, who had already been sent to the minors. After a few phone calls, a Sorensen model glove arrived. Little O then ritually sacrificed his own glove. In a spoof of Eastern mysticism, catcher Tim Laker decorated an empty locker stall like a shrine and placed the cursed glove atop it. With candles burning around the treacherous leather, and a roasted chicken above it, and a baseball inscribed "The curse is killed" below it, Vizquel sat before it in the lotus position and renounced the letter "E" and the number "6."

1. Thad Matta. He insists on thoroughly chewing a piece of Juicy Fruit or Orbit gum before each game (a ritual so essential that Matta does not blanch if it requires him to retrieve the gum off the ground to chew anew should it pop out of his mouth). He's always on the lookout for lucky pennies. Matta has his young daughters pick out his necktie before games. He laces his shoes at the same time at the same spot on the practice court every day and makes sure the shoelaces are exactly even after every loop. He stays with the same clothing ensemble as long as the Buckeyes are winning (although he does have managers launder his clothes after each game). He keeps a lucky Coke next to him after halftime. He stands in exactly the same spot for the national anthem, with the non-negotiable demand that his starting point guard always stand right next to him. Other than that, the Ohio State basketball coach is as normal as you and I.

Note: Always quick with a quip, former Browns head coach Sam Rutigliano (1978–84) was also a serious student of the game. His role in the re-casting of Ozzie Newsome as a tight end, and Ozzie's role in the evolution of the position, shouldn't be understated. Sam developed a lot of good players in his time here, though some were easier to bring along than others.

5. Clay Matthews. In 1978, we ranked him the 13th-best player in the draft, regardless of position. Detroit picked the defensive back we wanted on the 12th pick and we followed the board and took Clay. He went on to play 19 years—19 years!—at linebacker in the NFL. Was involved in red zone, short yardage, goal line and all situations as a linebacker. Could play on a tight end and play the run, could blitz, could do it all. Athletic enough to play in space and cover wide receivers and running backs. Very intelligent and high size/speed athleticism. Clay was a very good tackler in space and a great competitor. In my mind, he's a Hall of Famer.

4. Jim Plunkett. As offensive coordinator, I coached him in New England after the Pats Plunkett the first overall pick of the 1971 draft. Jim reported late because of the Chicago All-Star Game, and he was still Rookie of the Year. He ran for his life almost the whole year. Finally pulled a hamstring and we could then keep him in the pocket. The Patriots eventually traded him to the 49ers, who cut him. The Raiders picked him up as a free agent for $100,000 and he won two Super Bowls with them. You have to remember, no matter what all the scouts, coaches and draft analysts tell you, judging NFL talent is a crap shoot.

3. Ozzie Newsome. The Browns traded QB Mike Phipps to the Bears for a No. 1 pick, giving us two in the first round of the '78 draft. We took Clay Matthews with the first pick and Ozzie as our second. I sent (assistant) Richie Kotite to Alabama to find out how big a butt Ozzie had. He reported back: Ozzie has a big butt, which meant we would convert him from a wide receiver to a tight end. At our first mini-camp, I told him he could be a great tight end in the NFL. Ozzie said that Bear Bryant had told him that his best position in the NFL would be tight end. That sealed the move from wide receiver. He was smart, fast enough, tough, and had truly great hands. In seven years, I saw him fumble once. He was a clutch, big-play, pressure player and an adequate, willing blocker. He changed the position of tight end in the NFL. We used him as a wide receiver/tight end, much like the Browns now do with Kellen Winslow II. Ozzie disrupted defenses, so everybody around Ozzie caught passes, too. We had five players who caught 50 or more one year. He was a fantasy league player, playmaker, Hall of Famer.

2. Archie Manning. I had him while I worked as quarterback coach in New Orleans. He was a great athlete, instinctive, smart, the second player taken in the '71 draft. He survived the two years I was there (1976-77) only because he could run. Surround him with the group his son Peyton Manning has around him with the Colts, and Archie would have been better. He gave Peyton the mental assets and Archie was clearly the better athlete. He could have signed a major league baseball contract. Great competitor, team guy, and every bit the student of the game Peyton is.

1. Brian Sipe. The Browns had traded Paul Warfield to Miami for an early draft pick in 1970 and used it on quarterback Mike Phipps out of Purdue, who was heralded as potentially better than Len Dawson or Bob Griese. I arrived in 1978 and was told by the owner and the GM that Sipe was not the answer. I was working in TV at the time and spoke to Dawson, Griese and Fran Tarkenton about Sipe. They all said, as much as we overrate a QB's arm, we underrate accuracy. And they said Sipe was a very accurate passer. Judging a quarterback is at best a "seat of the pants" feeling. Some things are immeasurable and must be instinctual. You must crave the pressure as a quarterback. I always say playing quarterback is like being a tea-bag. You don't know what you have until you put it in hot water. With Brian Sipe, after the hot water, the rest was history.

Five Players Who Were A Challenge to Coach :: Sam Rutigliano

Note: Rutigliano faced unfair criticism that he was less interested in winning games than in the "Inner Circle," a groundbreaking substance-abuse program the Browns instituted while he was their head coach from 1978-84. But through his Inner Circle work, Sam saved lives. How many coaches can say that? The Brooklyn native also didn't back down from problem players, of which he had his share.

5. Lyle Alzado. We drafted him when I was an assistant coach in Denver from Yankton College in South Dakota. I left the Broncos and Lyle had a great career with them. The Browns traded for him in 1979. He was the toughest player I ever coached. He was a good person, but he was either coming in on Monday after a game swinging on a chandelier or crawling under the carpet. Extreme mood swings. I never knew what to expect. We traded him to the Raiders and he went to the Super Bowl. Once he retired, he got sick and tried for the first time in his life to help himself and other players to not take drugs to enhance their ability to play in the NFL. But it was too late for Lyle. After he died, I felt badly that this wonderful person and great team football player had virtually destroyed himself.

4. Chip Banks. He played outside linebacker at Southern Cal, before being moved inside for his senior year. The switch was a disaster. Marty Schottenheimer, Bill Davis and I went out there and sat with (SC coach) John Robinson and looked at every film from the past five years. Banks was better than Clay Matthews. He was an incredible talent. But he was different. He was not self-motivated. He did not fit in the locker room. He wanted to quit his first week of camp. I told Marty, "You get paid to coach Chip Banks, not Clay Matthews." Clay was fun; Banks was a pain in the rear. But he could have been a great one. After I left, they gave him away. He never reached his full potential.

3. Duane Thomas. When I was an assistant coach in New England, we traded Carl Garrett, a running back, to Dallas for Duane. He reported to camp, did not talk, dressed in Middle Eastern clothes, and would not eat any of his meals. Just a very strange person. Would not line up in the proper stance for a running back in the I formation. Actually turned his chair around in a meeting with his back to the coach running it (me) and was looking at his teammates. Players came to me and did not want to play with him. (General Manager) Upton Bell, who made the deal, left camp and instructed the assistant GM to send him back to Dallas and to call him when Duane Thomas was on the plane and it was safe for Bell to come back. Better do your homework before acquiring talent.

2. Hanford Dixon. A shutdown corner from Southern Mississippi, good athlete, very tough, excellent tackler. His personality fit the defensive back position in the NFL, although he did not have good hands. Dixon, Frank Minnifield, Chip Banks and Clay Matthews gave us the best group of perimeter defenders in the NFL—three No. 1s and a guy (Minnifield) picked up out of the USFL. But you could not tell Dixon anything. He changed or challenged the goals you would create for him. As a coach, you must find out where the button is located. You can't treat them all equally, only fairly.

1. Don Rogers. He was our top pick from UCLA. In my mind, he would have been one of the best strong safeties in the league. He played free safety, but his size and toughness would qualify him as a linebacker. We would have moved him to strong safety. Arizona of the USFL wanted to sign him. I sat down with him, told him we had selected him, and that I wanted to talk directly to him, and that I expected the same from him, instead of us communicating with each other through the media or his agent. He signed in right field at the Stadium during baseball season. He was an immediate starter and a future great player. I was fired in 1984. During the offseason in California, the night before he was to be married, Don was pronounced dead on arrival because of drug use. He was a great person and player, and I had no idea that he was using drugs. I think about Don Rogers a lot because of the work I did with the Inner Circle. I have always been puzzled and deeply saddened that we never saw signs of drug use.

The Seven Toughest Cornerbacks I Faced
:: Bernie Kosar

Note: One of the most popular Browns ever, quarterback Bernie Kosar won with his head more than his arm. Daring, confident, tough, resourceful and generous to teammates (he always deflected praise and money-making media opportunities to fellow Browns), if not opponents, the Boardman, Ohio native was everything you would want in a leader. A first-round pick in the 1985 NFL supplemental draft, Kosar guided the Browns into and through the franchise's last golden age. With the arrival of Bill Belichick as the new head coach, Kosar fell out of favor, which was high praise considering Belichick's inability to rate offensive skill players in those days. Kosar left the Browns in 1993 and played a few more years with the Cowboys and Miami, where he'd burst onto the national scene as QB of the upstart University of Miami Hurricanes in the early 80s. But with changes in the way the game was being played, he recognized, with remarkable clarity, that his future prospects in the league were no brighter than the Browns' chances under Belichick. He realized that in the new era dawning in the NFL, smarts, will and guts could no longer make up for a shortage of fast-twitch muscle fibers. He retired in 1996.

"The change to zone blitzes in the 90s made me feel like an old quarterback," said Kosar. "When everyone played bump-and-run, you could make sight adjustments and throw the fade. When zone blitzing came in, if you were an immobile quarterback, the pocket was not the place to be. You'd look for your passing lane and a lineman would be standing in it. The pocket passer is outdated. That's why Drew Bledsoe had a bad year in 2006. You cannot stay in the pocket anymore."

Kosar's smarts and audacity have, however, served him well enough in his post-football career. He has started successful restaurants and a magazine and owns parts of two pro sports franchises. He continues to oversee the Bernie J. Kosar Charitable Trust, which aids disadvantaged kids and young adults.

Kosar took advantage of plenty of overmatched cornerbacks in his day. But some of them won his begrudging respect and a place on this list.

7. (tie) Steve Brown and Patrick Allen, Oilers. They were on that Glanville team in Houston. The blitzes were something I loved because they played bump-and-run. They very rarely got to us on the blitz. Usually we beat those people.

5. (tie) Lester Hayes and Mike Haynes, Raiders. Dixon and Minnifield were better by the time I played against them in the L.A. Coliseum. But Hayes and Haynes were still very good.

3. (tie) Hanford Dixon and Frank Minnifield, Browns. I went against these guys in practice all the time. We played games in practice. We had fights. They used the bump-and-run coverage and really got in receivers' faces. Very aggressive going after the ball.

1. Deion Sanders, Falcons, 49ers, Cowboys, Ravens. He was clearly the best. He played games with you. I was stubborn, and I wouldn't throw away from him like other quarterbacks. Deion would make you think the receiver was open, but he was just so incredible at closing on the ball. He was cocky-slash-confident, and I like that in a guy. His closing burst—the last one or two yards when the ball was in the air—was something no one else had. But he only got one (interception) off me.

My Five Toughest Centers to Play Against
:: Brad Daugherty

Note: The former Cavalier had his career cut short by back problems. But he still ranks as best all-around big man in franchise history, as well as one of the most intelligent players of his era. Now a NASCAR analyst on ABC, Daugherty entered the University of North Carolina as a 16-year-old freshman. He lends the same precocious intelligence, along with his NBA experience, to rating the best centers of his day.

5. Kareem Abdul-Jabbar. Kareem was near the end of his career when I played against him. I never played against a guy so long. And he was still very strong. He was a methodical player by that time. He set up real well and established position by taking up so much space. Usually, I could put my body mass into someone and move him, but I had to go around Kareem. He was a master of the angles for the entry pass, too. If you let him get into a rhythm with the sky-hook, it was lights out. It was like playing Mark Eaton (Utah's huge, limited center), only with a lot of skill, like playing someone with a 7-foot-6 wingspan.

4. Patrick Ewing. I enjoyed playing against Patrick because he played so hard. He worked very hard at his game. By that stage, he was a good intermediate shooter. He was a menacing-looking guy, but he was not a dirty player. I really enjoyed my games against him.

3. Bill Cartwright. Bill had been a scorer earlier in his career, but most of the times I played against him, he was just supposed to get in the way. The Bulls always ran their first four plays through him. He was always flailing around out there with his elbows, so you had to be careful or you could pick up a cheap foul that would affect how you played. He was a guy who was always flopping around, creating havoc.

2. Hakeem Olajuwon. I usually played pretty well against Hakeem, but he was very tough to guard. Strength-wise, he was evenly distributed across his body. That's very unusual. He could go both ways with equal efficiency. One time, he might come across the lane and jump off his left foot on a fadeaway and the next time he might come across and jump off his right foot. He could jump to dunk with equal power off either foot. I had good strength and did pretty well against him. In part, that was because I wasn't a shot-blocker, so I didn't go for his pump-fakes.

1. Sam Perkins. It sounds funny, but it's not just the North Carolina background. He was a nightmare for me to guard. He had great range for a big man and could shoot the three so well. So I either had to stay in rebounding position and let him take a three or go out and try to bother the shot and get out of rebounding position. He presented you with problems that had no right answers.

You know that nail, for want of which the shoe was lost, for want of which the horse was lost, for want of which the rider was lost, for want of which the battle was lost? It was a Cleveland nail. Just a move or two different, a coach's arm windmilling here, a situational matchup that worked there, here a motivated superstar, there a last-play gamble gone awry, coulda' made us more than just contenders. It coulda' made us "chuh-chuh-chuh-champions," hard as that word is to say around here.

10. Joel Skinner shoulda' sent Kenny Lofton home. If Lofton had scored from first on Franklin Gutierrez's double with one out in the seventh inning of Game 7 of the 2007 ALCS, it would have tied the game, 3-3, and the Red Sox might have pressed, having wasted a three-run lead. Left fielder Manny Ramirez, jogging toward the ball, had no play except at second base. Lofton could have scored, standing up and moonwalking. But the Tribe's usually aggressive third-base coach Skinner held him up at third and the next batter, Casey Blake, grounded into a first-pitch double play to end the inning and the Indians' momentum. The Red Sox went on to win the game 11-2 and the pennant.

9. Robbie Alomar shoulda' stayed in bed. What can you say about a guy who jogs on double play grounders, takes first-pitch swings when Seattle's Jamie Moyer was fighting his control and basically played like he had fleas? And does it in the division series-deciding playoff game in 2001. It was inexcusable, and it is why Bill Livingston will not vote for Alomar for the Baseball Hall of Fame.

8. Anderson Varejao shoulda' given the ball back to LeBron James. With the Cavaliers down, 72-70 and LeBron James, who had scored 12 points already in the fourth quarter, flying in for a return pass and a game-tying dunk in the last 13 seconds of the third game of the 2007 NBA Finals, the "Really Most Sincerely Wild Thing" spun to the basket and airballed a layup. San Antonio won, 75-72, and went up, three games to none. You know the rest.

7. Bruce Bowen wanted to intentionally foul James, so the refs shoulda' called it. "If he tries to foul me, I'm shooting a three," James told teammates when the Cavs called time in the last 5 seconds of the third game of The Finals, with the score 75-72. Bowen grabbed James by the upper arm, as he took the inbounds pass. James shot a triple and missed. But referees Bernie Fryer, Bob Delaney and Dan Crawford swallowed their whistles. Where have you gone, Tim Donaghy?

6. Lenny Wilkens shoulda' guarded Brad Sellers making the inbounds pass. Give Wilkens credit for guts because he never doubled Michael Jordan, not even the night he laid 69 on the Cavs. But he did this time. Still, it was easier to make Warrensville Heights native Sellers beat the Cavs with a tough inbounds pass than to stop Jordan once he got the ball. Especially because Larry Nance, who gave Craig Ehlo brief, ineffective help, was playing on a bad ankle. Jordan's subsequent buzzer beater won the game and 1989 playoff series and established the teams' respective fates for seasons to come.

5. Brian Sipe shoulda' thrown it to the blonde in the first row. This is a tough one because Browns placekicker Don Cockroft was having an awful day with a ball that had all the elasticity of a sedimentary rock in the two-below cold. Still, Ozzie Newsome was too closely covered to risk a pass on a cold, windy day. The interception clinched a 14-12 loss and finally flatlined the Kardiac Kids.

4. Eric Wedge shoulda' hooked C.C. Sabathia after six innings. The chance to win a pennant at home in 2007 mandated that Wedge go to his best reliever (Rafael Betancourt) after six innings of Game 4 of the ALCS. Sabathia had pitched all game the way Custer generaled at Little Big Horn, with trouble all around him. He should have been done after six. As it was, Wedge tried to get another inning out of him. A double and a triple brought Betancourt in too late. The resulting 3-1 deficit against the overpowering Josh Beckett looked bigger than the midge infestation did to the Yankees' Joba Chamberlain. The Red Sox won, 7-1.

3. Webster Slaughter shoulda' run out his pattern. By standing and watching the play, Slaughter freed Jeremiah Castille, who would have had to cover him. Castille took the opportunity to force "The Fumble." Instead of tying the score, 38-38, the Browns went on to lose, 38-33.

2. Marty Schottenheimer shoulda' kept Dave Puzzuoli in on "The Drive." Nose tackle Puzzuoli had sacked John Elway for an eight-yard loss on second down, forcing a third-and-18 in the 1986 AFC Championship Game. Marty played prevent defense the rest of the game, rushing only three men. Elway was never pressured, and "The Drive" became part of Cleveland sports infamy.

1. Mike Hargrove shoulda' had Charlie Nagy up in the bottom of the ninth. Why is the closer sacrosanct? What, the man who has to get the three toughest outs of a game comes apart like cheap plaster at the slightest touch of pressure, even at the sight of activity in the bullpen? Jose Mesa was such a frail vessel for such huge hopes. Distrusting his own talent and best pitch, Mesa kept shaking off Sandy Alomar's call for the fastball in the bottom of the ninth inning of Game 7 of the 1997 World Series. The Marlins tied it at 2-2 and Nagy, who was bumped for Jaret Wright as the starter, lost it, in the 11th inning. The next day, in the airport departure lounge waiting to return to Cleveland, Indians' legend Bob Feller wrapped his hands disgustedly around his own throat. "I'm Mesa," he said.

Trying to create a new nickname is kind of like putting up a half-court heave at the end of the first half. Only one in a blue moon succeeds. But the potential reward justifies the minimal risk of damage to your shooting percentage. Sportswriters try to come up with them all the time (nicknames, not half-court heaves). And, oh, if readers could just eavesdrop on press boxes or get an X-ray of what's really going on inside the heads of reporters who cover their teams. Oh, wait. That's what you're getting here.

15. "The Penguin." Dates from Jim Tressel's days as coach of the Youngstown State Penguins.

14. "Badden." The flip side of the maddeningly inconsistent Drew Gooden.

13. "Injun Joe." A construct of *Plain Dealer* Indians beat reporter Paul Hoynes, who coined it for Joe Carter. Politically incorrect to the max, but fun. It was Hoynes who wrote of the Indians' retreat from contention in 1986: "The Wahoo war wagon has made a U-turn on its way to the Promised Land."

12. "Green Hamm and Eggs." For William Green and Asia Gray, respectively. Developed by Livingston when Green said he tripped going up the stairs and stabbed himself in the back, a move worthy of Olympic gold medal gymnast Paul Hamm, instead of being stabbed by his longtime girlfriend, Gray, who was also the mother of his two children.

11. "Toker Billy." For William Green, who played really well "on grass."

10. "The Pie Man." In keeping with the dining motif, Akron's Sheldon Ocker coined this one for Eric Wedge.

9. "Mumbles." For Bi—mutter-l Bel—mumble—ch — tongue tied in reverse half-hitch — k.

8. "Lyin' Butchie." On the day Butch Davis was hired, a Florida reporter familiar with him from his days at The U. told Bill Livingston: "Well, and there is no nice way to say this, Butch Davis is a liar. By the end of the day, his nose reaches Calcutta." After playing for him for a few years, Tim Couch agreed: "I think a lot of players would tell, if they're in a situation like I am, where they're not in the league, and they could really tell you that they've been lied to by him."

7. "Heckuva' Job." For Mike Brown, Cavs coach, in "honor" of his simplistic, Basketball 101 offense. Derived from George W. Bush's praise of his feckless FEMA director, also named Mike Brown, after the Hurricane Katrina catastrophe: "Brownie, you're doing a heckuva' job."

6. "Flop." DeSagana Diop certainly was here (0 for 5 from the line, 1.0 average his last season) in his attempt to establish himself as a legitimate NBA big man.

5. "Fritz and Hans." Based on the Katzenjammer Kids, but applied to Marty's use of brother Kurt. It was an example of nepotism that recalled Dick Van Dyke's tolerance for brother Jerry and his infernal banjo.

4. "Peter the Grate." For Peter Bavasi, whose czar-like view of power and abrasive style led to the coinage. Not Bill's best work, but useful as a burr under the saddle of Bavasi, which was the point.

3. Derrick "Miss" Chievous. Shot 35.4 percent from the floor in his two Cavs' seasons. Always the last one on the practice floor, first to leave.

2. "Magnum P.I." This coinage came from the magnum-size of Vitaly Potapenko and Zydrunas Ilgauskas, Cavs' draftees in 1996. Gordon Gund used it in one news conference after it appeared in print. Then, Potapenko was traded and that was that.

1. "Daddy Chargebucks." Because Al Lerner's empire was founded on MBNA credit cards, this take off on *Little Orphan Annie's* Daddy Warbucks seemed mildly amusing. *Plain Dealer* editors did not agree.

Funny ones, sad ones, wrong ones, right ones, dumb ones, dumber ones. Our sports figures usually come up short on the field. But they have always held their own coming up with memorable quotes in the interview room.

13. "If you can't make the putts and can't get the man in from second in the bottom of the ninth, you're not going to win enough football games in this league, and that's the problem we had today." Browns head (football) coach Sam Rutigliano, who went on to explain how critical it would be to box out on rebounding, only swing at pitches in the strike zone and choose the right club for the approach shot on the Road Hole to make it to the Super Bowl.

12. "A quarterback is like a tea-bag. You have to see how he does under heat and pressure." Rutigliano, setting the metaphoric precedent followed years later by Butch Davis when he explained why the receivers he drafted needed to be like sieves.

11. "The greater the fall, the higher the bounce. We will bounce." Owner Art Modell after the Browns' 3-13 season in 1991. The comment set off debates among Clevelanders about what object they would like to throw Modell off to see how high he bounced. Leading contenders included from the bleachers at the ballpark he hated and envied, Jacobs Field, Terminal Tower and off the roof of a boxcar filled with his usual b.s.

10. "I have a great legacy, tarnished somewhat by the move." Art Modell. The former Browns owner went on to point out that Art Schlichter had a great NFL career tarnished somewhat by the gambling, Roy Tarpley established a Hall of Fame-caliber legacy tarnished somewhat by the drug use and Saddaam Hussein had a great first Gulf War tarnished somewhat by his inability to hold an early lead.

9. "Those bottles are plastic. They don't pack much of a wallop." Browns president Carmen Policy on Bottlegate. Wouldn't you have liked to play "Beer Bottle Skeet" with Policy? You yell, "Pull!" and a guy in a thousand-dollar suit runs across the field while you, factoring in the wind, the heft of the bottle and the trajectory of the missile when heaved from the top row of the Dawg Pound, try to put a half-full Bud Lite in Carm's way.

8. "I didn't see anything. Did you, Lew?" Browns owner Al Lerner, on Bottlegate, like a pair of Sgt. Schultz clones from *Hogan's Heroes* (the show's theme song once served as the Cleveland State fight song), Lerner and Lew Merletti, the former head of the Secret Service and the Browns' security czar, "knew nothing!" about the hundreds of beer bottles fans tossed onto the field during the game.

7. "I must be the luckiest guy in Callahuga County." Tribe pitcher Dennis Cook, after winning a home game in which he did not pitch well. Asked the whereabouts of Callahuga County, he replied: "That's where we are, ain't it?"

6. "Don't put the cheese on the floor. The rats will get it." Cleveland State coach Kevin Mackey, advising his big men not to dribble. Mackey would later demonstrate that you also don't put the coach in a crack house with a hooker or those dirty rats the coppers will get him.

5. "See you next Tuesday. Spell it out." Cavs coach Paul Silas. Hmmmm: I get "C-U-N . . . " So, what's that really spell? Why, Carlos Boozer!

4. "Not Europe. Italy." LeBron James, when asked if he had ever visited Europe as the 2004 Olympic team readied for the Athens Olympics. LeBron's autobiography is unlikely to borrow the title of John McPhee's classic essay on Bill Bradley's years at Princeton, "A Sense of Where You Are."

3. "I call him 'The Maestro.'" James on 2004 USA Olympic coach Larry Brown—before Brown stapled his 19-year-old butt to the bench.

2. "Didn't have to drive him far, did you?" Indians manager Mike Hargrove on Albert Belle, after a reporter asked if the 415-foot center field wall in 1991 was being brought closer to home plate "because it was just driving Albert crazy."

1. "Kick field goals." Rutigliano as he left Alvy's restaurant at the old Stadium the day he was fired when Bill Livingston asked him if he would have done anything different.

Ten Examples of Charley Manuel Dexterity

Known as Aka Oni ("Red Devil") during his young, carrot-topped playing days in Japan, Indians' manager Charlie Manuel embraced the stringent conditioning and foreign culture of the Japanese game. But he never appreciated his Far Eastern hosts preference for linguistic precision. Charlie is known for maneuvering his tongue around some of the most enjoyable Stengelisms since Sparky Anderson, if not the Old Perfesser himself.

10. "Konerkle." For the White Sox' Paul Konerko

9. "Wrench." For White Sox pitcher Kelly Wunsch.

8. "Under Armor." A play on the athletic equipment and on Wunsch's submarine (underarm) pitching style.

7. "Hart Throb." Indians General Manager John Hart, when he was getting along with him.

6. "Hart Attack." When he was not.

5. "Ptomaine Poisoning." For Jim Thome, a Manuel favorite.

4. "Funky Cold Medina." For Luis Medina

3. "K-Love." For Kenny Lofton, another Manuel favorite whom he personally recommended as a leadoff man when Lofton was a minor leaguer with the Astros.

2. "Cameroncross." A combination of the first and last names of Australian-born Indian pitcher Cameron Cairncross

1. "Jughead." For Jaret Wright, "because he's got a big head that's kind of empty."

Note: A former Lorain Congressman, Sherrod Brown grew up in Mansfield, driving with his family to Indians games "up old Route 42." His father would have gone to the fifth game of the 1920 World Series at League Park, the game in which Bill Wambsganss turned the only unassisted triple play in World Series history, but Brown's grandmother wouldn't let him. "It was a Sunday (Oct. 10), and Sunday was for church," explains Brown, who won election to the U.S. Senate in 2006, and attended his first Indians game when was only four-years-old on Bob Feller Day in 1957. But the first game he really remembers came in 1959 when Rocky Colavito came out of the outfield to pitch an inning. A true Indians fan, the Senator knows his baseball.

14-4. (tied) The Indians of the 1960s: Sam McDowell, whom I met once in a hotel lobby as a kid. Sam was, let's call it, 'brash.' And Jim Perry, Steve Hargan, Sonny Siebert, Leon Wagner, Frank Funk, who had another name I liked, and Woodie Held, Max Alvis, Joe Azcue, Vic Davalillo and Gary Bell.

3. Calvin Coolidge Julius Caesar Tuskahoma McLish. I loved his name. I always used his full name when I talked about him.

2. Omar Vizquel. He's the only recent Indian on my list. The teams when you were a kid stick with you more. How fair is this? You reporters got to interview Omar and Joe Carter. I got to talk to Newt Gingrich and Dick Cheney.

1. Rocky Colavito. The arm was as big a part of why you watched him as the bat.

My 12 Most Hated Yankees :: U.S. Senator Sherrod Brown

Note: A lifelong Indians fan, Sherrod Brown understands that supporting the Tribe also means despising the Bronx Bombers. "Rooting for the Yankees is like rooting for the drug and insurance companies," says Brown. "You can do anything you want in baseball if you have enough money behind you." Brown called the Tribe's Game 4 Division Series victory over the Yankees in 1997 his biggest thrill. "Sandy Alomar, Jr. homered in the bottom of the eighth off (Mariano) Rivera to tie it, and the Indians won it in the ninth. I remember the Yankees' Paul O'Neill slumped against the right field fence (after the homer). It seemed like the season was over before that. And (to homer) off Rivera!" Brown said the toughest thing about composing his lists was "reducing to ten the number of my most-hated Yankees." He didn't quite succeed, but no true Indians fans could.

12-6. (tied). The Yankees stars of my youth, as a whole: Bobby Richardson, Tony Kubek, Whitey Ford, Moose Skowron, Mantle, Maris, Luis Arroyo. I was at a game Easter Sunday, 1962, at Yankee Stadium. Only time I was there until the 90s. Maris had broken the Babe's record the year before. First time up, he struck out. Second time he comes up, they booed him. It was New York.

5. George Steinbrenner. Three reasons: He closed the Lorain shipyard in my district. He was convicted of making illegal contributions to the Republican Party. And he owns the Yankees.

4. Reggie Jackson. I always felt the same way about him as I did about Clemens and Wells.

3. Phil Rizzuto. He never should have been in the Hall of Fame.

2. Roger Clemens. Just the arrogance of him. He threw at guys in the American League when didn't have to bat. And if he really thought (Mike) Piazza's shattered bat was the ball, why did he throw it at Piazza and not to first base?

1. David Wells. More obnoxious Yankee arrogance.

Herb was the "Voice of the Indians" on either TV or radio from 1964–97. He didn't sing "Take Me Out to the Ballgame" like Harry Caray or cry "How about that?" like Mel Allen. He didn't root like Phil Rizzuto and he never quoted from the "Song of Solomon" about the "Song of the Turtle(dove)" like Ernie Harwell. But the Old Lefthander taught us a thing or two about the game and left us with a thousand or two great memories.

5. Listening to Herbie, you never knew if the Indians were winning or losing. He never screamed, "The Indians win the pennant!" (even when they did, twice). He never let the team's 41 years in the wilderness or the losing get him down. Herbie knew you played to win the game, each day, every day, with a purity of effort and tightness of focus, long before Herm Edwards made that a rallying cry in the NFL.

4. He was the voice of summer in Northeast Ohio. Through all the player trades, the failed saviors, the under-funded owners, Score was always there, the soothing voice of a franchise that was fortunate to associate with him.

3. He knew the game. Whenever a controversy arose or a rhubarb broke out, Herbie was quick to tell us what it was all about.

2. He never blamed the end of his career on his eye injury, or the arm he hurt after he came back. "I lost my job because I quit pitching well," he said.

1. Herb never forgot how hard the game is to play. It was a rare and especially egregious blunder that would cause Score to criticize a player on the air.

Ten Inexactly Expressed Sentiments from Herb Score

Then again, he wouldn't be Herbie without the head-scratching malapropisms and endearing vagueness.

10. Herb often had trouble distinguishing between Oakland platoon catchers Mickey Tettleton and Terry Steinbach. During one game when the former was at bat, Herb called him "Mickey Tettlebach."

9. Carl Yastrzemski came to bat in his last game at Fenway Park against the Tribe in 1983, moving Herb to say: "A standing ovation here from the fans in Baltimore for their hero." Then he added: "Yaz played 23 years for the Orioles."

8. Once during the days when Score partnered in the booth with Steve Lamarr, Herb ended a broadcast with: "This is Steve Lamarr, signing off for Herb Score. Good night, Tribe fans."

7. When a player was on a hot hitting streak, Herb said: "He is 24 for his last 49, and even I know that is over .500."

6. With the Indians leading Baltimore, three-games-to-two and the sixth game in extra innings in the 1997 ALCS, Tony Fernandez homered in the top of the 11th inning to give the Tribe a 1-0 lead. Said Score: "And the Indians are going to the World Series . . . maybe!"

5. When a pitcher was working from the stretch, Score offered: "The pitcher checks the runner on first . . . .I beg your pardon, there is no runner on first."

4. On a double down the line, Herb said: "It's fair. It's foul. It is."

3. With Esteban Yan warming up, Herb identified him as "Ron Jantz" (pronounced, "Yontz"), a local weekend sports anchor.

2. With Efrain Valdez stalking in from the bullpen, Score identified him as "Efrem Zimbalist Jr."

1. This one requires a little backstory: The Indians, who had played in Kansas City the night before, were in Milwaukee, and next were headed for Boston. After a night of conviviality that included a libation or two with old friends but no sleep, Score arrived in the booth feeling well south of the fair-weather line. Partner Nev Chandler did the first inning, in which the Royals took a 2-0 lead. A game, but outgunned Herbie, called a six-pitch Tribe top of the second, the brevity of which kept him from getting into any rhythm. He then said: "And, after one-and-a-half innings, the score is: Kansas City two, Indians nothing."

A check of the outfield revealed no waterfall behind the centerfield fence, so Score nimbly recovered and said: "I beg your pardon. We are not in Kansas City. We are in Boston. And the score is: Red Sox two, Tribe nothing." A further check of the surroundings revealed no Green Monster in left.

"What city are we in, Nev?" asked Herbie, amiably.

"Milwaukee, Herb," Chandler replied, sotto voce.

"And the score is: Brewers two, Tribe nothing," Score concluded triumphantly.

When the Indians returned home at the end of the road trip, General Manager Phil Seghi asked Chandler before the game: "Does Herb know he's in Cleveland?"

Top Ten Revolting Developments Since 1964

When particularly disgusted about his latest setback, Chester A. Riley (as played by William Bendix in the 1950s sit-com *The Life of Riley*) would bluster: "What a revoltin' development this is!" A big-hearted blue-collar worker, Riley established the prototype for later TV characters like John Goodman's Dan Conner in *Roseanne* and even Fred Flintstone. Riley worked in Los Angeles at an aircraft plant, but his sensibilities and personality were pure Cleveland. As we watched with revulsion while neighboring cities and hated rivals won championship after championship in the long years since the Browns brought home Cleveland's last in 1964, we felt his pain.

10. Art Modell finally won a Super Bowl—after moving the Browns to Baltimore.

9. Bill Belichick won three Super Bowls.

8. The Pittsburgh Steelers won five Super Bowls.

7. The Detroit Pistons won three NBA titles and the Detroit Tigers won two World Series.

6. The Philadelphia Phillies won their only World Series title.

5. David Justice led the Yankees to a World Series title after the Indians traded him.

4. The Florida Marlins won two World Series.

3. The Chicago White Sox won a World Series.

2. The BOSTON RED SOX won TWO World Series titles.

1. That pretty much leaves the Cubs and the Tribe.

Top 18 Names That Sound Dirty, But Really Aren't

A friend of ours, who used to cover Virginia Tech, was complaining that Vernell Coles had kept him waiting for an interview, when he was told: "It is hardly the first time you have waited for a Bimbo." Of such low humor and hijinks are these names listed.

18. Bartolo Colon, Indians, 1997-2002

17. Jerry Ball, Browns, 1993, 1999

16. Phil Bedgood, Indians, 1922-23

15. Josh Booty, Browns, 2001-03

14. Dick Brown, Indians, 1957-59

13. Don Cockroft, Browns, 1968-80

12. Bimbo Coles, Cavs, 2000-03

11. Bill Contz, Browns, 1983-88

10. Steve Cox, Browns, 1981-84

9. Curtis Dickey, Browns, 1985-86

8. Fernandas Eunick, Indians, 1917

7. Thane Gash, Browns, 1988-90

6, Ben Gay, Browns, 2001

5. Boobie Gibson, Cavs, 2006-

4. Mel Harder, Indians, 1928-47

3. Woodie Held, Indians, 1958-64

2. Fair Hooker, Browns, 1969-74

1. Dick Pole, Indians pitching coach, 2000-01

The Dean's List: Greg's Ten Classiest Cleveland Sports Figures

As the longest-running sports radio personality in Cleveland, co-author Greg "The Dean" Brinda knows the roster of the city's sports figures like few others. And as a journalist, he knows which guys were easy to deal with, and which guys were tough. Here's his list of the ten classiest sports figures—guys who had time for you, win or lose—that he has dealt with during his many years on Cleveland's airwaves.

Honorable Mentions: Tom Cousineau, Hanford Dixon, Dick Ambrose, Mike Johnson, Brian Brennan, Chris Bando, Brook Jacoby, Eddie Johnson, Sandy Alomar, Ron Harper, Rick Manning, Mark Shapiro, Mike Brown, Ernie Accorsi, Carlos Baerga, Chris Palmer and Art Modell

10. Mike Hargrove. "Grover," as he was called, played and managed the Indians for parts of 16 years. As a player, Hargrove played on some pretty bad teams, so there were a lot of nights when talking about another loss wasn't very pleasant. Hargrove though always sat by his locker in the cramped Indians' clubhouse, answering everything until the media was finished. As the team's manager, he helped the team improve and, as the Indians got better, his time was stretched. Yet he made time for everyone and really protected his players.

9. Felix Wright. The Browns safety played eight years here from 1985-1992. Maybe because he went undrafted and spent three seasons in the CFL, Wright realized how fortunate he was to play in the NFL. He played in the Browns mid-80s heyday and also played on some horrible teams late in his career. But Wright always gave thoughtful and reasonable answers no matter how good or bad the game went for him and the Browns.

8. Omar Vizquel. Vizquel played 11 seasons for the Indians. Most of those years were very good times for Cleveland fans. Vizquel knew he was on stage and acted like the perfect showman. Of course, the Indians didn't win every night. On those bad nights, Vizquel shined even more. He often held court in the clubhouse and answered the tough questions when everyone else decided to hide.

7. Ozzie Newsome. Newsome is one the most beloved Browns players ever. He played in Cleveland from 1978-1990 and I had the privilege to cover his entire career. Even in the worst of times, Ozzie knew the media had a job to do and did his part to accommodate all of us. Never once did the "Wizard of Oz" believe he was too special for us. And when he didn't want to talk about a particular game or subject matter, he always answered in a humble truthful way without making anyone uncomfortable.

6. Bob Golic. A hometown boy who played at St. Joseph's high school and attended Notre Dame, Golic was very happy to spend most of his career in his backyard. Golic played with the Browns from 1982-1988. He played with such free spirit and seemed to enjoy being on stage. That's why he ended up on television. I don't think I ever saw Golic turn down an interview. Although he played for some pretty good Browns teams, there were still bad times. Golic, though, handled every win or loss the same way—with pleasantries and good answers to sometimes very hard questions.

5. Jim Thome. Thome was the definition of a good guy. He liked everyone and rarely did you see him angry. Thome played with the Indians from 1991-2002. Although a lot of fans hate him for leaving via free agency, they seem to forget that Thome was one of the reasons the team was so successful in the 1990s. For a guy that was so good and likable, it's hard to believe there's any animosity. Unlike a lot of players, most of us just saw the good side of Thome.

4. Mark Price. Price played with the Cavs for nine seasons. Because Price had to defy long odds to make it as a pro and perhaps because of his strong religious background, he had a solid foundation and knew what kind of person he was. I don't think Price ever had a bad word to say about anybody. He too was totally accommodating to the media, win or lose. All Price would ask is that he get dressed before he talked. Too many times, we in the media are in such a hurry to interview players when they are quite not ready. The best thing I could say about Price is that he's the kind of person you'd like to have as your brother.

3. Doc Edwards. Doc wasn't in Cleveland a long time. He managed the Indians for one full season and parts of two seasons. The team wasn't very good in the late 1980s, but it wasn't his fault. It's difficult enough being a manager and being the head guy on a bad team can't be much fun. But each and every night in a cramped office, Edwards answered every question good and bad. He respected the media and vice versa. Most managers, even the real nice ones get surly once in awhile. But not Edwards. He just loved being in the big leagues and he showed it.

2. Randy Smith. Smith played for the Cavs for just two seasons from 1979-'81. I was just getting started in the business and I couldn't believe it was this easy talking to professiohal athletes. Smith made it easy and it spoiled me. This guy took time and answered every question and I know there had to be some dumb ones in there. This is a guy who really enjoyed what he did for a living and it showed. He always had a smile and if you needed to ask him a question, on- or off-the-record, he didn't ever hesitate. The sports world would be a better place if everyone were like Smith.

1. Sam Rutigliano. Sam is by far the most entertaining manager or coach in Cleveland sports history. He spent six-and-a-half seasons coaching the Browns. They were some pretty good times, including the "Kardiac Kids" years, but also some lean ones. Sam, though, delivered his thoughts as if he were doing a one-man Broadway show. He was funny, articulate, down to earth and never demeaning. The media always looked forward to his Monday press conferences. To miss one would mean missing great sound bites for the week. He was deeply religious, yet never preached. He would do anything for anybody. And considering he had one of the toughest and most demanding jobs in sports, Rutigliano never let on that he was tired or mad, even when the situation would have justified it.

Ten Nicknames That Weren't Complimentary

A guy whose big head had nothing to do with ego. A problem breakfast gambler. Somebody with an over fondness for groceries. A pair who shared an unfortunate physical resemblance to varmints. A professional athlete trapped inside the body of a portly frat boy. Some players just beg to be rechristened.

10. Paul "The Human Garage" Silas. The power forward turned coach could box out an entire row of courtside reporters trying to watch his misconceived offense.

9. Greg "Flounder" Swindell. He disabused us of any hope that he would be the next "Sudden Sam" in his first game, which he lost 24-5. After that, we were left only with his resemblance to fat frat pledge Kent Dorfmann from Animal House.

8. Jamie "The Rat" Easterly. Much like former Indian Billy Martin, of whom it was said, "He looks like a mouse, studying to be a rat," Easterly had that rodent look. He seldom threw cheese, however, hard or otherwise. His career record was: 23-33.

7. Ken "Mouse" McFadden. Like Easterly, the CSU point guard of the 1980s seemed in need of cheese. Now!

6. Don "The Rock" Schulze. "Is the nickname because he throws hard?" Bill Livingston once asked manager Pat Corrales of the Tribe pitcher in the mid-80s.
"Nooo," said Corrales, as he stood on the bottom step of the dugout.
"Is it because he's so tough?" Livingston asked.
"Noooo," said Corrales, as he languidly stretched his arm up to the roof of the dugout and began to pound the concrete just above his head with his fist while pointing with his other hand to his head.
"Is it because he's a rock head?" Livingston said.
"Yessss," said Corrales.

5. "Dinner Bell" Mel Turpin. Spectacularly apt monicker for the Macy's parade float who preceded Shawn Kemp in the Thanksgiving parade for the Cavs.

4. Rodney "Buckethead" Craig. A size nine batting helmet made his the league leader in head circumference until Barry Bonds had to start wearing an American Tourister on his head during the steroid era.

3. Fredo. Browns players' derisive term for the owner's adopted son, David Modell. Probably would have been as feckless an owner, had Artie not sold the team, as the middle Corleone kid was a gangster.

2. Eddie "Special Ed" Taubensee. The Tribe's back-up catcher was so-called, not for his special athletic talent, as he thought, but for mental acuity that teammates thought made him a candidate for "special education" classes. Hey, we didn't make it up, we're just doing our jobs as journalists and reporting it.

1. Craig "Eggs" Ehlo. The Cavaliers played shooting games after practice, with the loser buying breakfast. Guess who paid for two over-easy the most?

Note: During Wayne Embry's tenure as General Manager from 1986-99, the Cavs rebuilt themselves from the rubble left behind by the Ted Stepien era into a perennial NBA title contender. Embry was the new sheriff in town, insisting on bringing in players of good character after too many of Harry Weltman's gambles crapped out. He built a top team that would have won it all except for that Jordan guy. He and the first coach he hired, Lenny Wilkens, wrote another proud chapter in Cleveland's history of racial progressivism as the first black GM-head coach tandem in the NBA.

But it wasn't all blue skies and green lights in the Embry years, especially for him. In 1989 he traded, at owner Gordon Gund's insistence, Ron Harper and two first-round draft picks for Danny Ferry and a sack of beads. But even though he didn't want to make the trade, Embry took the bullet. It was the way he operated. No excuses, no finger-pointing. His character, along with his shrewd personnel moves, helped the Cavs become a proud franchise during his time as general manager.

10. Losing Dell Curry in the expansion draft. Oh, boy, is it hard to find shooters. It was a very tough decision. We could have put Mike Sanders out there, but we thought we wanted to preserve the starting rotation. Dell played a long time in the league, but he was not established at the time. He was the key part of the trade with Utah to dump Mel Turpin. Then, lo and behold, the league decided to expand. We tried to make a deal with Charlotte to influence them to take somebody else. We gambled and we lost.

9. Dealing with Mel Turpin and Keith Lee. I inherited them, but Gary Fitzsimmons (former pro personnel director) and I made the decision to get rid of the whole lot of them, John Bagley, too. Harry Weltman (formerly the Cavs' GM, but by then the New Jersey GM) was dragging his feet on the deal. It was getting to be nine or ten at night, and the NBA office said they were going to close. I remember telling Gary to get on the phone and tell them, "Don't you dare let everyone leave."

8. My first season when we played the Celtics at old Richfield Coliseum. Not many people were going to our games in those days. But we had a big crowd that night and most of them wore green. That was disappointing. That told me we had work to do.

7. Well, of course, the Ron Harper trade. You make a decision and you live with it. Ronnie loved Cleveland. He still hugs me when he sees me.

6. The first time we made the playoffs (1988). It wasn't "The Shot" series, which was the next year. But it showed we had the capability to do something in the league.

5. Making the Eastern Conference Finals in 1992. Boston was aging, but they still knew how to win. I remember the fourth game (of the conference semifinals series) in Boston. Mark Price and Larry Nance got home court back for us. And I remember how Mike Sanders got into Bird defensively in the seventh game.

4. "The Shot." It was a little premature for us to make our run, due to the youth of our players. It was just a first-round series, but a lot is made of it today because it's seen as launching the Bulls. But they still had to get past the Pistons and wouldn't for a while. I remember Lenny Wilkens drew up a helluva' play to get us the lead on Craig Ehlo's layup. But it worked too well and too much time was left.

3. The premature end of Brad Daugherty's career due to back problems. People thought he was soft. It was ridiculous. He wasn't soft. He was big, wide and a tough guy to guard. He had one of the last real hook shots. He could beat you scoring or passing. Ask David Robinson, ask Patrick Ewing, ask any of the top centers of his era. Nobody liked playing him. And we hated to see him retire.

2. Dealing with Shawn Kemp. He was a likable guy who lacked self-discipline in a lot of ways. I tried to give him tough love. He had a "fat clause" in his contract, and when he violated it, I met with him to fine him $250,000. He said he didn't hold it against me, he knew it was what I had to do. I said: "No, Shawn. It's what I want to do. It's the only way you can get your life back together." He had needed tough love for a long time. By then, it was too late.

1. The death of Bobby Phills in Charlotte. One of my favorite players. A wonderful person. A guy who listened and made himself into an NBA player. I noticed that Z (Zydrunas Ilgauskas), when he was asked whom he would like to share the Finals' success with, if he could, said, "Bobby Phills." That tells you a lot about Z, and a lot about Bobby Phills.

As Bill said, he's a hoops guy. Don't expect him, in the LeBron James Era, to brook insults to his game.

6. They change the rules in the last two minutes. Yeah, so what? Helping the trailing team through a few rules tweaks makes games more compelling and keeps fans interested. When NBA teams advance the ball in the last two minutes from their own baseline to a spot 28 feet from the other team's basket, it costs a timeout. The NFL awards a free timeout (the utterly misnamed "two-minute warning") and nobody gets outraged about its bending of the rules. How about all those bunch-up-the-field yellow flags in NASCAR late in a race?

5. Only the last two minutes matter. This is the longest running canard of all. Have you considered that baseball makes the last three outs of a game—the toughest outs to get, we are always told—separate and unequal, compared to what went before? That is done both to justify overpaying pampered closers and to, unwittingly, devalue the first 24 outs of the game.

4. Nobody plays any defense. Actually, when the ball goes up for the center jump, teams like the Detroit Pistons fix bayonets. No team guided by someone from the Larry Brown coaching tree, including both 2007 Finalists, San Antonio (Gregg Popovich) and the Cavs (Mike Brown), plays anything less than nasty defense, usually from jump street.

3. It's a game for glandular cases. As long ago as the 1950s, Red Auerbach argued that it was a game of quickness, not size. Any league that has had a place for such mighty mites as Charlie Criss, Spud Webb and Central Catholic's own Earl Boykins is a league that puts a premium on quickness. You can't teach height, true. You also can't teach slashing penetrator quickness with power forward heft, as with LeBron James.

2. Too many timeouts in the last two minutes. Here's a scenario certain to create brain death. Browns score with eight seconds left in the first quarter, then kick the extra point. Timeout to sell cars on TV commercials. "Action" resumes. Browns kickoff, returner is tackled five seconds later at the 20. Timeout to sell beer. "Action" resumes. Off-tackle run gains one yard. End of quarter. Commercials now to sell Erectile Dysfunction products. Total: eight seconds of action in exchange for about ten minutes of your life you will never get back. And don't even get me started on the between innings "breaks" in the World Series.

1. The Golden Age is gone. Oh, puh-leeze. They said that after West and Robertson retired, after Wilt and Baylor hung them up. They said it about Bird and Magic and Dr. J. "This is a new Golden Age, declared NBA commissioner David Stern before the 2007 playoffs. He meant James, Dwyane Wade, Carmelo Anthony, Chris Bosh, the newcomers Greg Oden, Kevin Durant and Mike Conley Jr., and selected others. James would have been a rookie at the start of the 2007-08 season if he had played four seasons of college ball. Not even Oden's knee surgery before he played a game in the league could put a damper on that.

Your Name's Your Game: Seven Guys With Names That Matched Their Professions

We note only that our seventh selection seldom moved his team past midfield. Hah! What nominative irony!

7. Spergon Wynn, Browns quarterback.

6. George Winn, Indians.

5. Vic Power, Indians.

4. Chris Gatling, Cavs, not a real big gunner, but still perfect on a team full of them (Ricky Davis, Lamond Murray).

3. Michael Cage, Cavs big-man cager.

2. John Battle, undersized but hard-nosed Cavs' shooting guard.

1. Al "Bubba" Baker, Browns, defensive end and barbecue chef.

Not the Best Names for Sports: Seven Guys With Names That Created Mismatches

Not every athlete gets blessed with a distinctive, stylish name like LeBron James. Or a short, tough one like Kevin Mack that perfectly matches his talents and career intentions. But some get saddled with decidedly un-athletic names that sound like a kid's breakfast cereal or a character from an Emily Bronte novel, creating one more obstacle to their making it to the big leagues. We've had more than our share of name-challenged players in Cleveland. Or at least these seven.

7. Eppie Barney, Browns, 1967-68

6. Lloyd Bishop, Indians, 1914

5. Coco Crisp, Indians, 2002-2005

4. Bruce Flowers, Cavs, 1982-83

3. Milt Plum, Browns, 1957-81

2. Heathcliff Slocumb, Indians, 1993

1. Birdie Tebbetts, Indians, 1951-52

By the 1980s, Indians pride had become so impoverished that Clevelanders reacted to the 1989 film as if its story had really happened. It would become Cleveland's favorite movie, or at least its runner-up favorite behind *A Christmas Story*. For a time, the former "Jerry's Place" bar in Fairview Park held a party every year on the day pitchers and catchers reported to spring training. A showing of *Major League* was the high point of the revelry. Waitresses dressed as vendors in Tribe uniforms sold hotdogs with Ball Park mustard, peanuts and Cracker Jack. Local TV stations flocked to cover the scene as patrons stood and cheered the Tribe's victory over the Yankees as if they were watching a live broadcast of the ALCS.

10. Bill Livingston makes his movie debut. Sort of. A shot of a fake *Plain Dealer* sports page with Bill's column picture in the opening moments bore the headline: "Can ex-Vegas showgirl turn Tribe around?" As Livingston told anyone who asked, and many who didn't: No, he did not receive any pay for the plug. (He did, however, insist on rewinding the videotape to show the scene at least twice each year at Jerry's.)

9. Harry Doyle, everybody's favorite play-by-play man. "Friends of the Feather." "Chieftains of the Cuyahoga." "Sons of Geronimo." "The Yankees have beaten the Tribe like a tom-tom this year." "That one's off the reservation." The film used the signature phrases of Doyle (played by Milwaukee Brewers' announcer Bob Uecker) as deft send-ups of political correctness. In one perfectly played scene, the addled broadcaster, with five empty cups of Jack Daniels lined up before him, signed off after a loss to the Yankees by saying: "So, a tough start for the Erie Warriors, as they drop a heartbreaker to the Yankees, nine to nothing. The post-game show was brought to you by . . . (he searches for the promotional paper) . . . Christ, I can't find it. The hell with it. This is Harry Doyle saying, goodnight, everybody. And happy hunting." Doyle had become Herb Score—on bourbon and steroids.

8. It mocked Latin players as well as Native Americans and white guys. Impartial in its satire, the movie was a serial offender. It made the movie's Cuban refugee, Pedro Cerrano (Dennis Haysbert), no more effective at hitting the curveball than real-life Cuban defector and Tribe pitcher Danys Baez was at throwing one. That is, until Cerrano renounced the voodoo fetish doll, Jo Buu, with its taste for Cuban cigars and dry gin. The KFC chicken sacrifice in the film is a great, hilarious compromise by director David S. Ward between religious mysticism and having PETA protesters walk around the set with live chickens squawking under their arms.

7. It mocked the religious right, too. Eddie Harris (Chelcie Ross), the fundamentalist pitcher, denounces Cerrano as a "savage." But then Harris shows Rick "Wild Thing" Vaughn (Charlie Sheen) three smears of "Crisco, Bardahl, and Vagisil" on his chest. "Any one of 'em will give another 2-3 inches drop on your curveball," says Harris. He also swears by rubbing a jalapeno pepper inside his nose to start the mucus flowing. "You put snot on the ball?" asks a disgusted Vaughn. We didn't know it at the time of the movie's release, but Harris prefigured rumors about Orel Hershier, the "Doxology"-singing Indians pitcher whose "wet one" was considered a reliable weapon against drought in several states.

6. Koreans didn't escape. The groundskeepers, always conversing in Korean, required subtitles to translate their degree of belief. ("They're still shi**y," is what they are still saying at the midpoint of the movie.) By the playoff game, though, they are spotted enthusiastically banging together their shovels—inventors of the rally stick.

5. Or the press. "The local press," says manager Lou Brown (played by James Gammon), "thinks we'd save everybody a lot of time and trouble if we just went out and shot ourselves. Me, I like to waste sportswriters' time so I'm for hangin' around and seein' if we can give all these guys a nice big shi*burger to eat."

4. Small-market baseball, either. The smoking, rattling "Wahoo Express" team bus; the antiquated DC-3 airplane that leads the team to suffer from, as Doyle terms it, "a bit of propeller lag"; the ratty, cheap feel of the whole operation—the filmmakers only needed to insert a shot of Phil Seghi and Gabe Paul strolling through the clubhouse to capture the era perfectly.

3. Millionaire players got ribbed worst of all. Yelps Roger Dorn (Corbin Bernsen), whipping out his contract: "Those penalty sit-ups you want me to do? I got it right here in my contract that I don't have to do any calisthenics I don't feel are necessary. What do ya' think of that?" According to the original script: "Brown looks at the contract a second, then drops it on the ground, unzips his fly and gives it a golden shower."

2. Even the love scenes got the emotional-growth-stunting appeal of baseball (as Jim Bouton discussed it in Ball Four) just right. Says Lynn (Rene Russo) to Jake (Tom Berenger): "You like the life you've had, Jake. You like hangin' out with the boys, livin' in hotels, eatin' dinner at midnight, having girls send you their underwear in the mail . . . .I'm sorry, Jake. You'll always be the little boy who wouldn't grow up." Ouch.

1. Life didn't imitate art—it tops it. In the movie, Willie Mays Hayes (Wesley Snipes) scored from second on Jake Taylor's bunt to win the division playoff game against the Yankees. Nine years later in real life, Enrique Wilson scored from first base in the 12th inning with the go-ahead run on a bunt by Travis Fryman in a 1998 ALCS playoff game against the Yankees. True, Fryman got away with interference by running outside the "box" down the first-base line. But while the ball rolled to the edge of the right-field grass and Wilson circled the bases, Yankee second baseman Chuck Knoblauch, who was covering first, argued with the umpires and blithely blew a bubble with the gum he was snapping, inspiring a New York tabloid to label him, "Knoblockhead!" The Tribe went on to win the second game of the 1998 American League Championship Series, 4-1.

Problems with *Major League*

No one will ever mistake it for cinematic baseball classics like *Bull Durham* or *Bang the Drum Slowly*. But the 1989 film *Major League* did offer some good, lighthearted laughs, a story revolving around the Cleveland Indians, some free publicity for Bill Livingston and a reasonably accurate picture of life in the MLB. Well, not entirely accurate. Here are a few of the filmmakers' bigger flubs.

7. There is no such thing as a "red tag" placed in a player's locker to tell him he has been cut.

6. No one, not even Johnny Lipon, would put a sore-kneed, lumbering catcher like Jake Taylor (Tom Berenger) in the No. 2 hole in the batting order behind leadoff hitter Willie Mays Hayes (Wesley Snipes).

5. The scoreboard clock during one game reads 10:40 a.m. Not even the Cubs play games that early in the day.

4. If owner Rachel Phelps (Margaret Whitton) really wanted to destroy the team, she would have waived the players who began to flourish. Or brought in Joe Klein as her general manager.

3. *Major League III: Back to the Minors.* About the only thing they got right in this 1998 sequel to the sequel was the title.

2. Just as the climactic fight in *Rocky* took place at the Los Angeles Sports Arena and not the Philadelphia Spectrum, much of the on-field action of *Major League* was filmed in Milwaukee County Stadium, former home of the Brewers and a miniature version of Cleveland Municipal Stadium. In fact, some billboards advertising Milwaukee businesses can be seen in certain shots.

1. They didn't have the Indians win it all. No local team had brought home a championship to Cleveland since 1948, so it would have been nice of them to let us at least celebrate a cinematic triumph. So, while technically accurate, having the Indians fall short was still cruel. But six years after *Major League* came out, the real Indians did finally reach the World Series, then returned two years later. "Jerry's Place" changed ownership and stopped showing the movie at the start of spring training. Cleveland still hasn't hosted a victory parade. But bigger dreams than the movie's downsized ones really did come true.

Note: From the holiday lights on Public Square in *A Christmas Story* to the scenes at the U.S. Steel mill and Saint Theodosius Russian Orthodox Church in *The Deer Hunter*, Cleveland has always looked great on film—even if it is identified as a mill town in northern Indiana (in the former) or upstate Pennsylvania (in the latter). Our cinematic expert Tom Feran rated these Cleveland pics in no particular order.

10. *The Deer Hunter.* Cleveland served as the very recognizable shooting location for director Michael Cimino's 1978 winner of five Academy Awards. Unfortunately, it played Pennsylvania. The cast included Robert DeNiro, Christopher Walken, Meryl Streep, John Savage and, in his final role, John Cazale—forever Fredo Corleone.

9. *Antwone Fisher.* This autobiographical drama from 2002 explored the nightmarish Cleveland youth of writer Antwone Fisher, played by Denzel Washington, who also directed.

8. *Light of Day.* It's less fun than it sounds, but local references abound in director Paul Schraeder's 1987 blue-collar, rock 'n' roll drama starring Michael J. Fox, Joan Jett and Gena Rowlands.

7. *Telling Lies in America.* Dress sharp, drive fast, look cool, laugh last. Cleveland gets into the Six Degrees of Kevin Bacon game through this 1997 Bacon vehicle/coming-of-age movie set in the early 1960s and written by Clevelander Joe Eszterhas.

6. *Stranger Than Paradise.* Written and directed by Cleveland native Jim Jarmusch, this absurdist comedy from 1984 ranks as a classic of independent filmmaking. Earns extra points for featuring "I Put a Spell on You" by local R&B legend Screamin' Jay Hawkins.

5. *Those Lips, Those Eyes.* Set in the 1950s and shot at Cain Park in Cleveland Heights, this underrated romantic comedy from 1980 grows in stature as more and more people discover it on late-night cable TV. Stars Frank Langella, Tom Hulce, Glynnis O'Connor and the inimitable Jerry Stiller.

4. *American Splendor.* It's hard to get more Cleveland than this locally-filmed story of Cleveland-to-the-bone writer Harvey Pekar. The hit film became an unlikely Oscar nominee and launched the even more unlikely leading-man career of star Paul Giamatti.

3. *Welcome to Collinwood.* Written and directed by Clevelanders Anthony and Joseph Russo, this 2002 feature was shot in Cleveland and has George Clooney in it. Need more be said?

2. *A Christmas Story.* Yes, the setting is a fictitious Indiana mill town. But the winter shots of Public Square and Tremont practically make this authentic 1982 classic a home movie for Clevelanders. The Tremont house used as Ralphie Parker's home in A Christmas Story has even become a popular tourist attraction, complete with a museum devoted to the movie across the street from it.

1. *The Fortune Cookie.* This 1966 comedy with a movie Hall of Fame lineup served as the breakout feature for the North Coast. Directed by Billy Wilder (*Some Like It Hot, Double Indemnity*), it stars the original odd couple Jack Lemmon and Walter Matthau in their first screen pairing—plus Municipal Stadium and the Browns.

Note: Tom Feran is a walking encyclopedia of local entertainment history cleverly disguised as a longtime *Plain Dealer* reporter. He offers a random play version of our city's best songs. Says Feran: "Use any order you like, it's endlessly debatable—which is why I started the list title with 'Ten' and not 'Top Ten.' With notable omissions like Pere Ubu, Nine Inch Nails, Bobby Womack, Gerald Levert, Bone-Thugs-N-Harmony, the Dazz Band, Michael Stanley and some more-strictly-local groups, the list could have easily stretched to 100, and beyond. I cut it off in the late 70s, before music splintered into too many genres for stuff to be commonly familiar."

10. "Go All The Way" by Eric Carmen and the Raspberries reached No. 5 on the Hot 100 with this harmonic and brashly naughty power-pop masterpiece that ruled the radio in the summer of 1972.

9. "Time Won't Let Me" by The Outsiders. Driving guitars, powerful drumming, a great horn riff and Sonny Geraci's strong vocal shot this to No. 5 in January 1966 with a record that straddled the styles of the Beatles and Motown and became a pop classic.

8. "It's Cold Outside" by The Choir. The band only reached No. 68 on Billboard's national chart with this debut single But they owned Cleveland, where "It's Cold Outside" perched at No. 1 for seven weeks in early 1967. With three Top-40 stations in town—WIXY, WHK and WKYC—you couldn't go more than a few minutes without hearing this stunningly catchy and relentlessly driving single.

7. "Walk Away" by The James Gang. Calling the James Gang the Cream of Cleveland compliments Clapton & Co. With its fire-breathing guitar work and cascading drum, this Joe Walsh composition from 1971 was what hard rock was all about.

6. "War" by Edwin Starr. We flipped for his debut with "Agent Double-O-Soul." But Edwin Starr, who started singing in his years at East Tech High School, was No. 1 everywhere in 1970 with this growling anti-war song that became an anthem for a generation.

5. "With This Ring" by Sonny Turner. Cleveland's own Sonny Turner, a Rock and Roll Hall of Famer, was lead singer for the Platters on this, the group's final Top-40 hit, a soaring and sweetly soulful record that reached No. 14 in 1967.

4. "Born Too Late" by The Poni-Tails, a trio formed at Brush High School, were one of the first successful "girl groups" of rock and roll's first generation. They broke the Top 10 in 1958 with this song that went on to become a standard.

3. "Use Ta Be My Girl" by The O'Jays. The band had a boatload of hits. But we always remember Reggie Jackson saying he'd be truly happy if he could sing like Eddie Levert on this ever-fresh hit that sweetened the summer of 1978. Who wouldn't be?

2. "The Boy Next Door" by The Secrets. This Shaw High girl group with an attitude and a tight, tuff sound to prove it saw their debut single hit No. 18 and stick around Billboard's Hot 100 for ten weeks in 1963.

1. "Mr. Bass Man" by Johnny Cymbal. A worldwide hit in 1963, an oldies standard, and the signature song of Johnny Cymbal, who was born in Scotland, but started his music career in his early teens while growing up in Cleveland. A prolific songwriter, Cymbal recorded under many names and scored again as Derek in 1968 with "Cinnamon."

Since taking over as head football coach at St. Ignatius in 1988, Chuck Kyle has guided the Wildcats to nine big-school state championships. Along the way, his teams have played against the best that Northeast Ohio, as well as the rest of Ohio and nearby states, have to offer, and beaten just about all of them. Kyle always shows respect to other programs, but a few opposing players have impressed him above the others.

3. Ted Ginn, Jr., QB, Glenville. Oh, boy, I know he is going to make a lot of money in pro football. But if he had stayed in track, he'd be right there in the hurdles when the Beijing Olympics come around. He was the quarterback in the spread formation against us in 2003. That's scary, a guy that fast, in space. We distorted the whole defense to stop his running. We always had seven or eight in the box. We tried to latch onto their wideouts, who were flying down the field, and stay with them one-on-one. It was a matter of counting how many are in the box and then Ted had to hit some passes. We were fortunate he only hit one deep one. I don't know who would have won a 100-meter dash between Ginn and Robert Smith, but I would have wanted to see it.

2. Maurice Clarett, RB, Warren Harding. This guy was a great runner, but he could receive, too. I thought he would play 10 years in the NFL and average something like 4.8 yards per carry. He ran for 400 yards against St. Ed's the week before we played them in 2003. They defended him in theory, but they had the usual high school safety, 5-11, 180, coming up to tackle him, and Clarett would just—Bam!—run over him. We used a linebacker Justin Kazmarcik in the secondary. He had a little more size and could come up to clean up tackles. Clarett could make sharp cuts and break tackles. He wasn't blindingly fast, but he was fast enough on the football field. He reminded me of Emmitt Smith. With all our adjustments, he still had 185 yards at halftime on us, but we held him to 20 the second half and cooled him off. I don't think I can say we stopped him if he got 205 yards, though.

1. Robert Smith, RB, Euclid. The guy ran like O.J. Simpson. He was the first one we faced where you just said, "This guy is awesome. We have to do some radical things against him." He liked to bounce it to the outside when he got through the hole. If he got those long strides going down the sideline, all you could do was yell, "Kickoff return team, get ready!" You weren't catching him. In the Immaculate Reception game (1989 regional finals), we played with the entire goal of making him cut back to the middle. He played quarterback and ran the option. Every play, it was like that book, only we were saying, "Where's Robert?" instead of "Where's Waldo?"

The former *Plain Dealer* copy editor is the golden booter in our crowd. Along with a lot of Clevelanders, he took a shine to indoor soccer in the 1980s and '90s during the glory years of the Cleveland Force and Cleveland Crunch in the Major Indoor Soccer League (MISL) and National Professional Soccer League (NPSL). Here, he shines his light into the local history of indoor soccer to show us the gems that played in Cleveland.

10. Tim Tyma. Playing outdoors, he helped Brecksville High School win the 1975 state title and played one year at Cleveland State. Then he went indoors to start a pro career that included three consecutive NPSL Defender of the Year awards and championships with the Canton Invaders and Cleveland Crunch. The fearless defender blocked over 1000 shots to become indoor soccer's all-time leader and gain a starting spot on the All-Time NPSL Team. What he lacked in skill and pace, Tyma made up for in heart and toughness.

9. Andy Schmetzer. He and his twin Walter joined the Force in 1985 as 18-year-olds out of high school. While a knee injury ruined his brother's career, Andy made All Star teams with the Force and Crunch as a valuable midfielder, capable both on offense and defense.

8. George Fernandez. The first overall pick in the 1983 draft by the Force, the defender became known as "Captain Crunch." The friendly, yet intense and tough Hawaiian played the 1994 playoffs with a separated shoulder, which didn't stop him from dishing out hard hits to help the Crunch win the title.

7. Craig Allen. Though seldom journeying into the defensive zone, Allen's nose for the ball near the opponent's goal made him one of the Force's great scorers. Like NHL great Phil Esposito, he camped at the doorstep, tipped in passes, and basked in the glow of the red light signaling "GOAL!"

6. Tommy Tanner. The third member of the Crunch's attack trio featuring Hector Marinaro and Zoran Karic, Tanner did the dirty work to set up the superstars. The 1991-92 Rookie of the Year sacrificed his own points to serve as a feisty midfielder digging the ball out of corners and getting it to the Dynamic Duo, helping his team to dominate the MISL and NPSL for a decade.

5. Keith Furphy. His flowing blond hair, long legs and ability to leave defenders in his wake on the way to goal made him a Force fan favorite. Females, in particular, ignored his disdain for helping out on defense and swooned over Furphy's booming left-footed shots and memorable goal-scoring theatrics.

4. Otto Orf. The shaggy-haired goalkeeper paid his dues as a journeyman backup until 1992, when new Crunch coach Gary Hindley recognized Orf's powerful arm as a potent offensive weapon. A goalie triggering the attack with outlet passes after making courageous stops, Orf became a perennial 20-game winner and all-star for a decade.

3. Zoran Karic. Lou Gehrig to Marinaro's Babe Ruth, the tempestuous Serbian ranks as the indoor game's all-time assists leader and among its leaders in goals. When not in the penalty box for yelling at referees, he hung back in the offensive zone, ready to undress defenders one-on-one or set up Marinaro and other Crunch players for numerous goals in numerous blowout victories.

2. Kai Haaskivi. He combined a computer-like mind with incredible athletic ability. A multiple All Star (and MVP of the '87 game), he passed, scored, played defense, and was voted Cleveland's most popular athlete in a mid-1980s *Plain Dealer* poll. He served as leader of the Force teams that packed fans into the Coliseum for years.

1. Hector Marinaro. To call him the Michael Jordan of indoor soccer wouldn't do Marinaro justice. He was more like the sport's Michael Jordan and Wayne Gretzky combined. Indoor soccer's all-time points leader and 14-time All Star, he won eight scoring titles, six MVP awards and led the Crunch to championships in 1994, 1996 and 1999—Cleveland's only pro sports titles of any kind since the Browns' NFL crown in 1964. His career here started, oddly enough, with the Force cutting him after he played five games as a rookie defender. But Marinaro persevered, switched positions and developed into a great-shooting forward who notched more than 1,400 goals in his storied career.

Top Five Local Golfers

So we're not a golf hotbed? Then how has the Cleveland area produced golfers who have won three British Opens, two PGAs, a Masters and a U.S. Senior Open? Plus, our No. 2 guy honored Cleveland tradition by leading the Tour in heartbreaking losses to the superstar of his age and sport, that Nicklaus fellow. Here he is, along with four other masters of the local links.

5. Barb Mucha. A Parma native, Mucha learned the game on public courses like Little Met, Ridgewood and Mastick Woods. She played on an even level with the boys at Valley Forge High School, then conquered the LPGA's Futures Tour to make the LPGA Tour in 1987. Although often plagued with health issues, Mucha has won five LPGA Tour events.

4. Herman Keiser. The long-time Summit and Portage County pro won the 1946 Masters and four other PGA Tour events. In 1947, he played on the United States' victorious U.S. Ryder Cup team. Keiser gave three years of the prime of his career to the Navy in World War II. When he returned, he finished second in Tour events four times despite the long layoff. Two of those runner-up finishes were to Ben Hogan, whom Keiser disliked. Which made his one-shot victory over Hogan in 1946 at Augusta for the coveted Masters title all the sweeter.

3. Ben Curtis. Born and raised outside Columbus, Curtis graduated from Kent State and has a home in Stow. His one-stroke victory over an elite field in the 2003 British Open ranks as one of greatest upsets in golf history, a reversal on the order of Jack Fleck over Ben Hogan in the 1955 U.S. Open playoff. The gritty Curtis, at 1-under, was the only player in red numbers at Royal St. George's. He won twice on the PGA Tour in 2006, proving he was something other than a fluke who benefited from a tricked-up course at St. George's.

2. Tom Weiskopf. The Benedictine product honed his game hammering practice shots at Luke Easter Park after the Bengals football team finished practicing. Weiskopf's perseverance and talent paid off with 16 PGA Tour event wins, seven of them in 1973, his best year, and one of the better years anybody has enjoyed on the PGA Tour. His victory at Troon that year in the British was his only major, but the Ohio State graduate was a four-time runner-up at the Masters. He also finished second in the 1976 U.S. Open. A respected course designer, Weiskopf won the 1995 U.S. Senior Open, edging long-time nemesis Jack Nicklaus. Besides the slimmed-down blond from Columbus, he had to compete against: Arnold Palmer, still a threat; Lee Trevino, who had come boisterously onto the stage; Johnny Miller, the Tiger of his age, for a couple seasons anyway; and then there was also a kid named Tom Watson who won a few tournaments here and there. Weiskopf's sweet swing remains one of the most beautiful in golf history.

1. Denny Shute. Herman Densmore Shute was born in Cleveland in 1904 and died in Akron 70 years later. Often overlooked today, Shute actually won three professional majors—the 1933 British Open at St. Andrews and the 1936 and 1937 PGA Championships. He was the last man to win back-to-back PGA Championships until Tiger Woods matched Shute's feat in 1999 and 2000. Shute's repeat was actually much more impressive. Tiger's second straight PGA victory came in three-hole playoff in a newly adopted format (not to mention a helping foot from one of his fans in the gallery who kicked Wood's errant drive on 18 out of thick brush). But Shute won his two PGAs playing in the brutal, man-killer match-play format. Every day was an 18-hole playoff for him.

Note: Burt Graeff covered 11 U.S. Opens, seven Masters and numerous other PGA Tour events during a 40-year period of working at the *Cleveland Press, Columbus Citizen-Journal* and *Cleveland Plain Dealer*. He was on the 18th tee at the Champions Golf Club in the 1969 U.S. Open at Houston when Orville Moody looked at his caddy and said, "Son, somehow we have to make par on this hole." Somehow, Moody did make par to complete one of the great upsets in Open history. Graeff was on the first tee in the 1971 U.S. Open when Jack Nicklaus and Lee Trevino met in an 18-hole playoff. It was there where Trevino pulled a rubber snake out of his golf bag, tossed it playfully at a startled Nicklaus, and then went on to win.

Just missed the cut: Elyria Country Club, Boulder Creek Country Club, Sharon Golf Club, Glenmoor Country Club, Portage Country Club, Pine Hills Golf Club.

10. Sleepy Hollow Golf Course, Brecksville (Cuyahoga County). This public course where Charlie Sifford was once the head pro has the look and feel of a private club. And, it should. Designed by Stanley Thompson and sitting on land owned by the Cleveland Metroparks, it opened as a private club in 1925. It went public in 1963. This is not a course for the novice. It is a course that requires strategy, patience and plenty of game. If your game is not there, you can comfort yourselves with the spectacular views of the Cuyahoga River Valley to enjoy.

9. Good Park Municipal Golf Course, Akron (Summit County). Who says city-owned and city-operated golf courses have to be dog tracks? Good Park, designed by Bertie Way and opened in 1926, is as good as any city-owned, city-operated course in Ohio. Tight, tree-lined (and the trees are tall), fairways, more than make up for the lack of water hazards. A double-bogey, or more, is waiting to happen for those spraying shots off the tee. This beauty has been challenging some of Northeast Ohio's top amateurs for nearly a century.

8. Fowler's Mill Golf Course, Chesterland (Geauga County). A Pete Dye gem, which means plenty of railroad ties—roughly 2,000 of them. This wonderful layout opened in 1979 as a course for employees by TRW, who sold it to the American Golf Corporation in 1986. The golfing public was the real winner. This course is anything but boring, one that invigorates the soul no matter how many times it's played.

7. Barrington Golf Club, Aurora (Portage County). This Jack Nicklaus signature course opened in 1994. As with all Nicklaus-designed courses, you get generous, forgiving fairways. But the fairways are guarded by dense, mature trees and there are lakes—including several guarding the front of greens—with plenty of rolling hills on this well-manicured layout.

6. Little Mountain Golf Club (Lake County). Another relative newcomer to the Northeast Ohio golf scene, Little Mountain opened in 2000. Designed by noted architects Michael Hurdzan and Dana Fry, it features ample fairways, but some of the deepest sand bunkers—as deep as 25 feet below the green—seen anywhere in Ohio. It is a target layout, with some terrific views of nearby Lake Erie along the way.

5. Stone Water Golf Club, Highland Heights (Cuyahoga County). Opened as a high-end public course in 1996, it is now members-only. Another Hurdzan/Frye design, it sits on 170 acres of wooded wetlands. Sixteen of the 18 holes have water to deal with. Hosted three Nationwide Tour events and the pros loved it.

4. Kirtland Country Club, Willoughby (Lake County). An oldie, but goodie, opened in 1921. Standing on the 10th tee, which overlooks the Chagrin River valley, yields views on an October day unmatched in the Cleveland area. Don't be fooled by the beauty. This is a real test, where numerous U.S. Open and U.S. Amateur qualifiers have been contested.

3. Canterbury Golf Club, Beachwood/Shaker Heights (Cuyahoga County). Old school here. Tree lined, little water, lightning-like greens, this venerable club—opened in 1922—has been the site of two U.S. Opens, two Western Opens, two U S. Amateurs, one PGA Championship and one U.S. Senior Open. Enough said.

2. Firestone Country Club's South Course, Akron (Summit County). Since the mid 1950s, when it hosted the Rubber City Open, no course in the United States has hosted more PGA Tour events or gotten more television time than Firestone South. Included on its resume: three PGA Championships, the World Series of Golf and currently the World Golf Championship's Bridgestone Invitational.

1. Sand Ridge Golf Club, Munson Township (Geauga County). Merged with the Mayfield Country Club in 2006 and now technically called the Mayfield Sand Ridge Club.

This may be a surprise No. 1 pick to some, but not to those who have played it. Tom Fazio-designed and opened in 1998, it sits on nearly 400 acres of maple trees, wetlands and is considered by most to be the premier private golf club in the Cleveland-area. Built adjacent to a sandstone quarry, it is said to be tough enough to host a U.S. Open.

Instead of "The Forest City," Cleveland could be called "The Fastest City." Because no other U.S. metropolis boasts two Olympic gold medal winners in the 100 meters,(Owens and Dillard). Four members of our team gained entry into the USA Track and Field Hall of Fame (Owens, Dillard, Manning and Albritton). Another (Mack) should make the Hall as a single-event Olympic gold medalist. Only a drug controversy may keep out another (Reynolds). We did not rank Stella Walsh, South, who won the women's 100 meters, running for Poland, at the 1932 Olympics, then silver in Berlin in 1936. An innocent bystander slain in an armed robbery in 1980, Walsh, an autopsy revealed, had male genitalia and possessed both male and female chromosomes, a condition known as mosaicism. However, the controversy over the woman Olympian who was a man, sort of, is not why Walsh fell short of making our list. It's just that Cleveland also had Jesse Owens. We held to two rules: It's a co-ed list, and no one (not even Jesse) competes in more than one event.

100. Jesse Owens, East Tech. Who else? For variety's sake, we could have gone with Dillard, who won the 100 meters in London at the 1948 Olympics, four years before he won gold in his real specialty, the 110 high hurdles in Helsinki. But the "century" serves as track and field's iconic event—a celebration of speed and explosive power. All other sports begin with these two elements, and so we begin with one of history's greatest and most iconic athletes, a man whose records stood for decades, not years and who remains a symbol of triumph in the face of hatred and adversity.

200. LaShaunte'a Moore, Akron Firestone. Member of the 2004 American Olympic team, due to the drug suspension of Torri Edwards, Moore would be the event's "It" Girl with better starts. She flashes a radiant smile and an ability to pulverize the curve like a batter sitting on the Deuce. Was the object of intense interest from LeBron James at the opening ceremony in Athens.

400. Butch Reynolds, Akron Hoban. Silver medalist at the 1988 Seoul Olympics and world record-holder for 11 years, the powerful Reynolds might have been history's premier one-lapper, had he not become embroiled in a draining battle against the IAAF over what was probably a botched drug test. To trackies, the moment when IAAF Grand Dragon Primo Nebiolo presented Reynolds with the gold medal for his 400 victory in the World Indoors in Toronto was the sport's Pete Rozelle and Al Davis moment.

800. Madeline Manning, John Hay. Gold medalist in the 1968 Mexico City Olympics and a four-time U.S. Olympic Trials champion, Manning was one of the great Tennessee State Tiger Belles, who made women's sprinting an American fiefdom in the 1960s.

1,500. Treniere Clement, Monroe Falls HS, Stow. Three straight national titles for the Georgetown graduate position her as the top American middle-distance runner. Clement fell in the 2004 Olympic Trials 1,500, but came back more focused than ever. Also runs the 800.

Steeplechase. Mark Croghan, Green. Two-time NCAA champion at Ohio State, three-time Olympian, four-time national champion, Croghan really hasn't spent his life sloshing around in squishy shoes. It just seems that way.

5,000. Michelle Sikes, Lakewood HS. The surprise 2007 NCAA champion in this event and third-place finisher in the Nationals as a Wake Forest distance runner, Sikes is a Rhodes Scholar who majored in a field of mathematics so abstruse that it flies over our heads like a discus.

10,000. Katie McGregor, Willoughby South. Has a national outdoors 10K title to her credit and an NCAA cross-country championship, earned at Michigan. Titian-haired and freckled, McGregor is an aerodynamic version of Pepermint Patty from the Peanuts comic strip

100 Hurdles. Carmen Banks, John Adams HS. Running for coach Monica Gary (now coaching at Purdue, as well as serving as an assistant at the 2007 Pan Am Games), Banks set or tied 11 outdoor and indoor state records. Her PR of 13.50 placed her second in the 1994 Junior Nationals. Her 41.80 in the 300-meter hurdles ranked as the nation's best in 1994. She tallied 28 of the 40 points her school totalled to take the team title in the 1994 state track meet.

110 Hurdles. Harrison Dillard, East Tech. "Bones" idolized Jesse Owens, joining the crowd to salute him at a victory parade in Cleveland after the 1936 Berlin Olympics. Dillard grew up to become the greatest track star ever in these parts, except for Jesse.

400 Hurdles. Glenn Davis, Barberton. World record holder and the first man to win the Olympic gold medal twice in the event (at Melbourne in 1956 and Rome in 1960). He often outscored entire other teams with the Magics and competed in the long jump in addition to sprints at Ohio State. He won the Sullivan Award in 1958 as the nation's top amateur athlete.

High Jump. Dave Albritton, East Tech. One of the first high jumpers to use the straddle style, he had a background that was almost uncanny in its similarity to Jesse Owens. Both were born in Danville, Ala., went to East Tech and Ohio State, then competed in the 1936 Olympics. Albritton and Cornelius Johnson both jumped 6-9¾ at the Olympic Trials, becoming the first black athletes to hold the world record in the event. Albritton finished second to Johnson in Berlin. He tied for three NCAA titles and was a seven-time AAU outdoor champion.

Pole Vault. Tim Mack, St. Ignatius. Let's see. Narrowly made his first Olympic team at almost 32 years of age by brushing the bar but clearing it on his third try at 19-2¼ to avoid a seventh-place finish, then won the Trials; jumped 10 times, one of the heaviest workloads ever in the Athens Olympic final and won the gold on his third try at an Olympic record 19-6¼; and—whew!—also became the twelfth man to jump 6 meters (19-8¼). Not bad for a guy who didn't make the state meet and never jumped higher than 13-6˙in high school, and whose only scholarship was to Canton's tiny NAIA Quaker school, Malone College.

Long Jump. Tianna Madison, Elyria. It probably should be Owens, whose world record in this event lasted 25 years. But we seek diversity here, and Madison's victory as a University of Tennessee sophomore during a downpour, at the 2005 World Championships in Helsinki, at the age of 19, overcame long odds, including those set by the angry skies above.

Triple Jump. Milan Tiff, Shaker Heights. Slim pickings here, but we go with Tiff, who still holds the state record, set way back in 1968, of 49-11. World-ranked twice, nationally ranked for eight straight years in the 1970s, Tiff won two AAU titles.

Shot Put. Dan Taylor, Berkshire. The big man from the little school in Geauga County was one of Ohio State's all-time great throwers. He could have been world class in the hammer too, had he worked at it. Taylor was ranked third in the world in 2007.

Discus Throw. Frances Kaszubski, South HS. Another tough call. Our choice made the Olympics in 1948 and won a bronze medal in the 1951 Pan Am Games. Runner-up Mindy Wirtz (Medina) was NCAA runner-up in 1995 at Kent State.

Hammer Throw. Jud Logan, North Canton Hoover. Didn't quite make the seven-county limit, but does if we consider college choice. The fiery former Kent State football player from North Canton Hoover made four Olympic teams, created a world-class throwers program at Ashland College, and finished fifth in the 1992 Barcelona Olympics before being disqualified for using clenbuterol, a steroid given to prize live-stock in Europe. Still, Logan's was a remarkable rise, given the lack of attention the hammer gets in the USA and the fact that he had to scrounge practice fields from friendly farmers.

Javelin Throw. Kim Kreiner, Mogadore. The American record-holder and Kent State alumna dominated the sport in the United States in recent years. She cracked the top ten in the world in 2007 and was a member of the 2004 American Olympic team.

Decathlon. LeBron James, Akron St. Vincent St. Mary. Just kidding. Although once memorably described as "a decathlete playing basketball," James would never be able to find a pole that could support his 250-plus pounds.

Coach. Alex Ferenczy, Cleveland Track Club. A Hungarian who emigrated to the U.S. after his country's failed revolution in 1956, he developed four Olympians, including gold medal winner Madeline Manning and runners who set 15 national and seven world records.

Harrison "Bones" Dillard, so nicknamed because of his skinny frame, brought four Olympic gold medals back to his native Cleveland in 1948 and 1952. The East Tech and Baldwin-Wallace alumnus remains the only man to win Olympic gold in both sprinting (or "flats," as he calls them) and hurdling events. Dillard sped past an elite field to the top spot in the 100 meters race at the 1948 Olympics, where he also anchored the U.S. men's team's 4 x 100 triumph. Four years later, he prevailed in his specialty, the 110 meters high hurdles, at the 1952 Games, while picking up another gold for the 4x100 relay. After retiring from track and field, "Bones" worked as a scout and public relations official for the Cleveland Indians.

11. Renaldo Nehemiah, former world record holder in the 110 meters hurdles. Renaldo would be close to the top sprinters of all time if he had kept running the flats. He chose to specialize in the hurdles, then went to the NFL after the 1980 Olympic boycott froze the U.S. out of that year's Games in Moscow. We'll never know just how great he could have been.

10. Tony Dees, silver medalist in the 110 meters hurdles at the 1992 Olympics. People have to really follow track to know Tony's name. He didn't compete that much on the flats. But believe me, he could flat-out fly.

9. (Tie) Mel Patton, Lloyd LaBeach and Barney Ewell, who finished second, third and fifth, respectively, in the 1948 Olympic 100 meters final that Dillard won. These three had been swapping the 100 meters world record back and forth in 1948. They must have run four, five, six races against each other, taking turns winning while tying or breaking the world record. I don't know how many times I would have won if I had to run that Olympic 100 against these three again.

6. Ben Johnson, disqualified winner of the 1988 Olympic 100 meters. They threw out all his records because of doping. But when he ran that time (9.79 in Seoul), holding his arm up for the last three or four meters, it was one of the most amazing things I ever saw.

5. Justin Gatlin, 100 meters winner at 2004 Olympics. Because he's serving a drug suspension now, he might be disrespected like Ben Johnson. But Justin beat a great field in 2004 with an amazing time of 9.85.

4. Maurice Greene, 100 meters gold medalist in the 2000 Olympics. Maurice Greene was the only runner other than Carl Lewis I ever saw who could pick up speed midway through a 100 meters race.

3. Carl Lewis, 100 meters gold medalist at 1984 and 1988 Olympics. He might be the greatest, given his ten Olympic medals (nine of them gold). He was the first sprinter I saw who shifted speeds. Carl seemed to run faster as the race went on. Others would build up their speed in the first 15-20 meters, then maintain it to 40, 50, 60 meters, but after that, they started to slow down. Carl Lewis would actually accelerate at 40 or 50 meters.

2. Jesse Owens, the 1936 Olympic 100 meters gold medalist (and Dillard's hero). Given the pressure he faced at the 1936 Olympics in Berlin, up against the Nazi's master race theory and Hitler's presence, Jesse might be No. 1.

1. Bob Hayes, 1964 Olympic 100 meters gold medalist. I'm basing this on how he ran the final leg of the 4 x 100 for the U.S. men's relay team in '64. Bob went from three meters behind at receiving the baton to three meters ahead at the tape. People don't make up ground like that in the 4 x 100 against elite competition. (Some observers timed Hayes running that 100 meters in 8.5 seconds.) Then he went on to play football with the Dallas Cowboys and changed the game. Opposing teams had to pass him off from one defensive back to another because no single man could stay with him.

Ten Names That Require Spell Check

We gotta say, these are the toughest names we've come across since we learned to think: "i" before "e" except after "c." Or even: "Crazy" with a "K" not a "C" and no "a" then "zewski." See? "Krzyzewski" is easy compared to these.

10. Jhonny Peralta, Indians, 2003

9. Bill Romaniszyn, Browns, 1972-74

8. Ebenezer Ekuban, Browns, 2004

7. Desagana Diop (pronounced, naturally: "Sah-GAHN-uh Jop) Cavs, 2001-05

6. Geff (Not "Jeff." Not "Geoff." But "Geff.") Crompton, Cavs, 1983-84.

5. Errict Rhett, Browns, 2000

4. Bill Wambsganss, Indians, 1914-23

3. Pio Sagapoulete, Browns, 91-95

2. Adimchinobe Echemandu, Browns, 2004

1. Martinas Andryskevicius, Cavs, 2005-06 . . . sorry, wait, just double-checked, should be: Martynas Andriuskevicius.

Stop the Insanity: Seven New Rules for "Namecalling"

We will have rules in our Name Game. And they shall be hard and fast, subject to no appeal, worthy of no waivers. No reporter henceforth shall have to check a flip card on deadline to see which Bizarro named player just coughed up the big fumble or airballed a buzzer beater.

7. No one will be called "The artist formerly known as (fill in the blank)." Or rather, don't fill in the blank. With anything. Ever again. It's no longer legal. Nor will an ornate symbol be allowed to substitute for a name. (Note: We are fine with royal names such as Prince Fielder, King Hill and Baron Davis, not to mention Prince the artist before he rechristened himself with a hieroglyph.)

6. Shape up, Laveranues Coles! Spelling and pronunciation are no longer allowed to traipse, willy-nilly, down different forks of the pronunciation highway. If it is to be pronounced "Lavernius," then it is to be spelled that way.

5. No numeral greater than "II" shall suffix a surname. (So much for you, Davis Love III.) Also, a strict prohibition will be enforced against first names that look like they came from an elite prep school yearbook or yachting registry. We have already endured a "Chipper," and that was one too many. As such, admittance to a major sporting league, even the PGA, shall be denied to anyone named "Biff," "Thurston," "Skippy" or "Schooner." The high walls and strict membership standards surrounding country clubs protect us from trying to keep a straight face when we pronounce such names. Henceforth, so to shall this edict.

4. Punctuational whimsy must be limited to one instance per name. Je'Kel Foster, former Ohio State guard in basketball is okay; Butler By'not'e , former Ohio State running back, has exceeded the apostrophe limit and must choose between fore and aft punctuation. The Butler might have done it, but the By'not'e will not, at least not in our book.

3. Neither a colon nor a semicolon may be inserted into a name because that amounts to copying of body parts.

2. Mamas of America! This notice shall be posted on maternity ward walls around the country: "Only one spelling shall be permitted for Sean, Shawn, Shawne, Shaun, Shawon, Chaun and Chone." Everyone get together and vote. Majority rules.

1. Yo, Antoine! (Also, Antwan, Antwon, Antwaan, Ontiwaun, Antawn, and Antjuan) See Rule No. 2.

Frankly, we'll take the Cavs Dance Team (hubba-hubba) over all of them. Especially, the damn Duck.

12-9. Doggies. After the Browns returned in 1999, the Dawg persona became Disneyfied and turned into more a marketing tool than a rallying point for fans. No less than four people in dog suits now troll the field at various times. Their names are "CB" (not for "Chip Banks"), "TD" (hey, this way there's at least one per game), "Trapper" (beats us; probably not a tribute to Joe DeLamielleure's blocking) and "Chomps" (well, it wouldn't be "Champs," would it?).

8. The Baseball Bug. It was, said Indians Vice President Bob DiBiasio, "a red, furry thing." Supposed to look like a ladybug, a good luck charm, it was more appealing than the midges that would swarm in from the lake in the summer time. You know, the "swarm troopers" that beat Joba Chamberlain and the Yankees in the playoffs. But not by much. Told during a hitting slump in the 2007 season that the Bug should be brought back for luck, DiBiasio said: "I'd rather our bats be reincarnated."

7. Tom E. Hawk. *Plain Dealer* desk man Billy Piotrowski was the flapping raptor in the 1982 season. "It was hot inside and it stank," revealed the former Mr. Hawk, who also wore leotards and long white gloves, in the manner of a beauty contestant. "I put a cold towel on top of my head before putting the thing's head on. I needed that cold water dripping down on me." Tom E's best routine was an insouciant flip of his tail to the music of "Shake Your Tailfeathers." Wearing a "Country 11" slogan, in reference to the music format of WWWE-1100 AM, Piotrowski was especially unpopular with Toby Harrah, No. 11 in your Tribe program. In the Piotrowski incarnation, the job ended when he threw a football back and forth with Rick Manning one day. "They thought it advertised the Browns," he said.

6. The Duck. "I was better than the Duck," said Piotrowski. "I have no idea why it was a duck." The part of the Waddling One was played by Jean Trimpe—yes, a woman!—who was a graduate of the Ringling Brothers School for Circus Clowns (no, I didn't just make that up) in Fort Lauderdale. The Duck was destined for the orange sauce, however, after she injured her knee slipping on a wet dugout roof.

5. The Brownie. An elf used to occasionally represent (although never on helmets or uniforms) the Browns from the team's inception in 1946 through the mid-1960s when Modell phased it out. It reappeared on team bags and ponchos after the franchise was reborn in 1999. Fear the pixie!

4. Rover Cleveland. The last gasp of the Modell Bad PR Idea Barrage, this attempt to cash in on the Dawg Pound phenomenon came a-cropper when the team announced its impending move in midseason and the guy inside the pooch suit quit in protest.

3. Whammer. A polar bear who never caught on with the Cavaliers, not even with Joe Tait, despite being named for Tait's signature dunk call "Wham! With the left hand!" "When are you going to mention me on the air?" Whammer asked Tait, after rappelling down from the Gund Arena rafters before the game.
"The day you fall," Tait replied.

2. Moondog. Cute, like Slider, and athletic like Whammer, the Doggie specializes in over-the-head half-court shots. One night, when writers were trying to research LeBron's career-high scoring games on deadline, Cavs VP Tad Carper breathlessly relayed the news that Moondog had just hit his sixth such shot in a row.

1. Slider. Big, furry, fuchsia and beholden to Sesame Street's Cookie Monster, Slider is presumed to be the only married mascot. He has played hurt after falling off the center field wall while leading cheers in the 1995 ALCS vs. Seattle and tearing up his knee. It was a tough postseason for mascots. The Mariner Moose had crashed his All-Terrain Vehicle earlier, tearing his antler cruciate ligament.

It takes a lot to compete with Art Modell for sheer, craven deviousness. But the "Pinocchio of the Paint," Carlos Boozer gave it his best shot. So conniving, he rivaled Modell in the days of the secret knock on the secret door, Boozer-as-in-Loser repaid the Cavs for developing him from a second-round pick into a budding star, letting him out of the final year of his contract so he could become a free agent, then granting him a $41.6 million deal by bolting for Utah (where he signed for $68 million in Morman money). Said LeBron James, "[Boozer] had to take care of his family" as if the Boozers couldn't have scrapped by on $41.6 million with discount coupons and soda can refunds here. Braaack!

11. (Tie) Norm Van Lier and Mel Turpin. From the time he publicly questioned how good the Cavs' teams of the mid-'70s were, Van Lier was relentlessly booed at Richfield Coliseum, and rightly so. "Dinner Bell" Mel spent the millions the Cavs gave him as a lottery pick to eat himself into oblivion. Niiiice career. Have another Krispy Kreme.

9. Chris Webber. He established his credentials early, beginning as a punk freshman at Michigan when he stood with Fab Five teammate Juwan Howard outside the Ohio State locker room, screaming "Shock the world, baby!" after senior-laden OSU lost in overtime in the NCAA regional final. He hasn't let up since, regularly adding to his repulsive resume across the years and across the country. He blew his team's chance at the national championship by calling the timeout the Wolverines didn't have (right after getting away with a blatant traveling violation) in the dying seconds of the NCAA title game against North Carolina. He bludgeoned his college program into a coma from which it has yet to awake by thumbing his nose at NCAA rules and pocketing in the neighborhood of a quarter-million dollars in Ann Arbor while whining and complaining that college players should be paid. He found a kindred spirit in Latrell Sprewell during his first NBA season in Golden State, teaming up with the infamous Choke Artist of another sort to get their coach Don Nelson fired. After years of seasoning, jumping from team to team and getting more coaches fired, Webber seemed to have finally found a home in Sacramento and a chance to redeem himself by leading his team to the NBA title; but during the the seventh game of the Western Conference Finals against the Lakers, the 6-10, 245-pound manchild collapsed into a butt-cheeks-quivering state of fright and sucked his thumb as destiny slipped away from the Kings. As an elder statesman, he went to Philly, got another coach fired by refusing to play hard or well, then demanded out. He returned to his home state, which should have known better, clogging the Pistons' roster and offering little more than comic relief for opponents with his wheezy, over-the-hill, 2,000-Year-Old Man impersonation against the Cavs in the 2007 playoffs. Clevelanders should actually love this glib, phony coward because of all the damage he's done to our rivals. But Chris Webber just makes that impossible.

8. Allen Iverson. The fans got it. Even though Iverson played like a true believer on game days, he did not respect the game or the incredible talent he'd soaked up in his gene pool. He was nearly booed off the floor after being named MVP of the Rookie Game at the Gund in 1998. If only other fans had seen through Iverson and responded accordingly, he might have been forced to mature into a contender. "Practice?!! We talkin' 'bout practice!" Yeah, Allen, practice.

7. Larry Hughes. The long-term, trusty sidekick presumptive when he came here for over $12 million a year in 2005, Hughes instead turned into a porcelain figurine, too fragile to play Mike Brown's bruising defense, despite his reputation. How often did Z get hit with his third foul of the first half coming over to pick up Hughes' man after another one of Larry's reach-in tries for a steal 20 feet out? On offense, he demanded one side of the floor to go one-on-one. That's Dr. J treatment. As Bill said: "I knew Dr. J. Dr. J is a friend of mine. You, sir, are no Dr. J." More like something Dr. Scholl's was invented to eliminate.

6. Rasheed Wallace. During the "Witness" craze of the 2006 playoffs, a sign bobbed in the stands at The Q showing seedy 'Sheedy's face with the words: "Wit-less." Pretty much said it all.

5. Bill Laimbeer. Whiner and finessy three-point shooter, this "Bad Boy" was memorably saluted by a guy wearing a "Laimbeer" sign while running around the Coliseum stands in an adult diaper with a baby bottle in his hand. Pretty much showed it all, or would have if the guy had carried a crowbar in his other hand.

4. "Wrong Rim" Ricky Davis. Mr. Triple Double himself ripped Cleveland, calling it a "black hole" after the Cavs unloaded him to the Celtics. The only black hole in Cleveland during his time here was the one that the ball disappeared into whenever it was thrown to Wrong Rim. Nothing ever came back out.

3. Rick Mahorn. He liked hurting people, especially ones half his size when they weren't looking. The 6-10 power forward made a name for himself blindsiding opposing point guards with shoulder blocks in Washington. He went on to win the 1989 Central Division for the cheap shot artists up north by sticking out his elbow and concussing Mark Price as he came around his screen. To the end of his odious career, Mahorn demanded respect but deserved a lengthy jail sentence.

2. Michael Jordan. This was the one city, even more than New York, where the disconnect between the NBA rule book and the Jordan Rules, as refs interpreted them, was not only noticed, but denounced with leather lungs. Jordan was a great, great player, but he got a lot of help on the court from people other than his teammates. In the process, he might have won more contempt on the macro scale than any visiting player except John Elway—and, of course, the guy who beat him out for #1 on this list.

1. Carlos Boozer. Played false with a blind man (Gordon Gund), crossed every finger and toe on his own body and that of his charming wife Cece while swearing eternal fealty to the Cavs so they would let him out of the last year of his deal and grant him early-bird free agent status. Then he flashed all that spectacular Duke character that Coach K always preaches about (kind of like Christian Laettner did when he stomped a fallen Kentucky player). Boozer took the money, ran, and, sadly, was not upbraided for it by LeBron James, who wants everybody to like him too much. Sometimes, it's okay to hate. Sometimes, it's your moral duty.

Cleveland's best-loved and, in the past decade, most consistently feckless team, the Browns benefited from Dawg-slobber joy with their 1999 reincarnation. Fans were happy just to have an NFL team again, even one as bad as the expansion Browns. Their 2007 rise to a 10-6 record should portend a coming era of contention. But there's always the chance it's an aberration like 2002. You never know, but in Cleveland, you expect the worst.

5. The free pass. Local kid and national media sensation LeBron James had to prove he could play to Cleveland fans. The 1990s Indians had to prove they were contenders before fans spun the turnstiles. The Browns can throw any old bag of pus out there and people will show up in sellout numbers.

4. The lack of disgust with the Lerner family. Big Al owned the jet with the secret door on which the Baltimore team pirates made the secret knock. After he shuffled off to the Big Dais in the Sky—and even before that—Lerner was forgiven by most Cleveland football fans. Why? "Because he was willing to spend the money it took to win," became the standard reply. This just in: It's a cap sport! Other than money-whipping Butch Davis to wreck the franchise with a salary that didn't go on the cap, his fiscal philosophy didn't matter!! Al Lerner was even almost able to airbrush himself off that unfortunate dais shot in Baltimore. But some of us will never forget.

3. Using the first overall draft pick on Tim Couch. Looking for the perfect guy to lead your team for the next decade? How about one who played in a gimmicky college offense built to accommodate his bean-bag tosses? In addition to a weak arm, he's got the head of a hick making white lightnin' down in the holler. On top of that, he boasts a sense of entitlement that will make him resent competing for his starting spot. Oh, and he's emotionally fragile and will come apart if the fans get on him. Hard to pass up a package like that, eh? The Browns couldn't. The fans quickly caught on that Couch was Just Another Guy (JAG, as in "crying jag"). It took most of the media in town longer, and the Browns braintrust longer still. Didn't anybody on the Browns staff bother to put Couch through a basic psych eval, much less a drill to test his arm-strength before the draft?

2. Hiring Carmen Policy. Which part of this snake-oil salesman offended you the most? Okay, there's a lot to choose from. But my vote goes to his bringing Dwight Clark in from San Francisco as GM to ensure Clark's silence on Policy's salary cap violations while he was with the Niners.

1. Speaking up for "Mumbles." Shifty-eyed Monotone Man Belichick was not run off by the Cleveland media and was not a genius here. Bill Belichick was sacked by Modell because he was a PR disaster and Modell had to make nice with the fans in Baltimore, where he had put casters on history and moved it. Obviously, Belichick has a bright mind, and has gone on to become a great success with what he learned from his experiences here. But spare me that "Mumbles" was the football gods' gift to us and we dummies here in the Rust Belt spurned him. He was an abject failure here.

He's a very good game-day coach and recruiter. He's done a lot of good things for the program, including improving the academic commitment and fostering a family-ly atmosphere. He's won multiple Big Ten titles and he's a nice guy. Most of all to long-suffering fans in North Columbus—er, we mean Cleveland—he won the 2002 national championship with a 14-0 record. Ohio State football is the fourth major sport in Cleveland, so it was our chests that puffed with pride and our backs that straightened after a King Kong-sized monkey was removed. The Buckeyes had been just as close as any Cleveland team (in 1969, '70, '73, '75, '79, '93, '95, '96, '98), only to have a Michigan school or a bowl game end their dreams. No one can ever take away the sense of pride Tressel gave us with the undisputed national championship, nor reduce the thrills of that harum-scarum season by the Comeback Bucks, who won half their games by a touchdown or less. But just because of all that, Ohio State football head coach Jim Tressel shouldn't get an automatic free pass on the occasional scandal and his rare but memorable coaching blunders.

5. He knew nothin' about Maurice Clarett's problems, even though Clarett's high school coach, the respected Thom McDaniels, told Ohio State coaches Clarett was high maintenance and needed close supervision.

4. He gave "Dirty Little" Robert Reynolds just a one-game suspension for choking Wisconsin QB Jim Sorgi on the bottom of the pile, forcing him out of a game that OSU went on to lose to snap its 19-game winning streak. No one said much, although it was the most thuggish football act in a long time committed by somebody not wearing a Raiders' uniform. What do you need to do on the field to gain a two-game suspension? Discharge a firearm?

3. He threw away a national championship in 2005. Alternating Troy Smith and Justin Zwick at quarterback against Texas cost OSU the game and probably a national title, which, not coincidentally, was won by the Longhorns. Tressel had a terrific defense to protect the end zone while Smith meshed his gears after his suspension. Zwick, frankly, peaked in Orrville HS in the ninth grade, and got eaten alive by the Texas defense. Steve Bellisari in the Outback Bowl, Scott McMullen over Craig Krenzel, Zwick over Smith—Tressel's first QB choice rarely works out. I'll admit, he's great with the mulligan.

2. Why is beating Michigan with a tight-ass, talent-squandering coach like Lloyd Carr supposed to make everything okay? I still see Marquise Walker dropping the wide-open post pass in Ann Arbor when Tressel won in his first game against Michigan. And a legend was born.

1. The 2006 BCS Championship Game, the Debacle in the Desert. Well, maybe beating the Hideous Helmeted Horde doesn't make everything okay after all. Tressel's game plan for the 2007 title game loss to LSU had holes in it, too. But the Buckeyes were not so much outcoached as overwhelmed by superior athletes at most positions. They hung in until the very end against LSU, too. But the Florida loss? Not only did the Gators do nothing different while they dazed and amazed OSU, but Tressel, as the deficit mounted, did enough wacky stuff to have Brutus Buckeye scratching his enormous foam-rubber head. How about going for it on fourth-and-1 inside his own 30, down 24-14, in the final 5 minutes of the first half? How about, when the defense amazingly held Florida to a field goal after Beanie Wells was stuffed, sending an overweight, under-prepared Troy Smith out to run the two-minute offense in the shadow of his own goal line, down 27-14? The proper move was to run out the clock, still just down two scores, and try to figure something out at halftime. Instead it was strip-sack, Florida fumble recovery, Florida touchdown, Gator Chomp, game over. When a veteran team gets that badly outplayed by a young team with a young coach (Urban Meyer), tougher questions need to be asked.

Five Things Bill Doesn't Get About the Indians

Maybe it's a hangover from 41 years in the wilderness. When the Browns fled and left the market to the Tribe. Leading to 455 sellouts in a row, it really did look like Cleveland had become a town that loved its football and baseball equally. But then the 1999 expansion Browns were hailed like MacArthur returning to the Philippines. The Indians return to the playoffs two years later after rebuilding in the Oughts? Not such an ecstatic embrace. For doing what they have done in a relatively small market in a salary cap sport, the Indians deserve much better.

5. What have you done for us lately? Until the 2007 Indians came within one game of the World Series, there was no good will left over from the great teams of the 90s. The maligned Dolans made one playoff run with the team they inherited, just missed in 2005, then just missed the Fall Classic in 2007.

4. The Mike Hargrove infatuation. Say Charlie Manuel got Alex Ramirez and Manny Ramirez mixed up on his lineup card, a colossal gaffe that forced pitcher Charlie Nagy to bat against David Wells. And then he blamed it all on underlings? What do you suppose the reaction might have been? Or suppose Charlie lost track of Bartolo Colon's pitch count? Or imagine if Charlie had said he'd just as soon keep wearing his number, even though the club had plans to retire it to honor a beloved Hall of Famer like Bob Lemon who wore the same number? I have always thought that instead of the hotdog race, they should have dueling scorecards or competing 21s leaning for the tape.

3. Vilifying the Dolans while continuing to revere Dick Jacobs. The guy they named Jacobs Field for wouldn't have maintained a top-five payroll once the revenue advantage of the new ballpark waned either.

2. If it looks like a choke, wheezes like a choke, and turns red from embarrassment like a choke, then it probably is a choke. Few in the local media made it out to be what it really was because both the 2005 and 2007 seasons were pleasant surprises. After their dress rehearsal of spitting the bit in the wild-card chase in 2005, the Indians, with C.C. Sabathia and Fausto Carmona getting starts in Games 5 and 6, blew a 3-1 ALC lead to the Red Sox in 2007, getting outscored 30-5 in the bargain.

1. Little Red Sambo. Oops, I mean Chief Wahoo. I'll defend the nickname "Indians" as long as there are Celtics, Knickerbockers and Fighting Irish. But the racist caricature has to go.

Bill's Six Inconvenient Truths About Baseball

Billyball, for this Bill, is basketball. Or football. Do I hear soccer? (Well, except for the World Cup, um, no.) And I am not alone in excluding baseball from my shortlist these days. In a fast-food, instant-messaging, no-waiting culture, how is a traditional game in which pitching changes last three times as long as your average teenager's attention span going to grow with the younger generation. I guess there's always the infield fly rule to fascinate and attract.

6. The man who wrote (and it was Red Smith), "There are no dull baseball games, only dull minds," may have been a sportswriting legend. But he was also as fatuous an apologist for the game as anyone before or since the Fox Network's band of shills. You want dull, I'll give you watching Mike Hargrove bat. They didn't call him "The Human Rain Delay" because of the scintillating, sparks-flying, hot, hellzapoppin' times when he was in the batter's box.

5. If you want to watch people think, take up chess. If you want excitement, take up chess. The guy who said (it was former University of Texas Sports Information Director Jones Ramsey, actually) that "the only thing more boring than track is field" never considered watching pitchers bat. Except for when C.C. Sabathia is waggling the old wagon tongue, I guess.

4. In other sports, you have to be great to be a Hall of Famer. In baseball, you just have to be good and stick around too long. Seniority carries more clout in baseball than it does in a labor union.

3. Steroids tainted the game's most glamorous records. Years ago, when Philadelphia's Darryl Dawkins called another NBA player (it was Seattle James Donaldson) "American Tourister" because his head is as big as a suitcase," he never got a load of Barry Bonds, the Noggin By the Bay. Abnormal head size is an offshoot of steroid abuse, although there is a lot more evidence of Bond's dirty work than his Grow Beast cranium. (Can you say "perjury," kiddies? Marion Jones could.) Moreover, has any sport ever been as degraded as baseball was by the Roger Clemens Congressional hearing? (Hey, kids, be a Major Leaguer. But don't forget the gauze to bandage your butt when the needle punctures start to bleed.)

2. Inter-league play polluted the divisional races. And the Wild Card destroyed the concept of the "pennant race." And the elongated playoff system (after 162 numbing games!) means the best team doesn't win that much anymore. Other than that, everything's swell.

1. Seriously, can you imagine starting up a game now that requires 17 of your pals (19, if it's in the American League), that has no clock, that ends after midnight in its "finals," and whose biggest deal of this era, until the fraudulent home run chase, was a guy (Cal Ripken Jr.) who's heroic achievement was showing up for work each day? Good luck with that.

The 1960 Olympic gold medalist (and 1956 silver medalist) has coached at Lakewood's Winterhurst Figure Skating Club for 28 years. Unfailingly enthusiastic, Heiss Jenkins, now 68, dominated skating in the 1950s. Athletic for her time, she was the first woman to land a double axel. She married 1956 Olympic men's gold medalist Hayes Alan Jenkins and, after a brief film career (her husband was asked by Moe Howard when Carol starred in *Snow White and the Three Stooges*, "Can your wife take a pie?"), she turned to making Cleveland a figure skating mecca. In 2008, she was elected into the U.S. Olympic Hall of Fame. Her favorite pupils:

4. Lisa Ervin. Lisa was very talented. She had an axel the first time I saw her, as did Tim (an axel is the most demanding jump because it requires one-and-a-half revolutions). She medaled in Nationals when I had her. I always felt she and Tim Goebel had the most natural talent of my skaters.

3. Timothy Goebel. Tim was ten when I first coached him. He had a wonderful gift for jumping and became the first person to land a quad salchow in competition. He was not very tall and he had really tight, quick turns. He had a thin, lithe body that was perfect for jumping. I remember the very spot at the rink in Winterhurst where he landed his first quad. It was very much like seeing someone set a world record in track and field. No human had done that before.

2. Jenni Meno. Jenni was a very hard worker who skated in a very competitive era—Tonya Harding, Kristi Yamaguchi, Nancy Kerrigan were all out there. She loved to skate so much that she didn't want to give it up, so I suggested, "What about pairs?" Eventually she and her husband Todd Sand became national champions.

1. Tonia Kwiatkowski. Tonia was very steady and an extremely hard worker. She was my first skater to go to the World Championships. She had graduated from college and had more life experiences than the young girls. We went to Italy, Germany, France and England together and she always did well. Coaches gravitate to hard workers. Tonia worked hard every day. I have known her since she was eight, and she is coaching here at Winterhurst now. We have had wonderful experiences together.

The Plain Dealer's kingpin hosts his own charity fundraiser, the Sam Manoloff Memorial Tournament, named for his late father. Manoloff has a sanctioned 300 game on his record, and he knows the sport from the Brooklyn side as a lefty and has it dead to rights, too.

10. Goldie Greenwald. A Women's International Bowling Congress (WIBC) Hall of Famer, Greenwald rolled a 732 series—a world-record for women—while competing in a men's league in 1918. She amassed more than 50 medals in her career.

9. Jeanne Maiden Naccarato. This WIBC Hall of Famer bowled consecutive games of 300-300-264 for a 864 series that included 40 straight strikes in 1986. She won the WIBC Tournament open division doubles title in1983 and the team title in 1986, then added a classic division team title in 1996.

8. Dave D'Entremont. Entering the 2007-2008 Professional Bowlers Association (PBA) Tour season, D'Entremont already had six career PBA national titles and 47 PBA perfect games on his resume. Won 1996 World Tournament of Champions and was the PBA's Harry Smith points leader in 1995.

7. J. Elmer Reed. Reed was a whiz at the bowling alley, but did as much for the game away from it by organizing the Cleveland Bowling Senate and helping found the National Negro Bowling Association.

6. Walter Ward. An American Bowling Congress (ABC) Hall of Famer, Ward held six Cleveland Bowling Association and three Ohio Bowling Association titles. He shot a 700-plus series 317 times and gave exhibitions at military bases during World War II.

5. John Klares. The ABC Hall of Famer won two titles at the 1952 ABC Tournament and paired with Steve Nagy to win the doubles event with a then-record 1,453. He served as captain of the Radiart Corp of Cleveland team that won the all-events championship.

4. Walter "Skang" Mercurio. An ABC Hall of Famer, he averaged 238 during the 1934-35 season in the Tomasch All-Star League. He completed 60 games without a miss in 1929, with the streak finally ending the next year at 65 games.

3. Joe Bodis. Originally known for bowling in street shoes equipped with a special rubber heel, Bodis went on to win renown for a lot more than just his unique footwear. He won ABC team championship in 1924. Then between 1925-32, this ABC Hall of Famer set an ABC Tournament record with eight straight all-events totals of 1,800-plus.

2. Harry Smith. The original young "Tiger" who dominated a sport, Smith's ABC Hall of Fame career began in Cleveland as a teenager. He continued for decades and eventually established himself as one of best all-time competitors in ABC Masters, which he won in 1963.

1. Steve Nagy. One of the sport's legends, Nagy was known as much for his genteel disposition as his talent. The ABC Hall of Famer won the Bowling Writers Association of America Bowler of the Year award in 1952 and 1955. Bowling Magazine named Nagy to its All-America First Team in 1956 and 1958.

They came. We saw (though usually not too many of us). Some even conquered their respective leagues. But all of these franchises were eventually conquered themselves by fan indifference, bad management or changing times.

11. The Rebels. Long before the days of 6-foot-9 point guards and multi-million-dollar contracts for benchwarmers, the Cleveland Rebels became an inaugural franchise in the 11-team Basketball Association of America, the 1946 forerunner of what now is the NBA. The Rebels posted a 30-30 record during their first season and ended up in third place in the Western Division. They then lost 2-1 against the New York Knickerbockers in the playoffs. Coached by Red Dehnert and Roy Clifford, the team was led in scoring by 6-5 center "Big" Ed Sadowski, who averaged almost 16 points per game in 43 contests. Shortly after ending its first season, the Rebels folded and went out of business.

10. The Cobras. Founded as the Cleveland Stars in 1972 as part of the American Soccer League, this franchise played at a time when soccer trying to establish itself in the U.S. as a summer alternative to baseball. The team changed its name to the Cobras before the 1974 season and continued playing in Cleveland until 1981, when they moved to Atlanta to become the Georgia Generals. The Cobra's Herbie Haller won Coach of the Year honors in 1975 after guiding the team to a first-place finish in the Mid-West Division.

9. The Thunderbolts. Football in a hockey rink, or Arena Football, as they call it, came to and went from Cleveland over a decade ago with the Thunderbolts. The franchise actually began in Columbus, but failed to gain a single win or much of a following in the heart of Buckeye country. After one season, they took their act to Cleveland in 1992 to play at the old Richfield Coliseum. The Thunderbolts only struck for 8 wins in 35 tries in their three seasons here. They did make the playoffs in 1992 only to get hammered by Orlando in the first round 50-12. Major Harris and former Ohio State alum Greg Frey were the quarterbacks, with former Buckeyes head coach Earl Bruce guiding the team in 1994, their last season before going out of business.

8. The Stokers. Professional soccer is bound to make it in Cleveland some day, some way, somehow. Just not quite yet. An early martyr to the cause, the Stokers played in Cleveland for two years in two different leagues—in 1967 as part of the United Soccer Association, then the following year as new members of the North American Soccer League. The Indians' Vernon Stouffer and Gabe Paul owned the Stokers the first season, then sold it to Cleveland businessmen Ted Bonda and Howard Metzenbaum (future U.S. Senator)in 1968. The Stokers won their division in 1968, but lost in the playoffs. The highlight that year was an exhibition game played at Cleveland Stadium against top Brazilian club Santos, featuring the great Pele. Against all odds, the Stokers won that game 2-1. A difference of opinion over business philosophy between the team's owners and the NASL led to the team's demise in 1969.

7. The Pipers. Although professional basketball was still in relative infancy, some folks thought the country could use a second baby in the nursery named The American Basketball League (ABL). A charter member of the new league in 1961, the Pipers were owned by George Steinbrenner (yes, that George Steinbrenner). The Boss signed 6-3 forward and Ohio State grad Larry Seigfried out of the NBA, but he was their only notable player. Steinbrenner hired the great John McClendon, making him the first African-American to serve as coach of a professional basketball team. But McClendon quit midway through the season because of Steinbrenner's constant interference. The Pipers won the ABL Championship in 1961-62, taking out the Kansas City Steers 3-2 in the championship series. Steinbrenner wanted to move on to bigger and more profitable things, though, and petitioned to join the NBA for the following. When the league refused he disbanded the Pipers instead of playing another year in the ABL. The league itself disbanded during its second season.

6. The Nets. The tennis boom of the early 70s inspired some businessmen to try to move the game indoors and away from being played only by moody independent contractors. Started in 1974, the World Team Tennis (WTT) league featured 16 teams, including the Cleveland Nets. Owned by local businessman Joe Zingale, the Nets employed home court advantage at Public Hall. Teams consisted of three men and three women playing singles, doubles and mixed doubles on a multi-colored, no-line court. But despite having superstars like Bjorn Borg and Martina Navratilova, as well as Cleveland's own Clark Graebner, the Nets didn't gain much success or many fans. Their first season proved to be their best, with the Nets going 21-23, only to get bounced out of the playoffs by the Philadelphia Freedom. The franchise hung around town another three years before moving to New Orleans in 1978, the WTT's final season.

5. The Lumberjacks. It's been a long time since any active lumberjacks called the Forest City home. But after 14 long years without professional hockey, local fans of the sport still welcomed the Muskegon Lumberjacks to Cleveland for the 1992-93 International Hockey League (IHL) season, even if the club never bothered to change its nickname. The Cleveland Lumberjacks stuck around for nine seasons, its best coming in 1996-97 when they reached the third round of the playoffs. Jock Callander was the franchise's best player, as well as team's all-time leader in goals, assists and points. The Lumberjacks folded along with the IHL in 2001, shortly after the NHL had stuck a franchise in Columbus.

4. The Crusaders. The Crusaders played in Cleveland from 1972-1976 as part of the World Hockey Association (WHA). Like other upstart new major sport leagues of the era such as the WFL and ABA, the WHA competed with its sport's top league, the NHL, for big name players to attract fans. The Crusaders managed to lure goalie Gerry Cheevers from the Boston Bruins, as well as a lot of fans. Owned by Nick Mileti and playing their first two seasons at the old Cleveland Arena, the team did very well early on. The Crusaders made the playoffs the first season, only to lose to New England in the second round. After moving to Richfield Coliseum, the Crusaders failed to continue playing well enough to lure large crowds. When the Gunds put the NHL Barons in the Coliseum for the 1976 season, the Crusaders fled to Saint Paul, Minnesota and became the Fighting Saints.

3. The Force. Indoor soccer in Cleveland? Hey, why not? We had indoor malls. Starting in 1978 as one of the original six franchises of the Major Indoor Soccer League (MISL), the Force played ten seasons at the Richfield Coliseum. Things did not get off to a good start, with low attendance and the club only making it past the opening round of the playoffs once in its first five years. But by the 1983-84 season, the Force averaged 13,000 fans per game and sometimes brought in over 20,000. Named for the mystical phenomenon at the center of the *Star Wars* films, the Force started a good run of form, reaching five straight playoff semifinals, then the league finals in 1988. Owner Bart Wolstein brought in some good players, including Hector Marinaro and Kai Haaskivi, plus George and Louie Nanchoff. But just as things were starting to really look up for the Force, the relationship between the players and ownership went down the tubes. After failing to convince the players union to renegotiate their contracts with him, Wolstein closed up shop.

2. The Crunch. After a one-year hiatus, indoor soccer returned to Cleveland in 1989. Unfortunately a lot of fans didn't. The Crunch replaced the Force as Cleveland's MISL franchise, then went on to play 16 seasons in three different leagues. George Hoffman was the team's principle owner for years. Hector Marinaro and Zoran Karic the mainstays on the roster. The Crunch actually changed its name back to the Force its last three campaigns. It was a nice nod to nostalgia, or maybe just an act of desperation. Either way, it didn't really work. The Crunch, though, did something the Force couldn't do: it won championships, claiming the MISL title in 1994, '95 and '99. It also played in five other championship series. But greater success didn't translate to greater attendance. The Crunch/Force folded following the 2004-05 season, financially flattened by years of poor attendance and money problems.

1. The Barons (x3). Talk about a trinity of hockey. We have the old AHL Barons, the NHL Barons and the new AHL Barons. But maybe we should have stuck to just the originals because the elder Barons enjoyed the greatest success. In fact, they ranked as the most successful team in American Hockey League history. They played in Cleveland from 1937 to 1973, winning ten division titles and nine Calder Cups. During much of that time, the Barons were considered the seventh-best team in hockey after the six NHL clubs. They drew well during the 1940s and 1950s, playing to capacity crowds at the old Cleveland Arena. But when the WHA Cleveland Crusaders took to the ice in 1972, the old Barons' days were numbered. The following year, Nick Mileti, who owned both teams, moved the Barons to Jacksonville, where the franchise folded a short time later.

Debuting in the bicentennial year of 1976, the NHL Barons proved to be only biennial, surviving for just two seasons in Cleveland. Poor attendance and money woes plagued the franchise formerly known as the California Golden Seals. The Gunds, who bought the team for its second season, failed to secure a favorable lease from the owners of the Coliseum. They merged the Barons with the Minnesota North Stars before the 1978-79 campaign. The team played until 1993, when it became the Dallas Stars.

The new, but not necessarily improved AHL Barons played in Cleveland at the Quicken Loans Arena from 2001-06. Never finishing higher than fourth in their division and only making the playoffs once in five years, the franchise relocated to Worcester, Massachusetts.

Eleven Things You Didn't Know About the Cleveland Rams

Before there was a Browns' dynasty, there was another NFL Championship team in Cleveland, albeit only briefly. The team had a glamorous quarterback with a bombshell wife. They got all the breaks in winning an NFL Championship, the ones the Browns missed in the '80s. Then they moved to another city on the coast. You know the rest. But probably not a lot about what came before that.

11. The Rams became a member of the first American Football League in 1936, finishing their first season 5-2-2, second to the champion Boston Shamrocks.

10. They joined the NFL the next year, replacing the St. Louis Gunners.

9. They played at League Park, Municipal Stadium, and at Shaw High School Stadium, the latter for the 1937 season.

8. They did not play in 1943, due to a shortage of players in war time.

7. Bob Waterfield, a 25-year-old Rams rookie in 1945 after finishing military duty in World War II, became the last rookie quarterback to lead a team to the NFL Championship. That season, he also became the first unanimous NFL Most Valuable Player. The Rams beat the Washington Redskins, 15-14, at Municipal Stadium.

6. Waterfield also was the placekicker and punter. In the title game, he missed one extra point and a second teetered on the crossbar before falling over.

5. Waterfield married in 1943 his high school sweetheart—movie actress Jane Russell, buxom star of Howard Hughes' *The Outlaw*. Cleveland comedian Bob Hope called her "the two and only."

4. Although Waterfield threw two touchdown passes in the 1945 championship game, the difference in the game came when Washington quarterback Sammy Baugh faded into his end zone in the first quarter and threw a pass that hit the goal post and fell incomplete. Under the rules at the time, when goalposts were located on the goal line, it counted as a safety.

3. Redskins owner George Preston Marshall was so angry after the loss that he successfully lobbied to have the rule changed before the next season began. Thereafter, such a pass simply was ruled incomplete.

2. Baugh, a Pro Football Hall of Famer, was knocked out of the game in the second quarter with bruised ribs and backup Frank Filchock played the rest of the way.

1. A month after the title game, citing poor attendance and a high rental fee at Municipal Stadium, the Rams relocated to the West Coast. They also feared competition from Ohio legend Paul Brown and his new team in the AAFC. They essentially conceded the market to the competition, just as the Browns turned the city over to the Indians in 1996.

Martydumb: Five Stupid Quotes From Marty Schottenheimer

Marty has proven time and again, all over the NFL landscape, that he can't win the big one. He can, however, get you to it. That certainly doesn't look so bad in retrospect after the Browns run of futility since he left Cleveland. But recalling some of the quotes he spat out during his tenure as the Browns' head coach from 1984-88 might help you miss him a little less.

5. "As I told the squad, the most important six inches in football are the ones between your breastbone and your backbone." Marty in 1988, after a victory in the snowy regular season finale at the old Stadium over Houston that put the Browns in the playoffs. Alas, the Browns lost to the same Oilers the next weekend in the wild-card round. Perhaps the squad's backbone/breastbone area had gone flaccid by then.

4. "I'll tell you, those Cowboys are a pretty good team. If you don't believe me, look at the film." Marty in 1988, after a narrow victory over the Cowboys in Cleveland. The Cowboys went on to finish that season 3-and-13 and looked so bad doing it that they fired their beloved longtime coach and resident father figure Tom Landry. Marty was not Siskel in terms of critical thinking. Not even Roper.

3. "I wouldn't trade Earnest Byner for any running back in the league." Marty in 1988, after Byner came under fire as the "landfill of the NFL" from Bill Livingston for stat-padding in "garbage time" at the end of lopsided losses. Byner thanked Marty for rating him above Eric Dickerson, Herschel Walker, Roger Craig and all his other peers by drawing back-to-back personal foul/unsportsmanlike conduct penalties and taking the Browns out of field goal range in a 24-23 wild-card playoff loss to those pesky Oilers in 1988. My, wasn't loss of poise in Earnest unusual? (Although, to be honest, Byner turned out to be way better than Livingston thought. But still not nearly as good as Marty claimed.)

2. "Art Modell and Art Rooney are the best owners to work for." Marty in 1988, after he quit before Modell had a chance to sack him, Schottenheimer then took a job coaching the Kansas City Chiefs. Why, the next thing you knew, he was saying Chiefs owner Lamar Hunt and Rooney were the best owners to work for. We know every coach has to kiss about eight miles of ownership butt from time to time, but Marty was obsequious even by the shameless standards of his profession.

1. "Play-calling is overrated." Marty in 1988, while serving as his own offensive coordinator after going a little imperial on everybody in the aftermath of the departure of Lindy Infante. Lindy, we hardly knew ye!

Formations Innovations From the Wily Schottenheimer

If too much was made, in the Schottzie view, of play-calling, he also clearly didn't think much of the league rule mandating a coach put 11 men on the field for every play either. A visionary surrounded by dull, myopic men who could never think higher or lower than the number 11, Marty offered an unappreciative world these unique formations.

4. 12 Men on the Field. This happened late in the first half at Houston in 1988. Oilers coach Jerry Glanville was so mad refs missed the infraction, he revoked his offer to Marty to hang out with him and Elvis Presley after the game.

3. 10 Men on the Field, Offense. This happened late in the first half of a 1988 regular season game at Denver, with the Browns trailing 30-0. Some of us considered it a sporting gesture, a taunting "Hah! We scoff at your big lead!"

2. 10 Men on the Field, Defense. This happened during an unsuccessful goal-line stand against Denver in the first half of the 1987 playoff game (yeah, yeah, the one that ended with "The Drive"). The Broncos scored on the series and won, 23-20, in overtime.

1. 9 Men on the Field. This happened in 1988 against Dallas in a punting situation. "They never did figure out our 'Nine,'" said a smirking Schottenheimer.

In the Letterman Countdown tradition, these lists usually only cover a Top Ten. But for Cleveland fans, we reach up to 13 for this one.

13. Gold Gloves won by Indians in 1990s; Big Ten titles won or shared by Woody Hayes.

12. One-hitters by Bob Feller.

11. Blocked shots in one game by Larry Nance.

10. Straight AAFC/NFL title game appearances by the Browns.

9. Years, out of nine played, in which Jim Brown led the Browns in rushing and was named to the Pro Bowl.

8. Browns titles, AAFC and NFL; years, out of nine played, in which Jim Brown led the NFL in rushing.

7. Titles won by Paul Brown; games won in Ohio by the Browns between 1999-2001 in 27 tries.

6. TDs in one game by Dub Jones; PGA Tour events won in Ohio by Tiger Woods between 1999-2001 in six tries.

5. Indians pennants.

4. Homers in one game by Rocky Colavito; Heismans won by Cleveland players (don't forget Desmond Howard); Big 10 titles for Ohio State under Jim Tressel; Cuyahoga County Olympic gold medalists in track and field.

3. No-hitters by Bob Feller, touchdown catches by Gary Collins in 1964 NFL title game.

2. Indians World Series titles; Olympic 100-meter gold medals in track won by Cleveland athletes.

1. Unassisted triple play in the World Series by an Indian; NBA Finals appearance by Cavs; Ohio State National Title under Tressel.

Ever since "Shoeless Joe from Hannibal, Mo." showed up in Damn Yankees, leaking blood from the contract he had signed, and led the Washington Senators to the pennant, we have been fascinated by players who were overlooked and long unsung, only to take their turn in the spotlight.

13. Steve Stone. Self-described as "The best right-handed Jewish pitcher in Major League history, because I don't know any other," this graduate of Brush High School and Kent State (where his catcher was Thurman Munson) went 82-86 in the non-Cy Young award portion of his career. In 1982, bolstered by five readings of the autobiography of the best left-handed Jewish pitcher in Major League history, Sandy Koufax, plus a new, curve-heavy pitching repertoire, he went 25-7 for Baltimore, winning 14 in a row. His agent had renegotiated his contract with Baltimore to pay Stone $100,000 if he won the Cy Young, calming Oriole GM Hank Peters fears by saying: "It's like buying insurance in case an elephant sits on you." Oof!

12. Bobby Mitchell. A 1958 seventh-round draft choice out of Illinois by Paul Brown, who loved speed, Mitchell was a Big Ten sprint champion who made trying to tackle him as vexing as trying to catch the wind. He gained 232 yards on only 14 carries against Washington in 1959. Traded to the Redskins in 1961 for the rights to the doomed Ernie Davis, as Brown went for size in the backfield, Mitchell went on to become a Hall of Fame wide receiver.

11. Miguel Dilone. Purchased by the Tribe in 1980 from the Cubs, he enjoyed a Joe Hardy year, only without the power. Dilone hit .341, with 30 doubles, nine triples and 61 stolen bases over the course of a season so at variance with the rest of his career as to defy belief. This being Cleveland, there was no pennant. The 79-81 Indians finished sixth.

10. Asdrubal Cabrera. A 21-year-old with the poise of a 41-year-old, in the nice phrase of Tom Hamilton, Cabrera reduced free-agent acquisition Josh Barfield to a pinch-runner, played second base as if he had been born there and—with his combination of hitting, smarts and defense—became, for many, the presumed shortstop-in-waiting. The Indians roared to the 2007 division title once he was inserted into the starting lineup.

9. Ben Gay. One of Butch Davis' ultimate "non-traditional" pickups, Gay arrived from a junior college in the middle of nowhere (Garden City, Kan., which you just know is an oxymoron). He provided what little oomph there was to the 2001 Browns. The sensation of training camp, Gay won the nickname "The Legend." In a November game, Gay came in for an injured James Jackson and rushed 18 times for 56 yards and a seven-yard touchdown run as the Browns beat the hated Ravens. It turned out to be "The Legend"'s one and only shining moment.

8. Brian Brennan. A fourth-rounder in 1984, he was such a "feel" receiver that he played in the Arctic temperatures of December and January without gloves. Some of us still see him coming back to catch the pass in front of the fallen Denver guy and skipping into the icy end zone for the touchdown that should have meant a trip to the Super Bowl.

7. Earnest Byner. A tenth rounder from unknown East Carolina, he was the heart and soul of the overachieving Kosar teams. He and Kevin Mack each gained 1,000 yards in a mean, nasty backfield in 1985. Yeah, he once Fumbled (with a capital "F") at an unfortunate moment. But he came back to ground out the yards in the last game at Cleveland Stadium in 1995, a wrenching tearjerker of a win. Surrounded by blacked-out or inverted signs, with sobbing fans ripping out the seats they would never sit in again to take as souvenirs, he took a farewell lap, shaking hands with the tearful fans. It was redemption, it was a victory lap, it was *Auld Lang Syne*, a circle completed, despite the fracture caused by Art Modell.

6. Doug Dieken. A sixth-rounder in 1971, "Diek" stuck around almost forever, playing 14 years at the most important offensive line position, left tackle. Drafted as tight end from Illinois, he played all of three quarters of exhibition season at tackle. Injuries during a mid-season game against Atlanta forced him to fill in at right tackle, a position he had never played before. In addition to ably covering the blindside of Brown's QBs for the next 14 years, Dieken also served in the wedge on the kickoff return team and in the front row on the onside kick receiving team. "Somebody noticed my receiving talents," he smirked.

5. Reggie Langhorne. Taken in the seventh round of the 1985 NFL draft, he played nine years, caught over 400 balls and amassed over three miles in receptions. Three times he ranked in the Top 10 in receptions or reception yardage or touchdown catches.

4. Fausto Carmona. The Indians tried to ruin this highly-regarded prospect by making him their closer in 2006 after trading Bob Wickman. The results: four losses in a week, three of them on walk-off hits, two of them homers. He finished the season with a 1-10 record. The experience might have understandably reduced him to a gibbering wreck. But after starting the 2007 season in the minor leagues, Carmona emerged along with C.C. Sabathia to give the Indians the best one-two punch in the starting rotation since the days of Feller and Lemon.

3. Jaret Wright. Is it unfair to include a first-round draft pick (No. 10 overall) on a list like this? Not when the California surfer with the big arm came to the rescue of an underachieving team as a midseason rookie call-up, going 8-3, beating the Yankees in Game 5 of the 1997 Division Series, yelling "Boo!" at all the ghosts of failure past. With Mike Hargrove pre-empting Charlie Nagy's start for him, Wright went $6^{1/3}$ innings in the seventh game of the World Series, then turned the ball over to the bullpen with a 2-1 lead.

2. Brian Sipe. Taken in the 13th round of the 1972 draft; not good enough to get on the field his first two seasons, which he spent on the reserve squad; a 1-6 record the next two years as a sometime starter; a season-ending knee injury in 1977, after finally having a good season in 76. After all that, who could have guessed Sipe would go on to win the 1980 NFL Most Valuable Player award and become the one-man CPR unit for the Kardiac Kids?

1. Gene Bearden. Before 1948, the left-handed knuckleballer had been in one major league game and sported a spiffy 81.00 ERA. But he won 20 in 1948, including the one-game, winner-take-all playoff at Fenway Park. He won four of the Indians' last eight games. He had one day's rest before the playoff game. He also shut out the Boston Braves in the fourth game of the World Series and saved the clincher in Game 6. They pitched him to death—which is hard to do to a knuckleballer—and he was never the same afterward. Yet Bearden left us with proof that there can be "Once upon a time" stories in Cleveland, even if the "lived happily ever after" part still needs work.

We all know who's No. 1. But the list of scoundrels and poltroons, of arrogant know-nothings and greedy do-nothings, gets to the heart of Cleveland's long championship drought. Inadequate ownership lies at the root of most evils in sports, and we have had some beauts. And they have hired plenty of not-ready-for-prime-time coaches and GMs. Maybe someone will, Dagwood Bumdstead-like, grab the back of the clue bus as it leaves the station. Some day . . . .

10. Ozzie Guillen. Since you had your hands wrapped around your neck to give Tribe fans the "choke" sign on the last day of the 2005 season, why don't you just allow a volunteer or two from the stands to finish the job?

9. Mike Lombardi. The sinister pro player personnel director was blameworthy enough to get his very own imitator—a fan dressed up as a court jester for a home game during the 3-13 apocalypse of 1990. (GM Ernie Accorsi and Modell each had their own, as well.) Lombardi once said of Bernie Kosar, who was getting treated like the piñata at a Feliz Navidad party by DEs running through the two open gates named Ben Jefferson and Kevin Robbins that Lombardi had brought in to play offensive tackle during exhibition season in 1990, "What makes him a sacred cow?" Well, only that he was the franchise quarterback, you incoherent bag of wind. Later proved so inept that even clueless Al Davis fired him from the Raiders.

8. PutArtintheHall.com. This repulsive web site, dedicated to the Hall of Fame hallucinations of Benedict Modell provides us with proof of just how delusional he has become and just how shameless his lackeys can be in supporting his demented fantasies. What exactly has changed since this backstabber and kidney puncher didn't even make the first round cut by the committee that votes on the best and brightest for enshrinement? Don't worry, Artie, there's a reserved spot waiting for you in the afterlife. It's just not in Canton.

7. Peter Bavasi. He wasn't around long, but he left his mark, like a shot put hurled onto a wedding cake. The short-time Indians president ran off well-liked, long-time media schmoozer/favorite Bob DiBiasio. Tried to close the bleachers. Widely viewed as the point man for a subversive movement to take the Indians to Tampa. After leaving the Tribe amid glowing, *Sports Illustrated* cover forecasts of an imminent pennant (the team lost 101 games) Bavasi returned Bill Livingston's phone call by musing: "Why should I call this c—ks—k-r? All he ever did was skewer me." Ahh, but with reason. With reason. Something you never employed when running the Indians, Pete.

6. Bill Musselman. In college, combined the pop and sizzle of modern pre-game NBA show biz with a plodding, deadly dull playing style, enlivened only by outbreaks of violence—knees to the groin, stomps to the head, and everything but brass knucks and jumping off the turnbuckle on Ohio State players. As the Cavs' coach, Musclehead made you pine for the days of John Lucas or Randy Wittman. Hell, he made you pine for Keith Smart and Don Delaney. That's how bad he was. He took each loss like a football coach in a short season. Utterly unsuited to a long season or a position of responsibility.

5. Bill Belichick. We can still see the old, crummy interview area in the corridors of the old Stadium, where Bill the Boy Genius would discuss the latest loss while fans pounded on trash cans outside the tent flap and chanted in unison: "Bill must go! Bill must go!" Not before trashing the roster some more and kicking that field goal on the last play in San Diego when down by 21 points, though.

4. Carmen Policy. More spin than Rumplestiltskin with the straw, but damn little gold. Classic "ten-percenter" who acted like he owned the team because Big Lerner let him. Little Lerner cashiered the snake oil wholesaler, in one of the few bright ideas Little Lerner had until the team magically came together in 2007.

3. Frank Lane. Traded players, traded managers, traded Rocky, traded his brain for a baseball card collection.

2. Ted Stepien. "Come over to my house. We'll talk and watch porno films," he said to *Akron Beacon Journal* Cavaliers beat man Sheldon Ocker, upon buying the team. Hired Bill Musselman from the University of Minnesota after he masterminded the Gophers' motorcycle gang assault on Ohio State's Luke Witte. Rampant nincompoop decisions in front office led NBA to institute a trade embargo, basically saying: "You're too stupid to make your own personnel moves." The fight polka. The Teddy Bears. Made the city an even bigger laughing stock than it already was from Johnny Carson's *Tonight Show* monologues.

1. Art Modell. Hard to know where to start with such an impressive body of work. Fired Paul Brown, leading to, as Brown wrote in his autobiography, "two management styles, one based on knowledge and experience and one on the exact opposite." MOVED THE BROWNS!! Took the merger money and jumped to the old AFL, now the AFC, thinking it was the shortcut to the Super Bowl, just when the Steelers were getting good enough to slug the Browns' brains out. MOVED THE BROWNS!!. Thought the old Stadium, which he bought, was the shortcut to riches; it was a money hemorrhage. Meddlesome and emotional, posed as the moral pillar of the league when Al Davis put the Raiders' franchise on wheels. MOVED THE BROWNS!! Hired Bill Belichick. MOVED THE BROWNS!! Left behind "our team, our name, our colors," which he had seldom done anything except dishonor.

Note: Bob August was the slam-dunk first choice to do this. The veteran sports columnist of the old Cleveland Press boasts the grace, the knowledge and the appreciation for the craft of writing. But at the age of 86, he lacks the inclination to enter the fray and pass judgment on his colleagues. To find a back up, we turned to John Gugger, the award-winning, retired columnist at the *Toledo Blade*. John spent three decades covering Cleveland and Detroit teams, still reads papers in both markets voraciously, and once said: "I spent more time in beds at the Airport Marriott in Cleveland, covering the Browns, Indians and Cavaliers, than in any except my own bed at my house." Gugger did not rate the late Hal Lebovitz, out of respect for the dead.

10. Terry Pluto, *Plain Dealer.* This was a tough one. If the criterion is quantity, Pluto finishes No. 1. If it's quality, which it is, he's right here. Pluto writes so much and so often, and that includes books, that his stuff begins to read like 30-minute columns. Hurried, simplistic, no depth. When he takes his time, which is increasingly rare, he can be very good. He went into Washington Heights, a fungo from the Bronx, when the Indians played the Yankees in the playoffs in the late 1990s, and came out with the best quotes and best background story of a young Manny Ramirez that I've ever read.

9. Tom Reed, *Akron Beacon Journal.* An insatiable curiosity about Olympic sports allied with the writing skills of a polished pro on more familiar ones made Tom's columns go down easy before he moved to the *Columbus Dispatch* during the downsizing at the Beacon. His only flaw was a lack of desire to mix it up in controversy. But he was so imaginative that he made up for it.

8. Tony Grossi, *Plain Dealer.* A long time ago, Art Modell complained about Grossi on the Browns' beat and PD management sided with Modell. That should tell you all you need to know about PD management. Grossi lost something when that happened and has never been the same, though he still occasionally shows the reporting skills and knowledge that he used to show daily.

7. Paul Hoynes, *Plain Dealer.* You ever see Hoynes at work? His head is in front of a computer, pounding keys an hour before a game until an hour after. He'll never shortchange his employer for work ethic and he has above-average writing skills. Yet, after 25 years covering baseball, his knowledge of the game remains just average.

6. Bud Shaw, *Plain Dealer.* A true wordsmith and a good guy with a nice sense of humor. He's misplaced as a columnist because he writes more features than hard opinion. He stays in his comfort zone, which means Browns, Indians, Cavs, Browns. If he were a takeout writer and upped his energy level, he'd be near the top of this list.

5. Jason Lloyd, Lorain/Lake County. He's proven he can criticize Ohio State athletics. In a part of the state that absolutely fawns over everything Buckeye, that's a good thing and sometimes a very difficult thing to do. Trust me, I know. He can also write well and like Windhorst will find a larger newspaper that wants his services.

4. Brian Windhorst. *Akron Beacon Journal.* He gets it. He understands the NBA game and his stories reflect that on one of the toughest beats on a newspaper. High energy level and even writes a blog for stuff he couldn't fit into a story. It's a good blog, too. He wasn't afraid to criticize Larry Hughes or Mike Brown, which was easy, or LeBron James, which is a lot harder. The BJ is a shambles of what it used to be, and it won't keep Windhorst forever.

3. Doug Lesmerises, *Plain Dealer.* I'm tempted to rate him higher, but he's only been around a few years. He writes very well and has a knack for finding an angle that the other Ohio State beat writers missed or, more importantly, never thought about. He's going to need to show his cojones at some point the way former OSU beat writer Bruce Hooley did, because so far all he's had to write about Ohio State are nice wins. That'll determine whether he rises or sinks.

2. Jim Ingraham, Lorain/Lake County. The undiscovered gem of the northeast Ohio market. He's wasted on the Indians' beat because he has so much more to offer. Read one of his Indians' columns on Saturday. You get insight that can't be found anywhere else in this market, including from the other beat guys. There's always the question of how he'd do out of his comfort zone, but that wouldn't stop me from making him a full-time columnist.

1. Bill Livingston, *Plain Dealer* (Disclaimer here. We've shared cabs, busses, been to lunch, dinner, and Barcelona bullfights together. Livy fell and severely sprained his ankle on one of those two-inch Barcelona curbs while, Olympic athlete that I am, I negotiated it seamlessly.) With a Vanderbilt English major's command of the language, Livingston is a columnist for all seasons. He isn't afraid to tackle a sport—bullfighting, let's say—he's never seen before and by the end, it'll read like he grew up with a red piece of cloth in his hand. His energy is above average. His forte: he's a real columnist. He has hard opinions, not feature stories passed off as columns. And he's not afraid to rip the sacred cow that is the Browns. If he weren't so obsessed with Tiger Woods and LeBron James, I wouldn't be able to find any faults worth mentioning.

Note: Roberts covered every Kentucky Derby from 1973 through 2006. The great Secretariat won the first in when Roberts was serving as sports editor at *The Lake County News-Herald*. He worked as a full-time turf writer at the *Cleveland Press* from 1976 until it closed in 1982 and then at *The Plain Dealer* from 1985 until 2003. During the three years in between, Roberts covered Thistledown and Northfield for *The News-Herald*. The man knows the state's race-horsing history as well as anyone. Here's his field for a dream Ohio Derby.

10. (Tie) Cut the Cuteness and Tougaloo. Cut the Cuteness won over $400,000. Without a graded stakes, she did score in two added money events (Bryan Station and Furl Sail) outside of Ohio. Tougaloo was a home girl, but an outstanding one, winning nine stakes and $583,030.

9. Recitation. Voted Ohio Horse of the Year in 1980, he never raced in North America. Instead, the son of Elocutionist won the Group I Grand Criterium in France.

8. Smart and Sharp. A winner of 22 races and $422,374 inside and outside of Ohio, he was still good enough to win the Grade III Appleton Handicap at Gulfstream Park in 1985 as a six-year-old. Tried to repeat the following year and was third.

7. Safe Play. Records are sketchy, but this daughter of Sham may be the only Ohio-bred filly to win a Grade I stakes race. She did so at Santa Anita, scoring in the 1982 La Canada.

6. Phantom on Tour. Hard-knocking son of Tour d'Or won seven of 20 starts and $724,605. Biggest scores came in a pair of Grade III features, the Rebel at Oaklawn and New Orleans Cap at the Fair Grounds. Reached for the brass ring but finished sixth in the 1997 Kentucky Derby.

5. Too Much Bling. Sprint specialist was voted 2006 Ohio Horse of the Year after winning three graded stakes—the Carry Back in Florida, the San Vicente in California and the Bay Shore in New York. He's been retired to stud and is making babies in Florida at $10,000 an affair.

4. Brent's Prince. Known as the "Chocolate Soldier," this colt raced for Bainbridge physician Ted Classen and rocked Thistledown when he won the 1975 Ohio Derby. Also took honors in the Grade III Round Table at Arlington. A foot injury ended his career prematurely.

3. Air Forbes Won. Helped put Ohio racing on the map when he won the Gotham and Wood Memorial and went to the post favored to win the 1982 Kentucky Derby. No roses, though. He finished seventh.

2. Royal Harmony. A running machine from racing's glory days, this 1964 foal won 22 stakes races in six years, including one at the ripe old age of eight. Captured Keeneland's Fayette Stakes three consecutive years.

1. Harlan's Holiday. Hands-down the best of the Buckeyes. Victories in the Grade I Florida Derby, Blue Grass and Donn Handicap were among his nine scores in 22 starts, good for $3.6 million in earnings. Foaled in Medina, he ranks among North America's top 60 all-time money earners.

The passions always run hottest with the Browns. We'd like to take many of these guys and put them in a dunking tank, the way Sam Wyche once sat in one for charity in Cleveland. Only there wouldn't be a protective screen in case of wild pitches, and it wouldn't be water these louts would fall into, but some of the stuff from when the Cuyahoga caught on fire, combined with Chernobyl meltdown and a splash of Love Canal, and there wouldn't be a way out, just deeper into the mire, until the only fish they slept with glowed in the dark and have two mouths, both of them hungry. Otherwise, we're okay with the fellows.

10. Sam Wyche. He once scolded Cincinnati's debris-throwing fans (who maybe should've just pulled up chunks of that crappy Riverfront Stadium and heaved them) by saying: "You don't live in Cleveland." Known as Wicky-Wacky for trying to reinvent the wheel. When it all fell apart with the Bengals, he wondered why Cincy fans cared so much and noted life would go on and that there was tennis to be played. Deserved a backhand to the face.

9. Jerry Glanville. The great Bob August immortally described him this way: "In a field of archers, Jerry Glanville would wear an apple on his head." Behind all the relentless PR and fear-mongering, Glanville was nothing more than a self-aggrandizing Half-Pint in Black with a fatal attraction for incendiary comments and thuggish coaching tactics that made it harder for his Oilers to win. But we hated him anyway.

8. Sam Huff. Jim Brown called him the smartest player of his era. But to Cleveland fans, Huff was an overrated jerk because he played in New York and because one of the first sports documentaries, *The Violent World of Sam Huff*, glorified him.

7. Brian Billick. It's not that he spurned the expansion Browns for Modell's Ravens. It's that he was considered an offensive genius and yet has never developed a good quarterback and never orchestrated a top offense in Baltimore, which failed to score a touchdown for five straight games during the 2000 season and still went on to win the Super Bowl.

6. Ray Lewis. Probably the single most sickening example of a league losing its way—ever. The Ravens middle linebacker pleaded guilty to obstruction of justice in a double murder perpetrated after a Super Bowl party in Atlanta in 2000. Instead of doing time in jail or even on the league's suspended list, Lewis got to lead the Ravens to victory in the next Super Bowl and be named the game's MVP. This guy became the face of the NFL? What, Hannibal Lecter had previous commitments?

5. Joey Porter. The Steeler linebacker's pre-game fight with the Browns' William Green in 2004 was as much a knockout of Green as Kellen Winslow, Jr.'s play three years later against Porter was an overdue butt-kicking. Unfortunately, Porter had moved from the Steelers to the Dolphins by then. But it still felt good.

4. Franco Harris. Jim Brown was right. Stay inbounds and man up, you big sissy.

3. Jack Lambert. Nice teeth.

2. Terry Bradshaw. Maybe Chuck Noll was right when he said of the Dallas Cowboys' Thomas "Hollywood" Henderson, "Empty barrels make the most noise." But when Henderson made this noise, "Terry Bradshaw couldn't spell 'cat' if you spotted him the 'c' and the 'a,'" it was music to our ears. And, in all honesty, we loved it when Turkey Jones tried to plant Bradshaw's head so far into the Cleveland Stadium turf it would pop out in Tiananmen Square.

1. John Elway. Mr. Ed plays quarterback. Ever see so many teeth? The spoiled brat leveraged his way out of Baltimore and into Denver by saying he would take his baseball glove and go play minor-league ball for the Yankees instead of taking snaps in Baltimore. We would've loved to see Steinbrenner get hold of him and turn Elway into the Drew Henson of his era. Arguably, the trade Elway forced to Denver in 1983 so devalued the Colts in Baltimore that they moved to Indy at the end of the season. Which ultimately led to Baltimore stealing our Browns a little over a decade later. We blame it all on you, Johnny E! When the ball bounced off the hip of Steve Watson, the man in motion, and Elway snatched it just off the grass top and fired a 20-yard completion on third-and-18 in the first of the AFC Championship trifecta, we knew God had left the building. We do gain some comfort from ESPN's endless replays of the Cal guy taking the last lateral and knocking over members of the Stanford band as he scores on the last play on a rugby-style kickoff return. It was John Elway's last college game and it knocked him out of a bowl game.

Not That Guy: 21 Sports Figures With Names That Make Them Easy to Confuse With Somebody Else

These guys had names that made them sound like they were other guys—other, more famous guys. But they weren't. And the quality of their play in Cleveland didn't make them threats to eclipse (or preclipse) the renown of any of their namesakes. Still we're "Glad All Over" to recall them so we can make "Bits and Pieces" of references to the Dave Clark Five and a so-so Wahoo of the 1980s, among others.

21. Karim Abdul-Jabbar, Browns 1999 (not Kareem Abdul-Jabbar, the Lakers' Hall of Fame center).

20. Bud Anderson, Indians, 1982-83 (not Jim Anderson's son on Father Knows Best).

19. Milos Babic, Cavs, 1990-91, (not Milos Forman, the Oscar-winning director of One Flew Over the Cuckoo's Nest and Amadeus).

18. Ken Berry, Indians, 1905 (not the Mayberry RFD and F Troop actor).

17. Bill Bradley, Indians, 1901-10 (not the Princeton basketball star and former U.S. Senator from New Jersey).

16. Gary Brokaw, Cavs, 1876-77 (not Tom, the former NBC anchorman).

15. Garland Buckeye, Indians, 1925-28 (not Brutus' daddy).

14. Seabron Booles, Indians, 1909 (not LeBron's daddy, either).

13. Clarence Campbell, 1940-41, Indians (not the former NHL commissioner).

12. Dave Clark, Indians, 1986-89 (not the head of the British Invasion band the Dave Clark Five).

11. Andrew Declercq, Cavs, 1998-2000 (no relation to F. W. de Klerk, the South African Prime Minister who helped engineer the end of apartheid).

10. Ed Fisher, Indians, 1968 (not the guy Liz left for Dick).

9. Joe Frazier, Indians, 1947 (not "Smokin' Joe," the heavyweight champeen of the world).

8. Willie Horton, Indians, 1978 (not the key figure in a George H.W. Bush commercial).

7. Michael Jackson, Browns, 1991-98 (not "The Thriller" artist, moonwalker and plastic surgery uber-patient).

6. Randy Jackson, Indians, 1958-59 (not the American Idol judge).

5. Henry James, Cavs, 1990-92, 1997-98 (not the 19th-century novelist).

4. Jose Jimenez, Indians, 2004 (not the Bill Dana character).

3. Darryl Johnson, Cavs, 1995-96, (not the Dallas Cowboys' fullback, Daryl "Moose" Johnston, moonlighting as an NBA point guard).

2. Bob Kaiser, Indians, 1971 (not Kaiser Bob, former basketball coach at Indiana and Texas Tech).

1. Don King, Browns, 1954 (not the electro-haired fight promoter and native Clevelander).

A Dozen Names That Are Just Fun

We could go on for a few paragraphs about the sports world's long tradition of quirky poetry and how recent decades have dumped a spice rack full of new multi-lingual, multi-culti names and terminology into the mix. But sometimes, it's best not to overanalyze. Or say much more than: these names just make us smile.

12. Otto Orf, Crunch/Force, 1989-2004

11. Minnie Minoso, Indians, 1949, 1951, 1958-59

10. Jerry Upp, Indians, 1909

9. Mason Unck, Browns, 2003-07

8. DeSagana Diop, Cavs, 2001-05

7. Vitaly Potapenko, Cavs, 1996-99

6. Orpheus Roye, Browns, 2000-07

5. Smush Parker, Cavs, 2002-03

4. Sultan McCullough, Browns, 2004

3. Zendon Hamilton, Cavs, 2005-06

2. Ethdrick Bohannon, Cavs, 2000-01

1. Shin-Soo Choo, Indians, 2006

My Five Favorite Browns Players :: Tim Mack

Note: The Olympic pole vault gold medalist from Westlake is a fan of all Cleveland teams. But, like many Clevelanders, he loves the Browns first and foremost.

5. Clay Matthews. He had that old car that he drove and didn't seem to care about material things. He was just about football and hitting people. He worked hard and was very tough. He played a long time and didn't miss many games that I remember.

4. Eric Metcalf. His running technique was superb. He had great moves. But as a track-and-field guy, I also appreciated his running from a technical standpoint. He kept his knees up when he ran. If you keep your knees up, you cover more ground and it's easier to separate from pursuit.

3. Webster Slaughter. I always liked to play wide receiver in intramurals, so I liked him because he had great moves and because he was a little guy. I was smaller than Slaughter (listed at 6-0, 175 pounds) when I was watching him play.

2. Bernie Kosar. Bernie dug deep. He got it done, no matter what. He was so smart. He was the perfect leader of a Cleveland team.

1. Brian Brennan. I always thought of myself watching him. He wasn't super fast. He wasn't tall. He wasn't that strong. But he worked hard and got it done. He didn't even wear gloves, as raw as it gets here in football season. I don't know if I would go that far, but I know I don't when I play golf. I need the feel of the club. No matter how cold it got, he always had a great feel for the ball and the game.

LeBron's Ten Favorite Teams

Many Clevelanders fretted in 2007 when the Cavs' superstar said in a national conference call before guest-hosting *Saturday Night Live* in New York that he favored the Yankees over the Indians in their upcoming playoff series, adding that Cleveland fans "will have to deal with it." From covering James for eight years, starting when LeBron was a sophomore in high school, Bill has compiled material for this list of LeBron's favorite teams. James' rooting preferences show a mix of front-running loyalty to the teams that were champions when he first became a sports fan in the 1990s, along with a politician's savvy in tailoring his rooting interests to geography. His tenth and his top team shows where his heart, soul and future lie.

10. Akron St. Vincent St. Mary. At least he is true to his school and hometown. When James worked out with St. Edward's Delvon Roe, a Michigan State signee, he said: "Why are you going to St. Ed's? Do you like to wrestle? If you want to play basketball, SVSM is your only choice."

9. Florida State. "I've always been a Seminole," James says, although actually, of course, because he skipped college, he has not been. But at least he's rooting for one tribe.

8. Michigan State. Likes coach Tom Izzo and the way his teams play. Mentions the Spartans a lot when playing road games against the Pistons.

7. North Carolina. Before he declared for the NBA draft out of high school, James was thought to be considering three colleges: Ohio State, North Carolina and Akron. He still makes a point to praise the Tar Heels before road games with the Charlotte Bobcats.

6. Ohio State. During LeBron's recruitment, Buckeyes coach Jim O'Brien made signing James, who, after all, played only 100 miles or so up the road from Columbus, a must-have priority and had an assistant coach virtually living in Akron. It would have been interesting seeing how Obie, who preferred overachievers who never caused him trouble on or off the court, would have dealt with a mega-talent like James and his entourage.

5. Southern Cal. Always lauds the Trojans when the Cavs are playing road games against the Lakers. This inspired native Texan Bill Livingston, in the aftermath of the 2005 BCS championship game, a 41-38 Texas victory over the Trojans, to wear a burnt orange cap to the next Cavs' practice. "Texas Longhorns: 2005 National Champions," it read. "Awww, man," James said, upon spying the cap, as Livingston loitered by the locker room door.

4. Dallas Cowboys. What was not to like about the Cowboys' 90s dynasty? Oh, right. Jealousy in the executive suite, Barry Switzer on the sidelines, Michael Irvin on the field, drugs, busts, and Nate Newton with his truck holding 213 pounds of marijuana and, then a long slide into mediocrity.

3. Chicago Bulls. LeBron actually did want to be like Mike.

2. New York Yankees. "I'm not from Cleveland; I'm from Akron," he will tell you. Nonetheless, Cleveland fans help pay the Dauphin's salary. So, like, put the Yankee cap some place other than on your head inside Progressive Field, okay? Otherwise, you have the wrath of the world's most colorful old coot, Bob Feller, to face. "Tell LeBron, I'm going to sit right behind their bench in a Detroit Pistons hat. Let's see how he likes that," Feller said.

1. Cleveland Cavaliers. "He gave a sense of hope to the franchise, a sense of hope to the entire city of Cleveland," said Cavs General Manager Danny Ferry. For that, he ought to get cut some slack, millinery mishaps and all.

Not everything in Cleveland sports involves the Browns, Indians or Cavs. Just most things. But we also remember our mid-major giant killers, how Tiger Woods made Firestone South his playpen and our first glimpse of the greatness that was to come in LeBron James. And there is always Ohio State-Michigan, "The Game," the one that stops two states for three hours on a cold Saturday afternoon in November, no matter how often people in Ann Arbor—the ones who say they read Proust and keep their pinkies pointing to the ceiling when they drink their soy milk decaf lattes at Starbucks—say it doesn't matter

10. Akron St. Vincent St. Mary 70-Central Hower 60, February 25, 2001. The first time Bill saw LeBron James play, LeBron was a 16-year-old sophomore. Central-Hower had a great basketball legacy, giving the NBA (back when it was Central High) Nate Thurmond and Gus Johnson. The program still had some players. But no one like LeBron. In the last minute, in the midst of a comeback, Central trapped James in the side-court, forcing him to pick up his dribble. Keeping the five-second jump-ball clock ticking in his head, James pivoted, taking the ball out of harm's way, leaped above both defenders, threw an Unseldian outlet pass the length of the floor with a flick of his wrists and hit a streaking teammate for the lay-up that broke the back of Central-Hower. Livingston, a hoops junkie, left tingling.

9. St. Ignatius 34-Cincinnati Moeller 28, Division 1 Ohio High School Football Final, 1989. As the parent of a St. Ed's grad, Bill says it hurts to admit this. But the Wildcats staking claim to the USA Today poll national championship by winning this game provided balm for our long-suffering city. The championship game was still played at the Horseshoe at that time. The biggest stage in the state added a mystique neither Canton nor Massillon, now the title game sites, can match.

8. Kent State 78-Pitt 73 (OT), NCAA Sweet 16, 2002. The best MAC team ever became the conference's first team to reach the Elite Eight since 1964 by overcoming the Panthers' height and the zebras' myopia. Antonio Gates was called for a totally bogus jump ball in the last seconds of regulation, with the possession arrow giving the ball to Pitt. In fact, the future Pro Bowl tight end, then a Kent State power forward, powered the ball up through the Pitt player's grasp and hit a LeBron-like muscle jumper that should have won it for Kent State. Gates gave the Golden Flashes a tremendous advantage in almost every game because he was the toughest player to guard on the floor. Undaunted, Kent State didn't give up anything easy on Pitt's last possession of regulation, and then they took control in the overtime. We still see Trevor Huffman's driving lay-up kissing high off the backboard then dropping through the net to clinch it.

7. Cleveland State 83-Indiana 79, 1986 NCAA Tournament first round. The commuter school from the AMCU-8 ("Sounds like a motor oil," quipped their coach Kevin Mackey) "runned 'em and stunned 'em." CSU scored to make it 2-2, and then Lay-Up City rose from the floor of the Carrier Dome as the Vikings scored two baskets as fast as they could steal the ball on the full-court press and lay it in. They never looked back. "How many of you SOBs thought that was an upset?" said Bobby

Knight afterward. (Well, we did.)

6. Tiger Woods wins 2000 NEC. And how! By 11 shots. In the process, he added seeing in the dark to his resume of supernatural powers, finishing the rain-delayed tournament, as dusk turned to dark. Fans ringing the 18th green held lights and flashlights aloft, like rock concert groupies. Golf's Fifth Beatle, his approach shot "homing in the gloaming," left himself two feet for birdie.

5. Ohio State 20–Arizona State 17, 1997 Rose Bowl. Buckeyes backup QB and game MVP Joe Germaine, a bandage flapping from his chin since being busted in the chops in the first quarter, outplayed Jake "The Snake" Plummer, passing the Sun Devils dizzy. Arizona State, Phoenix native Germaine's childhood team, resorted to dragnets and tridents in the secondary, drawing two pass interference penalties on the drive. Germaine's throw to wide-open freshman sensation David Boston from five yards out won it in the last 19 seconds.

4. Tim Mack wins Olympic gold medal. Westlake's Tim Mack completed one of sports great Cinderella stories by winning the pole vault competition at the 2004 Summer Olympics in Athens on his third-and-last try, wriggling over the bar at 19 feet, 6¼ inches, for an Olympic record and the gold. Mack had made the U.S. team for the first time at nearly 32 years of age a few months before with another dramatic, last-chance vault of 19-2¼ at the U.S. Olympic Trials, a clearance that left the crossbar jig-gling. During his high school days at St. Ignatius, Mack did not even qualify for the state meet and only earned a scholarship to Malone College in Canton, an NAIA school.

3. Ohio State 25–Michigan 21, 2005. "The Troy Smith Bowl," as far as we're concerned. The Buckeyes were dead on that field Up North, down nine points with seven minutes to play, when Smith led two harum-scarum drives. He scrambled for gains that should have been losses; he threw one of the most famous passes in OSU history to Anthony Gonzalez, hang-gliding it over a defender's shoulder pads; he never let his team give up. His coach Jim Tressel summed it up best: "Years from now, little boys will run through the leaves in their backyards with a football, pretending to be Troy Smith,"

2. Ohio State 42–Michigan 39, 2006. Troy Smith threw a 39-yard touchdown pass to Ted Ginn, Jr. in the second quarter in what amounted to a season-long play-action fake on the Hideous Helmeted Horde. The Buckeyes broke the huddle quickly on second-and-1 at the Michigan 40. Smith took the snap on the first count and whirled to hand off to a diving Beanie Wells out of a three-tight end formation. The Buckeyes had run Wells all year in that short-yardage set and Michigan's defense swarmed toward him. BUT NO! This time, Smith faked to Wells, dropped back and fired to Ginn, who had lined up as one of the tight ends on the play and was running free from the line of scrimmage, putting a smile on Woody's face watching from the Big Horseshoe in the Sky.

1. Ohio State 31-Miami 24 (2 OTs), 2003 Fiesta Bowl. Sorry, Texas-USC, this is still "The Greatest College Football Game Ever Played." It served up the whole all-you-can-watch buffet of football drama—kicking, defense, strategy, devastating injuries, controversy, close calls and TWO different endings. It seemed Miami had won in the first overtime, and then the interference flag fluttered and the game raged on until OSU won for keeps in the second extra session. Out of a spread formation, the Buckeyes used quarterback and MVP Craig Krenzel like a running back effectively all game. The Buckeyes knocked Miami running back Willis McGahee out of the game with a knee injury and left quarterback Ken Dorsey dazed and ineffective at the end because of the beating he had taken. Miami tied it on the last play of regulation. OSU kept the game going by converting a fourth-and-14 in the first OT on a drive that was later resuscitated again on the pass interference call with Chris Gamble in the end zone. Maurice Clarett stole the ball from Sean Taylor. And on and on the thrills went. The nation's highest TV ratings for the game were in Columbus. Second highest: Cleveland.

As the so-called Dean of Cleveland Sports Talk Radio, I have seen numerous Browns drafts over the years. Here is my take on the dozen worst Browns draft failures in recent decades.

12. Charles White, 1980. A bizarre, four-team trade brought White, the 1979 Heisman Trophy award winner, to the Browns as their number one pick in 1980. Drug use and injuries plagued White during his five seasons with the team. Because of his drug involvement, the Browns began the "Inner Circle" program to help players deal with drug abuse and other issues. That certainly helped some Browns players, but White didn't help the Browns much. In his five seasons, the former USC star played in just 26 games for the Browns, rushing for 942 yards and ten touchdowns.

11. Clifford Charlton, 1988. The 21st pick overall out of Florida, Charlton was expected to bolster a strong linebacking corp, but never did. He spent most of his two years here on special teams. Perhaps the highlight of his career came on draft day. A disorganized Houston Oilers staff passed on the 21st pick, allowing the Browns to select Charlton, the guy they thought Houston would take. The Oilers ended up taking Lorenzo White out of Michigan State with the 22nd selection. As luck would have it, the Browns would have made out better if Houston had had their act together and taken White before Cleveland could.

10. Gerard Warren, 2001. "Big Money" represented a last-minute, ad lib by coach Butch Davis. The Browns intended to use the third overall selection in the draft on defensive tackle Richard Seymour out of Georgia. But Davis at the last minute had a brilliant idea (or so he thought). He passed on Seymour and selected Warren instead. Selected later in the round by the Patriots, Seymour and has gone on to have an excellent career. Warren never lived up to his lofty selection. In four seasons, Warren averaged 2.2 tackles and .2 sacks per game. Keep reading those stats and I guarantee you will cry.

9. William Green, 2002. Green was the 16th overall pick out of Boston College. He rushed for 887 yards and six touchdowns his rookie season. After that it was all down hill. Green played three more seasons for Cleveland, totaling just 1222 yards and just three touchdowns. He was his own worst enemy. Green, who was disciplined twice at Boston College for marijuana possession, was suspended in 2003 for violating the league's substance abuse policy. He was also stabbed by his girl friend in November of that year. The Browns released Green in September 2006 after reaching an injury settlement.

8. Courtney Brown, 2000. The overall first pick in the draft, the defensive end out of Penn State was supposed to be the foundation of the team's new defensive line. The All American finished his college career with an NCAA record 33 sacks and 70 tackles for a loss. His first season with the Browns seemed promising. He recorded 70 tackles and 4.5 sacks. The problem, however, was that Brown had trouble staying healthy. From 2002 until 2004, Brown played in just 26 games and recorded eight sacks. You'd swear he'd get hurt getting out of bed. The Browns released him after the 2004 season and he signed with Denver. Brown tore his anterior cruciate ligament in the 2006 preseason and hasn't played since.

7. Steve Holden and Pete Adams, 1973. The Browns had two number one picks that year and they were both busts. Holden was the 16th overall selection after a trade brought the choice from the New York Giants for defensive end Jack Gregory. The cold hard facts about Holden's career are not pretty. The wide receiver played four seasons, 48 games and with just 62 receptions, 224 total yards and no touchdowns. (UGH!) The Browns second first-round pick that year was guard Pete Adams out of USC who also was a bust. It wasn't until the team's third selection, the 30th pick, Greg Pruitt out of Oklahoma, that the team hit pay dirt.

6. Willis Adams, 1979. Nicknamed "The Burner" by Browns head coach Sam Rutigliano as a running joke between the coach and the media, this wide receiver didn't play a whole lot. He caught just ten passes his first four years in the league. That's right ten catches, four years. Injuries and lack of ability limited Adams to just 61 catches for 962 yards and two touchdowns in seven seasons.

5. Craig Powell, 1995. What was Bill Belichick thinking? The Ohio State linebacker was the Browns' first-round pick in 1995, the 30th selection overall-a pick the team got from San Francisco on draft day. The Browns did have a higher pick, the number ten selection. But when Mike Mamula, a defensive end out of Boston College, went to the Eagles at the seventh pick, and tight end Kyle Brady went to the Jets at number nine, Belichick decided to trade down. He got the 49ers' third and fourth-round picks that season and a number one in 1996—and Powell. He held out for 18 days before signing a four-year, $3.26 million deal—65 percent more money than Kansas City paid that draft's next pick, linebacker Trezelle Jenkins. For all that, Powell lasted just three years in the NFL and played 14 games. San Francisco used the Browns' pick to draft J.J Stokes. With the 1996 first-rounder, the Browns got from San Francisco, they selected perennial All-Pro linebacker Ray Lewis. Except, they weren't the Cleveland Browns any more by then. They were the Baltimore Ravens.

4. Tommy Vardell, 1992. "Touchdown Tommy" was the ninth overall pick in the first round in 1992. Out of Stanford, Vardell was thought to be the next Kevin Mack. Unfortunately he couldn't tie Mack's shoes or even wear Mack's shoes. Vardell played eight years in the league, three with the Browns. In those three years, Vardell ran for 1061 yards and caught 48 passes and scored 5 touchdowns. Numbers that weren't worthy of being the ninth pick much less of comparisons to Kevin Mack.

3. Mike Junkin, 1987. The Browns moved up 19 spots to the fifth slot in the first round through a trade with San Diego involving the disgruntled Chip Banks. Cleveland was more than happy to accommodate the Chargers and coach Marty Schottenheimer fixated on Duke's Junkin when most draft experts thought the team would surely tab Shane Conlan out of Penn State. "The Mad Dog in a Meat Market" (Junkin's nickname from Browns' scout Dom Anile) was utterly disappointing. He was neither big enough nor fast enough to play linebacker in the NFL. But other than that, he was great. Junkin lasted just three seasons in the league, two with the Browns. To make matters worse, Rod Woodson and Jerome Brown went later that year in the first round.

2. Tim Couch, 1999. The quarterback was picked as "The Man" to be the cornerstone of the new Cleveland Browns. And if you remember, he didn't have a playbook at Kentucky. I guess they just drew the plays up in the dirt. Statistically his numbers are not that bad, but considering where he was picked and the expectation that he would bring the expansion Browns back to respectability after a three-year absence from Cleveland, Couch disappointed. He lasted five seasons before the Browns cut him in 2004. He threw for over 11,000 yards and completed nearly 60 percent of his passes. He threw 64 touchdown passes and was intercepted 67 times. His quarterback rating was 75.1. Injuries especially took their toll. Shoulder problems plagued Couch after being hit hundreds of times during his short career. Who knows how a good offensive line would have changed things for him.

1. Mike Phipps, 1970. Phipps was going to be the quarterback of the '70s and continue the Browns string of playoff runs. Desperate for a new signal caller with a fading Bill Nelsen on his last legs, the Browns traded future Hall of Famer Paul Warfield to Miami for the Dolphins' first-round pick, the number-three selection overall. Phipps's numbers tell the whole sad story. He played seven seasons with the Browns, throwing for just over 10,000 yards. He completed only 49 percent of his passes, while tossing just 55 touchdowns and a ghastly 108 interceptions.

The Indians' front office, particularly in the dark days of "Trader" Frank Lane, won infamy for their many bad trades. But they've made their share of good deals over the last six-and-a-half decades, as well. Here are the best of them.

10. Grady Sizemore, Cliff Lee, Lee Stevens and Brandon Phillips from the Montreal Expos for Tim Drew and Bartolo Colon, 2002.

This deal stunned Cleveland because it signaled the beginning of a rebuilding movement. But Sizemore has blossomed into a fine player, averaging .286, 78 RBI and over 25 homers in his first three full seasons in Cleveland. He has also claimed a Gold Glove for his play in center filed and selections to two All-Star games. Lee has won 51 games here, including 18 in 2005. Had the Indians not given up on Phillips, who looks like a budding superstar since being traded to the Reds, this deal would be higher up the list. Drew won a single game in three years after leaving Cleveland and is now out of baseball. Colon started off like radar-gun busters (always a Colon obsession--he loved to see triple figures on the gun posted on the scoreboard at ballparks) and won the 2005 Cy Young Award with a 21-7 record and 3.48 ERA with the Angels. But he has struggled with arm problems of late. After averaging 18 wins the first three seasons after the deal, he has won just seven times in the last two years and pitched in just 29 games.

9. Jose Mesa from Baltimore for Kyle Washington, 1992.

Some people still have a sour taste in their mouths from Mesa blowing the 1997 World Series. . . . No, let's put it this way: most Indians fans still HATE Jose Mesa. They forget that without him, the Indians probably don't get to that 1997 World Series. The Indians converted Mesa to a long reliever in 1994, then, out of desperation, made him their closer the following season. Mesa responded in '95 by saving 46 games, 38 of them in a row, and posting a 1.12 ERA. He played a huge role in helping the Indians that season get to their first World Series since 1954. Mesa saved 39 games the next season, when the Indians bowed out in the first round of the playoffs. In 1997, Mesa shared closer duties with Mike Jackson, but still led the team with 16 saves and helped get the Tribe to its second World Series in three years. He saved the fifth game of the ALCS against the Yankees (despite Paul O'Neill's almost-homer with two out in the ninth) and the sixth game against the Orioles to win the pennant. Then came the bottom of the ninth in Miami, and several shakes of his head when he didn't trust the fastball Sandy Alomar, Jr. called for and lost the lead without using his best weapon.

8. The Frank Robinson Trade. This is about history.

This is about changing the face of Major League Baseball. Although Robinson played with the Indians at the end of his career, his acquisition led to the Tribe making him baseball's first black manager. The Angels traded Robinson to Cleveland on September 12, 1974 for cash, catcher Ken Suarez and outfielder Rusty Torres. A month later, Robinson became the Indians' manager replacing Ken Aspromonte. On opening day 1975, Robinson smacked a home run in his first at bat. The Indians finished the season with their best mark in seven years. In 1976, the Indians went 81-78, finishing over .500 for the first time since 1968. Unfortunately the Indians unraveled the next year and Robinson was fired. But for those two seasons, the Indians were the talk of baseball.

7. Gaylord Perry and Frank Duffy from the Giants for Sam McDowell, 1971. Like the Cavs' World B. Free, Perry brought fans to the game all by himself. The right-handed starter won 70 games in his three-plus seasons with the Tribe. He also won the Cy Young Award in 1972 when he posted a 24-16 record. In 1974, he won 15 games in a row. Whenever he pitched, Perry put an extra 10,000 to 20,000 people in the stands, which is particularly dramatic when you consider that the average attendance at Tribe games in those days was between 5,000 and 10,000.

6. Kenny Lofton and Dave Rohde from the Astros for Willie Blair and Eddie Taubensee, 1992. Little did anyone know at the time what a huge role this trade would play in shaping the Indians in the '90s. Lofton led the American League in steals with 66, He went on to play in five All-Star games and win three Gold Gloves with the Indians. He was traded to Atlanta before the 1997 season when the Indians feared he would leave for free agency at the end of the campaign. Ironically, he resigned as a free agent with the Indians the very next season. Cleveland acquired Lofton again in 2007 and he helped the team make the playoffs for the first time in five years.

5. Omar Vizquel from the Mariners for Felix Fermin and Reggie Jefferson, 1993. Vizquel became one of baseball's best defensive shortstops, not to mention a pretty decent hitter (he hit as high as .333 one season). His eight Gold Gloves and timely hitting helped the Indians win a whole lot of games in the 1990s and to gain five straight division titles and two World Series appearances. He and Robbie Alomar made for one of the game's great double-play combinations from 1999 thru 2001. On top of all that, Vizquel is still considered one the biggest fan favorites in team history.

4. Sandy Alomar Jr., Carlos Baerga and Chris James from the Padres for Joe Carter, 1989. The Indians traded one of their better players in the game in Carter, but felt they had to part with him to get the young talent they needed to jump-start their rebuilding program. And guess what? It worked. After years of disastrous deals, the Indians finally made a trade that helped. Alomar was the American League's Rookie of the Year in 1990 and went on to spend 11 seasons with the Tribe. Alomar was recognized as the leader of a team that won five straight AL Central titles and two AL pennants. In 1997, he batted .324 with 21 homers and 83 RBI. Baerga played six-and-a-half seasons with the Tribe and was also an integral part of the team's growth in the 1990s. Switching to second base, Baerga batted over .300 in four straight years, while also averaging 19 homers and 97 RBIs. After helping the Indians get to their first World Series since 1954, Baerga gained weight, stopped getting to balls in the hole at second and fell out of favor with sinkerballer Orel Hershiser and General Manager John Hart. He was traded in late July 1996 to the Mets. Baerga never again enjoyed the same success he had with Cleveland.

3. Joe Gordon from the Yankees for Allie Reynolds, 1946. This is a deal that benefited both teams. Reynolds went on to help New York win six pennants, while Gordon teamed up with shortstop Lou Boudreau to form one of baseball's best double-play combinations. He also helped the Indians win the World Series in 1948, their first title since 1920. In 1948, Gordon batted .280 with 32 home runs and 124 RBIs. He was also a three-time All Star during his tenure with the Indians and eventually managed the Tribe during the tumultuous Frank Lane era.

2. Early Wynn and Mickey Vernon from the Washington Senators for Joe Haynes, Eddie Klieman and Eddie Robinson, 1948. Wynn, who should have changed his name to "WIN," notched 163 Ws over the next nine years for the Indians. He won 20 games four times, including 23 in 1954's pennant winning season. Wynn was part of one of baseball's best starting staffs, along with Bob Feller, Bob Lemon and Mike Garcia. He was also a three-time All Star. The Hall of Famer came back to Cleveland to win his 300th game in 1963 before retiring.

1. Gene Bearden, Al Gettel and Hal Peck from the Yankees for Sherm Lollar and Ray Mack, 1946. A lot of people might debate whether this was Cleveland's best deal. But without Bearden, the Indians probably don't win their first World Championship in 28 years. Bearden won 20 games in 1948 and then the most important one: a one-game playoff with the Boston Red Sox to give the Indians the pennant. The knuckleballer also led the American League with a 2.43 ERA in 1948. Bearden put an exclamation mark on the season by shutting out the Boston Braves 2-0 in Game 3 of the World Series and saving game six to the Tribe on top of baseball. The bad part; like most Indians, he faded into oblivion after that. But it was a wonderful season.

The Dean's List: The Dozen Worst Cavs' First-Round Draft Picks

The NBA Draft is always a bit of a crap shoot. Here's twelve cases of the Cavs crapping out in a big way with their first-rounder.

12. John Morton, 1989. The 25th selection overall out of Seton Hall, Morton was one of that school's greatest players. He averaged over 17 points per game his senior season and helped the Pirates reach for the national championship final against Michigan, only to see his team lose by one point 80-79. Morton played just a little over two seasons with Cleveland, getting into only 107 games. He never quite found his niche and averaged just 4.8 points per game.

11. Stewart Granger, 1983. That's right, that Stewart Granger. Granger was the #24 overall pick, but the Villanova grad and Canadian played just one season here, averaging 4.5 points and 2.5 assists per game.

10. Chad Kinch, 1980. The #22 overall didn't stay around long and didn't play much either. The reason: he wasn't very good. Kinch averaged 2.8 points per contest in 29 games his first season in Cleveland. Cavs' owner Ted Stepien sent Kinch and a 1985 first-round pick to the Dallas Mavericks for Geoff Huston and a third round pick in 1983. Huston actually turned out to be a very good player. Kinch, unfortunately passed away from AIDS-related complications in 1994 at the age of 35.

9. Randolph Keys, 1988. The 22nd pick, Keys came to Cleveland via the Cavs-Suns trade that sent Kevin Johnson, Tyrone Corbin and Mark West to Phoenix for Larry Nance, Mike Sanders and the pick. He played five seasons in the NBA, but only a year-and-a-half of it in Cleveland, where the 6-7 forward out of Southern Mississippi averaged 5.9 points and two rebounds. The Cavs traded Keys to the Charlotte Hornets for a 1991 second-round pick that turned out to be yawner Jimmy Oliver.

8. Brendan Haywood, 2001. Cleveland's second first-round pick that year, the Tar Heel Haywood didn't fit into the team's plans because the Cavs had so many good players back then. Just kidding! Still, the Cavs wasted no time trading him to the Orlando Magic for Michael Doleac. He was then dealt to the Washington Wizards, where he's enjoyed a decent career. The end result for the Cavs: Doleac for one season. Could we start over again with this one and just keep Haywood?

7. Chuckie Williams, 1976. Talk about a long and fruitful career. NOT! Charles Leon (his middle name) lasted one season. He scored a whopping 37 points in 22 games. He shot 30 percent from the field and averaged 1.7 points per game. Amazingly, Bobby Wilkerson, Richard Washington and Terry Furlow-all picked before Williams in that draft-also played for the Cavs at some point.

6. Shannon Brown, 2006. Brown has not adapted to the NBA. Too many mental mistakes, bad shots, and not enough defense kept him in coach Mike Brown's dog house for most of two years, and he was traded before the 2008 deadline.

5. Dajuan Wagner, 2002. There were high hopes for the number six overall. A prolific scoring guard out of Memphis, Wagner played just one season of college ball, averaging 21.2 points per game and setting a school single-season scoring mark with 762 points. Wagner also scored 100 points in a high school game. The NBA proved to be a different animal. Wagner played in just 102 games in three seasons. He averaged only 9.4 points per game after averaging 13.4 points per game his rookie season. Wagner was plagued by debilitating health problems. He suffered from ulcerative colitis and played just 11 games in his final season with the Cavs. A year later, Wagner had his colon removed and is trying to make a professional comeback in Europe. A healthy Wagner might have been a different story.

4. DeSangana Diop, 2001. The Senegal native was drafted eighth overall out of Oak Hill Academy High School, where he averaged almost 15 points and 13 rebounds in an undefeated 33-0 season. Unfortunately he was the rawest of raw basketball players who needed a lot of tutoring. The seven-footer played in 193 games in four seasons with the Cavs averaging just 1.6 points, 2.6 rebounds and 0.8 blocks per contest. The problem with Diop was conditioning and weight problems. Too much weight and not enough conditioning. On top of that the Cavs were just reluctant to give him more playing time because of his limited offensive skills. The Cavs let him go after the 2004-2005 season. He then signed a free agent contract with the Dallas Mavericks.

3. Luke Jackson, 2004. Very simply put, Jackson was easily forgettable. The tenth overall pick, the 6-7 guard had a great college career at Oregon. He is one of only two PAC 10 players to score 1900 points, grab 700 rebounds and dish out 400 assists during his college career. Injuries have dogged him professionally. In two seasons, he played in just 46 games, scored 125 points and averaged 2.7 points per game. Jackson was sidelined multiple times with patella tendinitis and underwent surgery for a herniated disc in 2005. He was traded to the Boston Celtics just prior to the 2006-2007 season for center Dwayne Jones.

2. Trajan Langdon, 1999. A Trajedy. The 11th overall pick in the 1999 draft, Langdon's biggest accomplishment remains that he was the first Alaska-born NBA player. Is that really an accomplishment? He could hit the three-point shot, but not much else and lacked consistency. Langdon missed most of his rookie season with inflammation of the right knee that required arthroscopic surgery to fix cartilage damage. "The Alaskan Assassin" lasted just three seasons, averaging 5.4 points per game.

1. Keith Lee (through Charles Oakley), 1985. Talk about screwing up a pick! Lee came to Cleveland in a draft-day deal. The Cavs selected Charles Oakley with the ninth pick and traded him and Calvin Duncan to Chicago for the 11th pick, which was Lee, plus Ennis Whatley. The Cavs also considered drafting Karl Malone with the pick, but GM Harry Weltman felt Malone wouldn't fit in with his team's style of play. Boy was he right on the money! Weltman also thought Lee would be a better all-around player than both Malone and Oakley. Again, another great call by Weltman. Lee came to training camp out of shape and never recovered. The 6-10 forward out of Memphis State played just two seasons with the Cavs, averaging 6.7 points. He was also hampered by leg pain and other maladies. Oakley went on to be a solid 20-year NBA player. Malone went on to be one of the 50 greatest NBA players ever.

Sometimes big-name players turn out to be little more than names by the time they come to play for your team. Cleveland has hosted more than a few once-great players who came here to play out their string and cash a few last paychecks.

10. Jim McMahon. You remember him on the Browns, right? Yes, the Jim McMahon who helped the 1985 Bears to a Super Bowl win actually played in Cleveland. McMahon became the Browns third-string quarterback in 1995 or, should I say, its designated sitter. He was active, but didn't play one down. McMahon slipped away to Green Bay late in the season as the Browns were preparing to move to Baltimore and threw one pass for the Packers. He played one more season in a backup roll for the Packers before retiring. Not many people even remember him wearing a Browns uniform. Then again, why would they?

9. Jack Morris. Morris' last hurrah came as a Cleveland Indian in 1994.
The Tribe had just moved into Jacobs Field and Morris was signed as a free agent after a 7-12, 6.19 ERA season in Toronto. Morris battled all season long and won 10 games in 23 starts. That was actually pretty good. However, on August 7, he pitched his final game for the Indians and his final game in the big leagues. He then went home to farm. I guess it was better than baseball. During his career, Morris pitched a no-hitter, won 254 games and three World Series. He deserves a spot in the Hall of Fame, according to some.

8. Jack McDowell. McDowell was signed as a free agent at the end of 1995 following a 15-win season with the New York Yankees. McDowell looked like a significant piece of the starting pitching puzzle that included Charles Nagy, Orel Hershiser and Dennis Martinez. General manager John Hart thought he had figured it out and struck gold. McDowell pitched the 1996 and 1997 seasons with the Indians, winning 16 games, but only three of them in '97. Some said he was beginning to tire of baseball and spent more time playing guitar for a band he had started than working on his delivery. Plus, when talking to McDowell, you never got the sense he thought that he ever pitched a bad game. He experienced arm problems that season and became a free agent at the end of the year. He retired two years later after winning just five more games.

7. Phil Niekro. The 47-year-old Niekro came to the Indians in 1986 for his 23rd season in baseball. He was a young 47, I guess. The knuckleballer had won his 300th game on the last day of the season in 1985 and went on to win 11 games for the Indians in 1986, then add seven more Ws in 1987 before being dealt to the Blue Jays in August. Those numbers weren't that bad, but couldn't we have signed him when he was 40? Win number 314 in 1987 gave Phil and his brother Joe the all-time victories mark for a brother combination. Phil Niekro retired at the end of the 1987 campaign.

6. John Jefferson. A four-time Pro Bowl selection with the Chargers and the Packers, Jefferson played eight seasons in the NFL, his last one with the Browns in 1985. The speedy wide receiver had caught 348 passes for nearly 5700 yards and 47 touchdowns in his seven previous NFL seasons. He hadn't even turned 30 when he showed up in Cleveland. But there was very little football left in him. Jefferson caught just three passes for 30 yards in 1985, then called it a career.

5. Dave Winfield. Winfield was more than done when the 43-year old joined the Indians in April 1995. Actually, Winfield was traded to the Indians on July 31, 1994 for a player to be named later, 12 days before Major League players went on strike. Winfield didn't play for the Indians before the strike and re-signed with the Tribe as a free agent right after the strike ended in April 1995. Winfield had banged out ten homers in 1994 in just 77 games. But in 46 games with the Tribe in 1995, he produced just two homers and four RBI. Yes, those numbers are correct. He didn't make the team's postseason roster and retired after the season. One interesting note, the Twins never got that player to be named later for Winfield. The deal was settled over dinner with the Indians picking up the tab. Thus, Winfield was traded for dinner. The tab remains a secret to this day.

4. Steve Carlton. After spending his first 21 full seasons with St. Louis and Philadelphia, the future Hall of Famer decided to take one last tour. In 1986, Carlton pitched for Philadelphia, San Francisco and the Chicago White Sox. He then signed with the Indians right as the season began in 1987 at the ripe old age of 42. He must have liked the Terminal Tower. The season was forgettable and uneventful. Carlton won just five games while losing nine to go along with his 5.37 ERA. On July 31, the trading deadline, Carlton was dealt one last time to Minnesota for Jeff Perry. Carlton finished the year with the Twins, who won the World Series but didn't include him on their postseason roster. "Lefty" pitched nine-and-two-thirds innings the next year and tried one more comeback in 1989 before calling it quits. The only notable event for Carlton as an Indian was teaming up with Phil Niekro at Yankee Stadium. It was the first time two 300-game winners had pitched in a game as teammates.

3. Walt Frazier. He was "The Man" in New York for ten seasons with the Knicks. A seven-time All Star, the guard helped the Knicks win two championships in 1970 and 1973. At the age of 32, New York thought he was done and dealt him to Cleveland in October 1977 as compensation for the Knicks signing free agent Jimmy Cleamons. Frazier, however, hurt his foot and was limited to 51 games, although he did average 16 points per game. At one point, the Cavs went 13-5 with Frazier in the lineup. Many thought "Clyde" couldn't play with pain. Many knew Frazier also hated Cleveland because its nightlife couldn't compare to New York's. Frazier played just 15 games the next two seasons, scoring only 139 before hanging it up. His only highlight took place one night in New York, his old stomping grounds, where he lit it up for 28 points. Does New York really have better nightlife than Cleveland?

2. Juan Gonazalez (the second go-around). Trying to catch lightning in a bottle twice, the Indians signed Juan Gonzalez prior to the 2005 season. Gonzalez already had one great year with the Indians in 2001, when he hit .325 with 35 homers and 140 RBI. The Indians rolled the dice four years later, even though Gonzalez hit just five homers with 17 RBIs in 127 at-bats with the Royals the previous season. Juan's second tenure here ended after just one at-bat when his back gave out in May. Then he tore a hamstring, ending any hope he would make it back that season. At press time, Gonzalez was trying to make a comeback at the age of 38 with the St. Louis Cardinals after having not played for almost three years. I think he got hurt again. What a surprise.

1. Keith Hernandez. Hernandez was signed as a free agent on December 7, 1989. It was a bold and expensive move by the Indians. The Tribe desperately needed leadership and thought the 36-year-old Hernandez would be a perfect addition for a young team. The Indians gave the former MVP a two year, $3.5 million guaranteed contract. That was a lot of bucks for the time. It was money the Indians didn't really have either. For all that cash, the team got 43 games, 130 at-bats and a .200 batting average. Hernandez had been plagued by back, knee and hamstring problems the previous few seasons, leading to a significant decline in his production. The Indians obviously looked past that and in the end all those injuries came back to haunt the franchise.

Brinda sends a shout-out to the guys who often made listening to Cavs, Browns and Indians games more rewarding than watching them.

10. Harry Jones. A former newspaper writer turned broadcaster, Jones called the Indians on TV and radio from 1961 thru 1974 and in 1977. Jones did a solid job of talking about the game and reporting. When he teamed up with Jim "Mudcat" Grant in '73, '74 and '77, they formed the most entertaining Indians broadcast partnership ever. It didn't matter what was going on during the game, Grant and Jones had better stories.

9. Jim Donovan. Donovan has been the voice of the Browns on radio since 1999. He is as solid as you'll find for a play-by-play guy. Donovan has also done a lot of TV play-by-play, including the NFL on NBC in the 1990's. He currently calls the Indians' TV games on Channel 3. Donavan sounds like he's having a good time when he does games. When the Browns made the 2002 playoffs and William Green keyed the clinching final-game victory over Atlanta with a long second-half touchdown run, Donovan screamed: "Run, William! Run!" It was what thousands of Browns fans were shouting in their living rooms.

8. Michael Reghi. One of the area's most versatile broadcasters, Reghi served as the voice of the Cavaliers on TV for 12 years and did college football and basketball play-by-play for 21 years, including tenures with ESPN and FSN. Reghi has a great up-tempo style with a creative vocabulary. You knew you were watching the Cavs when he was doing the game. "Flight 23, cleared for landing!" was his trademark call for a dunk by LeBron James, or "the deluxe All-American from Akron Saint Vincent-St. Mary," as he called him. When Cavs owner Dan Gilbert let him go after the 2005-2006 season, Cavs fans lost their TV voice. It was one of Gilbert's few mistakes.

7. Ken Coleman. Coleman did Indians baseball on TV from 1954 through 1963. He also broadcast Browns football on radio in 1952 and 1953. Coleman did Browns football on TV from 1954-67. He was a smooth, polished play-by-play voice. He gave you what you needed. What set him apart from some of his peers was that he did not try to make himself the center of attention, just the game. He left Cleveland to do the Boston Red Sox on radio and later the Cincinnati Reds on TV. His son Casey Coleman's signoff when he was their ABC-affiliate's sports anchor ("We're rounding third and headin' for home") was an affectionate tribute to his dad.

6. Bob Neal. Neal did Tribe baseball off-and-on from 1949 to 1972. Neal broadcast Browns' football on the radio in 1950 and '51. He missed some years in the '50s due to national radio commitments. Neal had a strong baritone voice that got him a lot of work doing baseball and football nationally, most of it on the Mutual radio network. His crooner voice and abrasive personality made him the complete opposite of partner Jimmy Dudley. The pair didn't speak to each other when they worked together. Neal was about as good and complete a broadcaster as there was in that era.

5. Jimmy Dudley. Dudley broadcast Indians baseball on radio and TV from 1948 thru 1967. He could be defined as smooth and cool. His Southern drawl made it easy to listen. A lot of Baby Boomers grew up listening to Dudley do baseball and it didn't matter if the Indians were good or bad, they still listened to every game. Like Red Barber in New York, Dudley brought a Southern accent and a fine appreciation of the game to the booth. "Lotsa' good luck, ya' heah" was his sign-off. We were always lucky to listen to him.

4. Tom Hamilton. Tom has done Indians baseball on the radio since 1990, earning the right to be the Indians radio voice as long as he wants to stay in the booth. "A SWINNNNNG and a DRIVE! WAAAAAAY BACK!" is his defining phrase. Tom can also go on memorable rants. He ripped Derryl Cousins, a former umpiring scab, in 2008, saying, "Some people get jobs because they work hard for them and others break rules to get 'em. Some umps are qualified to be in the Majors and some are there because the league is afraid to remove them." It was strong stuff from a very strong personality in the booth.

3. Nev Chandler. The most versatile play-by-play voice Cleveland has ever had, Nev did everything and everything well. That was due to preparation and hard work. Chandler's touchdown countdown "He's at the 30 . . . the 20 . . . the 10 . . . 5, 4, 3, 2, 1, TOUCHDOWN, CLEVELAND BROWNS!" was a classic. He also served as Herb Score's sidekick with the Indians for years. Chandler could do a spot-on, off-microphone impersonations of Modell, Score and almost anyone else. But it was not in his nature to be mean. Nev's mimicry was always done affectionately.

2. Gib Shanley. No one has called football on the radio better than Gib. For 24 seasons, he was the voice of the Browns on the radio. His call of who caught the ball and where remains unmatched. His performance for the 1964 NFL Championship game is a civic treasure. Gib also called it as close to as it was permissible in the Art Modell era, once dryly noting as the Browns ran to the locker room after a first half of being pounded one forlorn Sunday, "And that is the first time the Browns have crossed midfield today."

1. Joe Tait. Tait has served as the voice of the Cavaliers on radio and TV for all but two of the franchise's 39 years. He also broadcast Indians games on radio for seven years beginning in 1973 and eight more years on TV in the 1980s. Simply put, Tait is the best at what he does. Close your eyes and you know exactly what's going on. "Fasten your seatbelts. . . . Here come the Cavaliers!" "WHAM! With the left hand!" He brought an excitement to play-by-play every game.

Note from Greg Brinda: This list represents a collaborative effort from two gentlemen who played a big part in covering the Cleveland Browns. Hank Kozloski reported on the team for the *Lorain Journal* from 1964 through 1978. The late Gib Shanley served as the voice of the Browns on radio for 24 years from 1961 through 1984. Shanley passed away in April of 2008. He was working on his list when he got sick. About two weeks before he died, Gib tried to get a hold of me but I didn't get his call. He wanted me to come to the hospital so he could tell me what to write. What he did was dictate some notes to his wife. It is remarkable that he thought about this book and wanted to finish his part while he was dying. Words cannot express my gratitude. He was one of a kind and a wonderful person and we will miss him always. The list excludes the Browns' greats from the 1940s and 1950s because both Gib and Hank didn't start covering the team until the 60s.

10. Dante Lavelli. One of the best receivers of all time, Lavelli was elected to the Pro Football Hall of Fame in 1975. He led the Browns in receiving for four years. His 526 receiving yards in the postseason ranks him first overall in team history. He had the best set of hands you'll ever see. Lavelli would catch anything thrown near him and was smooth going down field.

9. Ozzie Newsome. The Wizard of Oz could catch anything. He made Brian Sipe's and Bernie Kosar's job very easy. When he got open, which was most of the time, you threw him the ball. And he caught it and started running and it took a lot to bring him down. Newsome led the team in receiving five straight years from 1981 through 1985. Ozzie was also one of the most decent human beings you'll ever meet. He was duly elected to the Pro Football Hall of Fame in 1999.

8. Gene Hickerson. This is the guy who cleared the way for Jim Brown, Bobby Mitchell and Leroy Kelly. It's a mystery as to why it took so long for him to get elected to the Hall of Fame. Thankfully, he finally got his just due in 2007. Hickerson was big and strong with speed to burn and just punished would-be tacklers on those famous sweeps. Ask anyone of those great running backs who should get the credit for all those yards, they will all say "Gene Hickerson." And what a treat it was to see those three great running backs with Hickerson at his induction ceremony in Canton.

7. Gary Collins. Although Collins's best year came in 1966 when he caught 56 balls for 946 yards, he will always be remembered for his three-touchdown performance in the 1964 NFL Title game, a 27-0 rout of the Baltimore Colts. Collins also punted. Yes, they did that back in those days. He still holds the record for the highest punt average in one season of 46.7 yards per kick. He was so smooth, but had a workman-like attitude. Sometimes, he just doesn't get the credit he deserves.

6. Frank Ryan. That's Dr. Frank Ryan. He has a PhD in math. He could also throw the football a little bit. Ryan was exactly what the Browns needed in the early-to-mid-1960s. He could throw the ball with some zing but he also had incredible touch. Like Collins, Ryan will be best remembered for the three touchdown passes he threw in the second half of the 1964 NFL Title game. He played about as well and was as accurate as any quarterback in that era. As you can imagine, the good Dr. Ryan was pretty smart, too.

5. Paul Warfield. It's just too bad Warfield didn't spend his whole career in here. The Browns definitely needed a quarterback in the 1970s, but trading Warfield wasn't the answer. He led the team in catches, receiving touchdowns and yards his rookie season in 1964. Getting hurt in the College All-Star game the next season set him back a bit. But in 1968, he gathered over 1,000 yards in receiving. Although he had great years with the Dolphins, this future Hall of Famer would have caught far more balls had he stayed with the Browns. He was also one of the most humble and nicest guys in the game of football.

4. Lou Groza. "Lou the Toe" was a kicker and an offensive tackle, then after a year of retirement in 1960, he came back to just place kick for seven more seasons. In his early days, Groza was an excellent offensive lineman. But, boy, could he kick. He had a number of field goals over 50 yards. A nine-time Pro Bowl player, Groza was a rugged guy and looked the part when he played. The Pro Football Hall of Fame took him in 1974.

3. Leroy Kelly. This guy could do it all. Kelly could run with the best of them. He could catch. He could run back kickoffs and punts. What didn't he do? When he saw a hole, he literally disappeared through it. He was quick and elusive. He was the answer to Chicago's Gayle Sayers. Kelly had some of the softest hands I'd ever seen on a running back. He was also tough as nails. As good as Jim Brown was, the team didn't miss a beat when he retired after the 1965 season. Kelly went into the Hall of Fame in 1994.

2. Brian Sipe. Say "Kardiac Kids" and you say "Brian Sipe." He wasn't bad for being a 13th round draft pick out of San Diego State University in 1972. The stats on Brian say a lot. He threw for 154 touchdowns and almost 24,000 yards. He was just fun to watch and in 1980 directed some of the most amazing comebacks in Browns' history. He just knew how to win. Sipe might have been the gutsiest quarterback the team has ever had. He was a great leader and just got it done.

1. Jim Brown. Did you think there would be anyone else at this spot? Arguably the greatest player in NFL history is what it's all about. We had the great pleasure of watching Jim Brown play in Cleveland. He just didn't play long enough.

Note: He is smart and quick and willing to tweak a player's image in his "How Come Quickies." (Samples: When Larry Nance, Brad Daugherty, Mark Price, and Hot Rod Williams missed a lot of games due to injuries. How Come . . . Danny Ferry never gets hurt. And, How Come . . . if they listed weights in Roman Numerals, C.C. Sabathia would be C.C.C. Sabathia? Cleveland media veteran Les Levine has interviewed most of the sports figures in the area and many of national stature who passed through town. Levine happily confesses, for example, that "I think I fell in love with Mary Lou Retton" after she was his guest for an hour. Suffice it to say, he did not hold such warm feelings for these guys.

5. Andy Geiger. The former Ohio State Athletic Director had an uneventful appearance on my radio show in the mid-'90s, but he makes this list for a letter he wrote to me in 2003. On the night before two local football stars were going to announce their decision about their choice of schools, I stated that I hoped they would be choosing OSU. Geiger sent me a 'cease and desist' letter, saying that as an alumnus of Ohio State, I could lead the NCAA to look at me saying that as a recruiting violation. If that, indeed, is true, you would think a polite phone call might have been a better idea.

4. Butch Davis. Absolutely would have rather been somewhere else. The only time a smile came to his face is when a question was asked that he could answer honestly without having to be creative in his wording.

3. Chris Palmer. At best the fifth choice of Al Lerner and Carmen Policy to coach the expansion Browns, Palmer seemed extremely insecure, even though he had the job already. After the show, he wrote me a nasty letter complaining that I put him on the spot for the entire hour. His lack of understanding of what coaches have to do beside coach came out clearly in his tenure with the Browns, as evidenced when he compared his second team to an "out of control train."

2. Bob Huggins. At the time, he was under criticism for poor academic results and legal problems with his players. He took offense to every question that was asked, even if it concerned basketball strategy. He acted as if he were in front of a jury, and didn't realize that the Cleveland audience he was playing to had no understanding of references he was making, although they may have been relevant to a Cincinnati audience that was familiar with the situations.

1. Barry Switzer. I might have caught him on a bad day on radio in the mid-'90s. But when he was promoting his autobiography, he sat three feet across the table from me and still hasn't looked me in the eyes.

These folks had made it a joy to flip on the radio in Cleveland, and keep it on all day long.

10. Jeff and Flash. From 1977 until 1994, Jeff Kinzbach and Ed "Flash" Ferenc hosted the morning show on WMMS. It was one the premier morning drive radio shows in the country. Re-titled "The Morning Zoo" in 1983, the show was a ratings hit. It had everything. There were interviews with rock stars, there were contests and comedy bits. The best music of the day was also played. It was a full service destination for the audience and Kinzbach and Ferenc were the straws that stirred the drink. It might have also been the greatest marketed and promoted show in the history of radio.

9. Mike Trivisonno. Triv, or "Mr. Know It All" as he's sometimes called, has had tremendous ratings and staying power. He began his radio career as a caller to the Pete Franklin show in the 1960s and '70s. His debates with Franklin were legendary. He parlayed that into a radio career. He first hosted a show on a classic rock station, then headed to the 50 thousand watt 1100 signal in 1994, taking over "Sportsline," ironically the show that Franklin had hosted. Triv is loud. He is opinionated. He doesn't have the best command of the English language. But his audience doesn't care. He doesn't even talk much about sports anymore. Some think he appeals to the lowest common denominator. Well, then that must be a pretty big niche because his ratings are consistently big.

8. John Lanigan. Lanigan's career began at the old WGAR in 1971. He later left for Florida before coming back in 1985 to host the morning show at WMJI. Lanigan has a devilish sense of humor and is a terrific interviewer. Sometimes he can come off as an old curmudgeon. But his audience loves him. As co-host of "Lanigan and Malone," he has enjoyed ratings that made him the top-paid radio personality in the market. He even held his own when Howard Stern was in the market. I could reveal his salary but I'm sure he would kill me. Let's just say I'm REALLY JEALOUS!

7. Martin and Howard. Specs Howard and Harry Martin were an incredible morning drive team in the 1960s in Cleveland on the old KYW 1100 channel. The show ran from 1964 until 1967 before the pair moved to Detroit. These guys did more bits than anything heard at the time. The production value of the show, considering the technology available, was at a very high level. These guys were funny and of course played the best Top 40 hits of the day. I started my school day with these guys every morning.

6. Allan Douglas. He was "Mr. Talk Radio" before talk radio became a part of the radio industry. He's one of the reasons I got into the business. He was on at midnight on WKYC 1100 for years. He talked about everything. He was one of the smartest people I've ever heard in the media. I especially enjoyed when he talked UFOs. I didn't know that many people were abducted by aliens. This was great radio. He talked politics and history. I really learned a lot as a kid listening to the radio after midnight. Douglas was also the original host of the "Morning Exchange" on Channel 5 in 1972.

5. Merle Pollis and Joel Rose. These were my buddies for years at WERE Radio. Pollis was the liberal. Rose was the conservative. Neither one liked sports very much but that was OK. At least they didn't have an opinion about the teams everyday of the week. But, boy, did they have opinions about politics and the world. Pollis came to town in the early '70s during the WERE People Power Days with Gary Dee. Pollis, at times, could be bombastic, but he knew his stuff. Rose first cut his teeth in television and worked at Channel 5 for many years. In the mid-1980s both Rose and Pollis did shows on WERE. They were polar opposites, but were incredible radio personalities.

4. Larry Morrow. He was the "Duker" and the king of Top 40 radio for years at WIXY. Morrow came from CKLW Radio where he was known as the "Duke of Windsor." The year was 1966 when Morrow arrived. The city was in the middle of riots. But WIXY became the town's king of Top 40 music and Morrow commanded half of the listening audience. He had a smooth style and played into records as good as anybody in the business. Besides, he was one the most generous and nice guys you will ever meet. I worked with Larry when he hosted afternoon drive on WERE when it was news-talk. Morrow also wrote and produced "Come On Cavs," the theme song for the Miracle of Richfield team.

3. Bill Randle. Randle dominated the Cleveland airwaves during the 1950s and early '60s. In the '50s, if you wanted to know what music everyone was listening to, Randle was playing it on WERE. He was the first disc jockey north of the Mason-Dixon line to play and promote Elvis Presley. That should tell you everything. In 1955, he brought Presley to Brooklyn High School for a concert. Presley, by the way, was the opening act. Pat Boone and Bill Haley and Comets were the headliners that night. Randle was also instrumental in bringing talk radio to Cleveland. He started shows like "Swap and Shop" and "Ask Your Neighbor." He might have been the most educated man I've ever known. He had a doctorate, three masters degrees and a law degree.

2. Gary Dee. Dee literally changed the face of radio in Cleveland. He came to town in 1972 and turned the town on its head with his shocking style as People Power Radio on WERE. Dee was crude, hilarious, mean-spirited, confrontational, clownish, but, in the end, incredibly entertaining. His best days were in the 1970s with WERE, but he also came back to do stints on WHK and 3WE in the '80s and '90s. The guy might be the most entertaining radio talk host ever. I probably listened to him more than I should have, but some of his stuff shaped my venture into the business.

1. Pete Franklin. He is the king of sports talk radio in the market. He started it all in the mid-1960s at WERE. And if you were a sports junkie like me, you had to listen to Franklin. "Sportsline" was the name of the show. Pete was opinionated and quite knowledgeable. And if you called him, you had better be on your "A" game. Pete hated kids and usually dismissed them out of hand. The teams always listened to Franklin. They knew when they made a bad deal or were playing poorly, he would show them no mercy. On many occasions, Franklin would bury a Cleveland team in a funeral like setting. I had the distinct pleasure of competing with Franklin and he would always call me "The Kid." I probably watched 600 Browns and Indians games at the old stadium with Pete. Those memories will live with me forever.

The Top Ten Things I Miss About Cleveland
:: Dick Feagler

Note: The most honored newspaperman in Cleveland, Feagler did not write for *The Plain Dealer* until the 1990s. Before then, he wrote for his beloved *Cleveland Press* from 1970 until it folded in 1982. He has also drawn suburban paychecks and worked for the *Akron Beacon Journal*. Feagler was a war correspondent in Vietnam; a proud graduate of Ohio University, where he was an English major; a Clevelander proud of his city, warts and all; and a tireless and ever hopeful Indians fan. Feagler has won a Peabody award, a Dupont-Columbia Award, and more Associated Press and Ohio journalism doo-dads than you can fit on a wall at his beloved Jacobs Field. He probably doesn't think much of the new, economic-engine name, Progressive Field. But we asked him for the things that have vanished that he did love, and he answered with this list:

10. When the Cleveland Public Schools were arguably the best school system in the country.

9. The sight of the streetcars screeching around Public Square in a shower of sparks that was like a fireworks display. And the sights and sounds of Cleveland Union Terminal when real trains ran there and train announcers bawled their destination.

8. Remembering when the slogan of Cleveland was "The Best Location in the Nation" and believing it.

7. Electing Carl Stokes as the first black mayor of a major American city. And how we felt at midnight 40 years ago that we were close to solving the race problem in America.

6. 1948 when we won the series. 1954 when we didn't.

5. Paying fifty cents to go to the observation deck of the Terminal Tower and getting a bird's eye view of the town. Things looked different from up there. The broadest, straightest street in the city was Woodland Avenue. It probably still is, but who would know that now?

4. Walking all the way to the foot of Ninth Street before there was a Captain Frank's (restaurant) and seeing a sign on the wharf that said "Speedboat Rides, 25 cents," then pooling your funds with your buddy and taking a bouncing speedboat all the way out into the lake. High drama.

3. All the Christmases with all the storefront windows, with all the mechanical toys. The movie *A Christmas Story* didn't do it justice. In the old days, when your mother brought you downtown, you could walk from Ontario to what is now Playhouse Square and press your nose against a half dozen stages of magic. And then of course, the last stop was to walk into Sterling Linder and see the biggest Christmas tree in town.

2. The chicken croquettes at the Clarks restaurants topped with cream pea sauce. I thought it was the best place downtown that your mother could take you to lunch. Especially the Clarks at Ninth and Euclid where there was a Treasure Chest of cheap toys awarded to any kid who wanted one. And what kid didn't? Even though I seem to have lost them all.

1. Euclid Beach Park. It was two transfers from my house to the St. Clair streetcar line. And when the trolley stopped at the park, you stepped out of real life and into magic. I know it didn't compare to the huge Theme Parks of today—Cedar Point or the Six Flags etc. But it was in our town. You could walk in for nothing. You could sit on a picnic table beneath the Flying Turns and eat the breaded pork chops your grandma had put in a picnic basket for you. Finally the park closed and the magic stopped. But the memories didn't. Anybody my age still thinks of Euclid Beach as a dream park. We can hear the rattletrap noise of the old Thriller clanking up the hill and the screams of its occupants as it made its breathtaking plunge. That's my favorite memory.

Teammates dissing each other. Teammates throwing punches at each other. A remake of *Diamonds Are Forever,* starring a pitcher's earring. A reliever who literally went to the bush leagues. The quarterback and the madam. Yikes, time to head to the Panek, er, panic room.

17. Omar Vizquel and Albert Belle. After Vizquel charged in his autobiography that "all Albert's bats were corked," Belle, by then retired, went screeching over the cuckoo's nest again, saying: "I'm sure he didn't write about all his escapades on the road and in Cleveland. That didn't come up, did it?" Then he added: "Since when did Omar Vizquel become good enough to write an autobiography? He hasn't done anything yet." He ended with: "If I ever write a book, it sure as hell isn't going to be about Omar Vizquel."

16. Omar Vizquel and Arthur Rhodes. In a game at Seattle, Vizquel and Rhodes (a future Indians reliever, then with the Mariners) began screaming at each other because Vizquel claimed the reflection of the sunlight off Rhodes' huge diamond earring was blinding him. Rhodes became so incensed that he was thrown out of the game. "He was pointing at my head, like he was going to hit me or something," said Vizquel, who was presumably more sedately accessorized, if not much more sedate.

15. Omar Vizquel and Jose Mesa. What is it with the Little O? How did he end up in more Odd Couple episodes than Jack Klugman? In the same autobiography, Vizquel said of the seventh game of the 1997 World Series: "Jose's eyes were vacant. Completely empty. Not long after I looked into his vacant eyes, he blew the save." Said Mesa: "If he comes to apologize, I'll punch him right in the face. And then I'll kill him."

14. Albert Belle and the Biblical Omega Man. David "The Biblical Omega Man" Henry, a 38-year old North Ridgeville Man at the time of the 1997 incident, was arrested at the White Sox spring training camp in Florida after climbing a fence to berate Belle for leaving the Indians. Charged with trespassing, he showed up again the next day and was jailed. "He says he's the Biblical Omega Man and he's out to make Albert Belle atone for what he did to the fans of Cleveland," revealed a Sarasota cop. Said Henry: "They think I'm crazy. They're afraid of me. I can sense it. They've run into something they have never met before." Now what gave him that idea?

13. LeCharles Bentley and Tyson Walter. In February 2000, Ohio State football center Bentley, a human development and family science major, broke Walter's nose and knocked out a few of his teeth with a single punch during a dispute between the two at an off-season Buckeyes' team workout session. Walter's subsequent lawsuit against Bentley hit the papers during preparations for the Buckeyes' dismal Outback Bowl loss to South Carolina at the end of the 2000 season. "I'm going to have to find out about these so-called problems," said the Buckeyes' so-called coach John Cooper before the 24-7 loss to South Carolina that led to his dismissal.

12. Shawn Kemp and women of childbearing age. A *Sports Illustrated* story said Kemp had fathered seven children by five different women.

11. William Green and Asia Gray. In 2003, Browns' running back William Green was arrested for felonious assault and domestic violence in a dispute with Asia Gray, his girlfriend and the mother of his two children. Despite a nasty stab wound in his back, Green denied that he and Gray had been fighting, claiming he stabbed himself in the left shoulder blade when he tripped going up the stairs in the couple's home. Police were unimpressed with Green's explanation. But gymnastics judges worldwide awarded his alleged roundoff backstabber handspring a unanimous "10."

10. Carmen Policy, Al Lerner, and the press. In the wake of the "Bottlegate" fiasco on December 10, 2001, when angry Browns fans littered the field with thousands of beer bottles after a bad call in a game against Jacksonville, Lerner said to security chief (and former head of the Secret Service) Lew Merloni: "I didn't see anything, Lew, did you?" Policy, who appeared to have emptied a few bottles of his own during the game, added: "Those bottles are plastic and don't pack much of a wallop."

9. Scott Sauerbeck and Lily Miller. At 3:45 in the morning on May 30, 2006, Sheffield Village police followed a 1966 Lincoln Continental that was weaving through Lorain County like a Phil Niekro knuckleball through the strike zone. The driver, Miller, a waitress at a bar in Westlake, made a sudden turn into a driveway, then fled on foot along with Sauerbeck, an Indians relief pitcher. They hid in the bushes behind a house until discovered by police. Miller was charged with DUI after registering a mellow .253 in blood alcohol content, three times the legal limit. Sauerbeck, who had handed the keys to Miller, was charged with wrongful entrustment, mainly because he had entrusted his car to a Foster Brooks' dream date.

8. Stan Jackson and Eddie George. After backup quarterback Joe Germaine guided the Buckeyes downfield in the fourth quarter in 1997 to beat Arizona State and give Ohio State its first Rose Bowl triumph in a generation, Jackson, the starting QB, sat on the bench, weeping. As Buckeye running back and Heisman Trophy winner Eddie George patted him on the back, Jackson, the ultimate team guy, sobbed, "I should've been in there, man."

7. Kellen Winslow, Jr. and a Suzuki GSX-R750. The "Crotch Rocket" motorcycle launched the Browns tight end at escape velocity out of what looked like a budding Hall of Fame career. Winslow had seen his rookie season cut short when he broke his leg during an attempt to recover an onside kick in the final seconds against Dallas in the second game of the season. Then the following May, Winslow decided to take himself and his recovering right leg for a ride on a motorcycle far too powerful for a novice. Hitting a curb going approximately 35 mph, the young tight end was thrown over the handlebars, leading to serious internal injuries and a tear of his ACL in his right leg-the same one he had broken earlier. Winslow's recovery from the crash was slowed by a serious staph infection.

6. Lassie, Rin Tin Tin, Beethoven, Rover, Fido, Marmaduke, Lady, the Tramp and the Dawgs. Haven't our four-footed friends been through enough? Fleas, mange, distemper, drinking from toilets, licking unsavory body parts, Michael Vick. And now the Browns rip off their species!

5. Albert Belle and Malley's Chocolates. More a case of "we can't keep not meeting like this." When Malley's Chocolates called a press conference to unveil its new Albert Belle Bar in 1995, Belle overslept. Later, *This Week in Baseball* invaded the clubhouse to ask players if they would comment on the bar. "I wouldn't lift a finger for that guy," said reliever Eric Plunk.

4. Bernie Kosar and Karen Panek. When police broke up a prominent local call girl ring in 1989, they found 100 names in the little black book of Karen Panek, the ring's madam. Among the names: Bernie Kosar, Hanford Dixon, and the Indians' Mel Hall. Kosar claimed he only lived in the same condominium with Panek, that he changed his phone number a dozen times, and that, so help him Alexander Graham Bell, he had no idea how she got his current number.

3. Dwayne Rudd and triumphant joy. You've got to tip your hat, or make that your helmet, to a man who can lose a game just after he thought he'd just won it. After sacking Chiefs QB Trent Green in the dying seconds of the 2002 regular season opener, Browns linebacker Dwayne Rudd celebrated by pulling off his helmet and tossing it in the air. The only problem: Rudd never, you know, actually got Green, um, well, we believe "down" is the word. Just before hitting the turf, Green had lateraled the ball to his 328-pound lineman John Tait, who then rumbled upfield for a 28-yard gain. But it didn't much matter, because the clock had run out during the play, ending the game. Or did it? Rudd's helmet fling mandated an unsportsmanlike conduct penalty and continuation of play because football games cannot end on a defensive penalty. So referees tacked on 15 penalty yards for Rudd's helmet fling and awarded the Chiefs another snap. The 43-yard gain and extra play allowed the Chiefs to bring on their kicker Morten Andersen to make the chip-shot, game-winning field goal. So Cleveland 39, Kansas City 37 magically became Kansas City 40, Cleveland 39, with no time on the clock. Rudd's debacle cost the Browns the game. It also inspires a paraphrase of Yogi Berra's theory of definitive cessation: "It ain't over WHEN it's over."

2. Jeff Garcia, Carmella DeCesare and Kristen Hine. Let's see. Garcia was dating DeCesare, his future wife and former Playboy Playmate, when she found out he had cheated on her with Hine, another Playmate. So there DeCesare was, minding her own business at a Cleveland nightclub while dancing on a table (hey, doesn't everybody from time to time?), when all of a sudden, here comes Hine and one of her female friends at "full-force, swinging like a guy," said Decesare. The former Playmate of the Year and future WWE pro wrestling diva responded by dropkicking either Hine or her friend in the head. The September 2004 incident wound up in all the papers just as the Brown's season was stumbling out of the gate. The nightclub in question was called "Tramp." You can't make this stuff up.

1. Chuck Finley and Tawny Kitaen. In April 2002, Kitaen, the soon-to-be-divorced wife of Indians' pitcher Finley, was placed under a judicial restraining order after she attacked Finley while he was driving the couple's car. Reportedly, she even kicked him with the spike-heeled boots she was wearing. En route to a domestic assault and battery charge, she also twisted Finley's ear. In court documents, Finley listed a whole pharmacological pill-a-palooza of prescription drugs to which he claimed his wife was addicted. The couple's nanny later testified that their two children often asked: "Is Mommy whacked out today?"

The 10 Best Seasons Cleveland Athletes Ever Had

Maybe the best way to start this list would be to peek at the astounding honorable mentions. One Baseball Hall of Famer (Bapoleon Lajoie), a Pro Football Hall of Famer (Paul Warfield), two baseball shrine probables (Manny Ramirez, Roberto Alomar) and an almost certain future Track and Field Hall of Famer (Tim Mack) get only a sniff of the top 10. We have to go at the tip of the tip with James Cleveland Owens. Why, he even had the city in his name. Maybe we love sports so much here because we have seen them played so well, particularly in these years by these athletes.

Honorable Mentions: Manny Ramirez, 1999 (.344, 44 homers, 165 RBI as the clean-up man for the Thousand-Run Offense); Hal Trosky, 1936 (.343, 42 homers, 124 runs, 162 RBI); Napoleon Lajoie, 1904 (.376, 102 RBI, 92 runs in the horse-and-buggy days of the game); Roberto Alomar, 1999 (.323, 24 homers, 138 runs, 120 RBI, 37 steals and Gold Glove defense); Paul Warfield, 1968 (back when receivers were treated as they left the line in a manner that would risk incarceration for assault and battery today, Warfield came up with 50 catches for 1,067 yards, a 21.3-yard average, and 12 touch-downs-topping Ozzie Newsome's best years as a Browns receiver in TDs and yardage, despite catching over 30 fewer balls); Luis Tiant, 1968 (a Gaylord Perry-like 21-9 record and 1.68 ERA, though in the "Year of the Pitcher" those numbers didn't earn him a single Cy Young vote); former Buckeye Robert Smith, 2000 (1,521 yards, 7 touchdowns, and 36 catches for 348 yards and 3 more TDs for the Minnesota Vikings); Steve Stone, 1980 (the Euclid-born Kent Stater was 25-7 with a 3.23 ERA for the Baltimore Orioles, winning the Cy Young, while for the rest of his career he was just 82-86); Tim Mack, 2004 (the Westlake native and St. Ignatius grad was unbeatable in the summer leading up to and following the Athens Olympics, becoming the first pole vaulter to win his sport's "Triple Crown" of the Olympic Trials, Olympic Games and World Athletics Finals); Braylon Edwards (80 catches-but too many drops-and 1,289 yards, plus a team-record 15 touchdowns) and Kellen Winslow, Jr. (82 catches, 1,106 yards for a team tight ends record, and 5 TDs, with some critical drops too), both in 2007 for the Browns.

10. Tom Weiskopf, 1973. The Benedictine grad and Bedford resident won seven golf tournaments around the world, including the prestigious Colonial, Canadian Open and World Series of Golf, plus a major with the British Open, He finished third in the U.S. Open, sixth in the PGA and helped the U.S. win the Ryder Cup.

9. Gaylord Perry, 1972. Won the Cy Young with a bad Indians team, going 24-16 with a 1.92 ERA over 343 2/3 innings, while only surrendering 253 hits.

8. Brian Sipe, 1980. Captain Pacemaker of the Kardiac Kids completed 60.8 percent of his passes, for 4,132 yards, with 30 touchdowns and just 14 interceptions. Sipe provided more excitement than Browns fans had experienced since the '60s.

7. Tris Speaker, 1920. The player-manager hit a mere .388, scored 137 runs, drove in 107, walked 97 times and only fanned 13 times while guiding the Indians to their first pennant.

6. Lou Boudreau, 1948. He served as both the Indians' top player and manager while guiding them to a World Series title. The "Boy Manager" in his MVP year hit .355, best in the league, with 106 RBI, cracking all sorts of crucial hits under pressure and hatching unorthodox tactics to win games.

5. Bob Feller, 1946. Bobby came marching home again and proved that his years away fighting for his country as a gunnery mate in World War II hadn't diminished his game. He went 26-15 with a 2.18 ERA, notching a staggering 348 Ks over a more staggering 371 1/3 innings.

4. LeBron James, 2005-06. He was 21 when the season began, yet he averaged 31.4 points, 7.6 rebounds, 6.6 assists, shot 48 percent from the field and 73.8 percent from the line. He almost single-handedly beat the Pistons in the playoffs and was on his way toward becoming the greatest prodigy since Mozart.

3. Jim Brown, 1963. The best year by the best running back ever featured these abacus figures: 1,863 yards and 12 touchdowns (in a 14-game season), with a career-best 6.4 yards per carry.

2. Jesse Owens, 1935. One day can a season make. One hour can last forever. At the Big Ten track meet in Ann Arbor, Owens shook off the effects of a back injury, incurred earlier in the week when he fell hard on his tailbone while playing a prank on his Ohio State teammates. He said he could not touch his toes before settling in for his first race. "Then, the pain miraculously disappeared," he said. The next 45 minutes were full of miracles. Owens set world records in the 200-yard dash, the 220-yard low hurdles and the long jump, as well as tying the world mark in the 100-yard dash. Owens' only long jump attempt set a record of 26 feet, 8_ inches that lasted 25 years - or two more than Bob Beamon's altitude-aided leap at the Mexico City Olympics in 1968

1. Jesse Owens, 1936. In a performance that transcended sports, Owens, of East Tech and Ohio State, won four gold medals in the Berlin Olympics for the 100, 200, long jump and 4x100 relay. In the process, Owens forced Adolf Hitler and his Nazi thugs to choke on the racist bilge they spewed as they watched a black man best their Aryan uber-mensches on their home turf.

This is THE list of the book, and a lot of horse trading took place between the co-authors over the people who would be included and what order they would be presented, especially the order of the top three. Suffice it to say, we expect reader debate, too.

The criteria: eligibility is limited to athletes from the seven-county (Cuyahoga, Lorain, Lake, Medina, Summit, Portage, Geauga) area, as well as those who played on professional teams in town. With one player from the Barons and two from the Force, you'll note that we included athletes who did not play on "major" professional teams. Athletes in team sports who became famous elsewhere, but at least have played high school sports here also made the criteria cut. In individual sports, we loosened the requirement. We think anyone who won an Olympic gold medal and grew up in the area, even if the athlete competed in college outside of Ohio, is aces.

We included players from 1900 to the present. There was some sentiment to restrict the list to post-World War II to cater to today's fans more. But if we excluded players who excelled before 1945, we would have cut many of the greatest players in the history of the Indians, and they were the only team that mattered in Cleveland in those years. We could not limit ourselves to choosing players from the awful 60s, 70s, and 80s to fill out the 100 when Hall of Famers were available who played before the war.

When in doubt, we afforded more prestige to those who won championships and brought glory to the city. Staying longer than to have a sip of coffee (which excused Nate Thurmond) was also required. And, naturally, we were biased toward the more recent athletes, because those are the ones we saw and the ones most readers remember.

In an effort to be open-minded about women's sports, we included five females on the list. Native Clevelanders who won it all got the most love. In 10 years, LeBron James will probably be a slam-dunk No. 1. But at press time, he hadn't won anything in the pros but a conference championship.

100. Buddy Bell. This pick may have been even tougher than the top three, because it came down to a bunch of worthy people who would either make the list or not. St. Edward's linebacker Tom Cousineau, an overall top pick in the NFL draft pick out of Ohio State, enticed us, but Cooz never lived up to the hype with the Browns after a stay in Canada. And Walsh Jesuit's Mike Vrabel has made a lot of impact plays with the Patriots after a terrific career at Ohio State. But Buddy Bell got the nod over both. Bell did not win any of his Gold Gloves with the Tribe, but he was steady, he made an All-Star team here, and in a particularly forlorn era for the Tribe, his good looks and sure hands made him popular with both casual fans and purists. Mike Hargrove, a former teammate, said Bell was the best third baseman he ever saw, which seems like an oversight of George Brett, but is testimonial enough for us to go with Buddy.

99. Tianna Madison. What does she have in common with Jesse Owens? Well, the Elyria track-and-field star matched him (and Zanesville Susan Nash) by winning four events in the Ohio state meet two years in a row. Madison's long jump victory in a monsoon at Helsinki in 2005 made her the first teenager to win a World Championships field event (where technique is so vital that it usually comes only after painstaking years of repetition) sinnce Ukranian pole vaulter Sergey Bubka in 1983. A Jill-of-all-trades, Madison competed as a sprinter/long jumper/relay runner for both Elyria High and the University of Tennessee. She is now training in Los Angeles with Jackie Joyner Kersee's husband and former coach Bobby Kersee and may climb up this list in year's to come with additional achievements.

98. Ken "Mouse" McFadden. The leading scorer in CSU history, "Mouse" (nick-named less for his diminutive frame than those Mickey ears on the sides of his head) was the archetypal non-traditional Kevin Mackey recruit. He did not play high school basketball and did not have a high school diploma. But McFadden got a GED and used the skills that made him a legend in New York's AAU circles to help CSU to the 1986 NCAA Tournament Sweet 16. He probably wasn't even the best player on that team (a distinction belonging to Clinton Smith). But Mouse was the face and driving force of Mackey's Run 'n Stun team for four years.

97. John "Hot Rod" Williams. A great 1989 radio skit, noting the Browns' Thanksgiving Day game in Detroit one night after the Cavs played there, revealed that the Browns had signed shot rejecters Larry Nance and Williams to one-game con-tracts. "While the pair make no tackles, they do block two field goals and one extra point," quipped WMJI funnyman John Lanigan. A second round (45th pick) selection who could not play for a year until he was cleared of involvement in the Tulane point-shaving scandal, "Hot Rod" was one of GM Harry Weltman's great steals.

96. Steve Nagy. The area's top bowler has to be included, given the sports local popularity and Nagy's national stature. Lucille Perk, Mayor Ralph Perk's wife, famous-ly declined an invitation from First Lady Pat Nixon to visit the White House because the event fell on her regular bowling night. The Big Lebowski should have been filmed here.

95. Charles Nagy. Old reliable, he should have been called. Took the ball every time it was handed to him from the last game in Cleveland Stadium until May 2000. Won 15 or more games for the Tribe seven times.

94. Gus Johnson. "Honeycomb," so named at the University of Idaho for his sweet play, was an Akron Central (later Central-Hower) teammate of Nate Thurmond. Gus was about style—he was considered as flashy swooping to the rim as Connie Hawkins, Elgin Baylor and Dr. J. And his Bullets teams won, too. Gus broke three backboards with ferocious dunks. The 11-foot, 6-inch high spot he slapped at a Moscow, Idaho bar called The Corner, was commemorated with a nail in a rafter. Bill Walton, among many others, tried from a standing start to touch it and failed.

93. Ted Ginn Jr. Taken out by "friendly fire" in the celebration after his touchdown return of the opening kickoff in the debacle against Florida, Ginn was 60 percent of the offensive game plan and all of the Buckeyes' speed in that forlorn title game. His absence showed just how important he was to the Buckeyes. Compared to Jesse Owens for his technique and effortless speed by Olympic sprint champ Harrison Dillard, Ginn was also a good receiver—an Eric Metcalf with a deadlier burst on kick returns. Even a bumblebee couldn't pilot his 82-yard zigzag return TD against Michigan.

92. Matt Ghaffari. An Iranian-born Greco-Roman wrestler out of Cleveland State, Ghaffari's outsized personality and fervent patriotism made him a big hit at the 1996 Atlanta Olympics. In the gold-medal match, he lost in overtime, 1-0, to Alexander Karelin, the nearest human approximation to the Russian bear.

91. Franklin Edwards. The best player in Cleveland State history, Edwards was personally scouted by Philadelphia 76ers GM Pat Williams, who, during one trip to Cleveland, happened to see Lenny Barker's perfect game. Edwards, who was part of the Sixers' bench rotation, scored a lot of points for Philly, including a buzzer beater basket to take out the New York Knicks in a playoff game during the Sixers' 1982-83 championship season.

90. Tonia Kwiatkowski. She was part of Carol Heiss Jenkins' impressive array of skaters who made competing in the Figure Skating Nationals a common occurrence for Winterhust Ice Rink skaters in the 90s. After a disastrous qualifying round prevented her from even skating in the finals of the World Championships in 1993, Kwaitkowski gained redemption with top ten finishes in 1996 and 1998. Holder of a college degree from Baldwin-Wallace, she was an elegant, mature woman, compared to the prepubescent Tinkerbells who came to dominate skating.

89. Mike Garcia. The "Big Bear" went 79-41 in four straight seasons in the 50s for the Tribe. He had one of the big leagues' best fastballs, along with one of its best senses of humor. As far as hitters were concerned, the "Big Four" of Feller, Lemon, Wynn and Garcia was a Final Four years before *The Plain Dealer*'s Ed Chay coined the term for the end of the NCAA basketball tournament.

88. Joey Maxim. This Cleveland light heavyweight (who was born Giuseppe Berardinelli), knocked out England's Freddie Mills in the 10th round to win the world title in 1950, hitting the Englishman so hard that three of his teeth were later found in Maxim's glove. His ring name came from the Maxim gun, a rapid-firing weapon, but he was almost out of ammo in his second title defense against Sugar Ray Robinson. Trailing badly on points in a bout held at Yankee Stadium in 1952 during a record heat wave, Maxim prevailed when an exhausted Robinson failed to answer the bell for the 14th round. It was scored as technical knockout for Maxim, the only time Robinson was ever stopped.

87. World B. Free. Major bone of contention among hoopaholics. Putting this selfish gunner among great athletes recalls "Send in the Clowns." ("Don't you love farce?/My fault, I fear/I thought that you'd want what I want/Sorry, my dear. Send in the clowns.") Face paint or not, Free averaged a LeBronian 26.3 points in the 1984-85 season, the only time he got into the playoffs here, carrying the Cavs from the ashes of a 2-19 start after coach George Karl turned him loose. The Cavs lost, 3-1, to defending champion Boston, but aggregate points were equal and the Cavs had the ball in the air at the final buzzer to win or tie in every loss. Where are the clowns? Maybe not here.

86. Tim Goebel. He was developed by local skating guru Carol Heiss Jenkins, though she was not his coach when he won the bronze medal at the 2002 Salt Lake City Olympics, Goebel became known as the "Quad King" after he landed the first quadruple jump in a figure skating competition.

85. Mike Mitchell. A very explosive scorer for the Cavaliers until the lights dimmed in the Stepien Era, Mitchell was capable of blowing up for 40 points at any time. His best years were in San Antonio, where he became the only player other than George Gervin to lead the team in scoring during the Iceman's era there.

84. Kai Haaskivi. Playing for the Force from 1982-87, he finished as Major Indoor Soccer League's fifth-leading career scorer and second-leading assist man. Haaskivi also excelled outside in the North American Soccer League. The midfielder was a creative playmaker and a passer who could make the ball sit up, roll over, curtsy, and scream "Gooooallllllll!"

83. Satchel Paige. Not only still a fine pitcher at some Methuselah age or other when he arrived here in 1948, Paige was one of the game's great showmen. He used: a triple windup, a double windup, and no windup; a hesitation pitch, a trouble ball, a bat dodger, and a B-Ball ("when I throw it, you be out"). He avoided fried foods, lest they "angry up the blood." Go on and look back, Satch. Ain't nothing ever gonna gain on you.

82. Diana Munz. This Chagrin Falls swimmer broke her back and leg in an accident in 1999 before her senior year in high school, but made a remarkable recovery. After not qualifying for the finals in her favorite event, the 800 freestyle, she won a silver in the 400 free and a gold as part of the 4 x 200 relay team. In Athens, she came back to win a bronze medal in the 800 free.

81. Mac Speedie. Had the game to go with the great name. Speedie became a great collegiate hurdler, despite walking with a slight limp after a childhood disease left one leg slightly shorter than the other. He led the NFL in receiving in 1952. He caught a screen pass in the Browns' own end zone and took it for a touchdown against Buffalo in the 1948 AAFC title game. Speedie would be in the Hall of Fame, but for leaving the Browns to play in the Canadian Football League for more money, thus earning the wrath forevermore of Paul Brown.

80. Luis Tiant. "Herky jerky" just doesn't cover the conniption school of pitching developed by Tiant. He went 75-64 with the Indians in the 1960s and was 21-9 with a get-the-microscope 1.60 ERA in the Year of the Pitcher, 1968.

79. Roberto Alomar. Twice hit well over .300 with over 100 RBI and at least 100 runs scored during a florid, yet flawed, stretch with the Tribe. When he felt like playing, which excludes Game 5 of the 2001 ALDS at Seattle, a win-or-go-home game, he could dominate a game at second base. Had a shortstop's arm which allowed him to stay out of harm's way on the double-play pivot, as he would fire while falling away. We never got his head-first slide into first, but there was no convincing Robbie that every track coach who ever lived would advocate running through the base instead of diving.

78. Sam McDowell. "Sudden Sam"—what a nickname. And what a long, not-so-sudden climb to finally reach his potential. McDowell was the ultimate proof that the old Yogi Berra comment, "Full head, empty bat," could also apply to the mound. McDowell would try to get a poor fastball hitter out with his curve, just because it was no challenge blowing his heater past him. He invented challenges for himself, but often, the artificial challenges held him back. There is no other reason for his having won 20 games only once.

77. Brad Friedel. The Cleveland area's greatest outdoor soccer player, this Bay Village native began playing on the North Olmsted Soccer Organization fields as a youngster. He went on to make more appearances in international play than any other American. After leading UCLA to an NCAA title as the goalkeeper, he backstopped the Blackburn Rovers in the English Premier League and once scored a goal by moving up into the attacking zone. In World Cup play, he became known as the "Human Wall" during the USA's run to the quarterfinals in 2002. He became the first man to stop two penalty kicks (as opposed to penalties in a shootout). He is the greatest American keeper ever.

76. Zydrunas Ilgauskas. Should be a Cleveland icon for playing after years of injuries, when surrounded by inept teammates, and sticking with it until he and LeBron James yanked the team up to new heights. Z has endured plenty of tragedy off the court, too, with the stillborn twins his wife delivered. A finesse-oriented guy from Lithuania, he can put up a double-double at will because he's 7-3 with game. It's been a long time since Z was the MVP of the Rookie Game (1998). Because of his role as a veteran leader, because he stayed the course, no matter how hard it was, Z was the first teammate LeBron hugged when the Cavs made the NBA Finals in 2007.

75. Earnest Byner. He only gained 1,000 yards once and then just barely (1,002, to go with Mack's 1,104 in 1985) and was out with injuries much of "The Drive" year of 1986. But Byner still served as the competitive heart of the 80s Browns. Upon stopping by the team bus after a pre-season game in D.C., Byner was bear-hugged by Mike Johnson, who said: "Now that we've got you back, we're not going to let you go."

74. Kevin Mack. Came out of the USFL and teamed with Byner to give the Browns two 1,000-yard rushers in '85 in a running game so mean, nasty and primitive that both should have won saber-tooth tiger skins and carried clubs. Mack served time in prison during the 1989 season after being caught with cocaine, then, in one of the great, redemptive moments in Cleveland sports history, returned to the team in time to gain the big yards that won the division over the Oilers in Houston.

73. Mel Harder. He won 223 and lost 186 in 20 years with the Tribe, and after that, developed Bob Lemon into a Hall of Famer as the team's pitching coach. Every Major League city has an overlooked player deserving of Hall of Fame inclusion, and ours is Mel. His only fault was that he pitched in an offensive era in which many suspect the ball was juiced to give Depression Era spectators a bigger bang for their buck. "I never noticed that," Harder once told Bill Livingston, although alleging the reverse would have helped his candidacy. Mel's ERA was a high 3.80. But the 1930s were a time when all the RBI records were set and when the National League, as a whole, batted .303 in 1930!

72. Doug Dieken. We use the baseball longevity formula here. Anyone who toils 14 years at a critical position like left tackle in the NFL had to be pretty good. One of the really fun guys in sports, too—just check out the list he contributed to this book.

71. Les Horvath. The first of the Cleveland area's three Heisman winners at Ohio State, Horvath missed the 1943 season to concentrate on dental school and even sometimes missed practice to study during his Heisman season in 1944. He played with the Los Angeles Rams and the Browns before becoming a professional dentist. He was about as much fun to other teams in college as getting a filling without Novocaine.

70. Hanford Dixon. Part of a lock-down corner combo with Frank Minnifield, "Daddy Dawg" created the junkyard persona for the team that lasts to this day by barking after good plays in practice. A three-time Pro Bowler, Dixon guarded one rear flank of a defense that stopped whatever was thrown at it, unless, of course, it was thrown by John Elway late in a playoff game.

69. Frank Minnifield. A member of the NFL's All-Decade Team for the 1980s, Minnifield made four straight Pro Bowls. Undersized, he still excelled by employing the athleticism that got him a scholarship at Louisville as a 5-9, 140-pound walk-on.. He was another USFL defector who allowed the ever-rebuilding Browns to reload instead.

68. Clay Matthews. He could blitz, he could cover tight ends, he could tackle, he could do it all, including lateral. Something of an independent thinker, he drove a beat-up Mercury Capri from his home in Southern California to training camp for years "until maintenance became a problem. You know. Oil was expected to last 10,000 miles," he said. He lasted 19 years in the NFL, making the Mercury Capri look like a short-timer.

67. Hal Trosky. Hit .330 with 35 homers and 162 RBI while playing every inning of his rookie season. His run production over his first three seasons topped that of Lou Gehrig, Jimmy Foxx and Hank Greenberg. His accomplishments came despite being plagued by excruciating migraine headaches throughout his career.

66. Troy Smith. Remember, bringing fame to the city counts a lot. Smith dominated the college football highlights his senior season of 2006 at Ohio State. The Glenville High School grad beat Michigan three straight times for Ohio State, once while running for nearly 200 yards and passing for almost 300; once when the Buckeyes were done, down 9 with 7 minutes to play—only Smith didn't know it; and once in the greatest shootout in the history of the game's greatest rivalry. He outplayed Brady Quinn in the Fiesta Bowl. He made a touchdown throw against Penn State after a scramble worthy of Fran Tarkenton or maybe Roger the Dodger. He won the Heisman in a landslide. Not bad for a guy who was the last player given a scholarship his freshman year.

65. Al Rosen. "The Hebrew Hammer," and, boy, they don't make nicknames like that anymore, drove in over 100 runs five straight seasons. In 1953, he hit .336 with 43 homers and 145 RBI and missed the Triple Crown on the last day of the season by one point, when Washington teammates of the batting race winner, Mickey Vernon, conspired to make deliberate outs in the ninth inning so Vernon would not have to bat one last time. Rosen's numbers dipped in 1954, the year after he was named league MVP, but then the third baseman was playing with a broken finger from midseason on. He is the third-greatest Jewish player ever, behind Sandy Koufax and Hank Greenberg.

64. Tom Jackson. An Ohio State recruiter took one look at this John Adams product and told him he was too small to play in the Big Ten. So he helped turn around the Louisville teams of Lee Corso (yeah, the ESPN guy who recently put the Brutus Buckeye head on during a telecast, in happier, saner days) and then played 14 years with Denver, intercepting 20 passes and making 40 sacks with a game built on speed at the linebacking position. He went on to become a member of ESPN's Countdown to Kickoff crew.

63. Brian Sipe. It is hard to remember now how much the Kardiac Kids meant to the city in the wake of bankruptcy, mayoral recall, the burning river and Johnny Carson's mocking monologues. But we shouldn't forget that Sipe was the lead cardiologist who revived the city's spirit. A 13th-rounder in the draft, Sipe was still proving the doubters wrong when the Browns let him jump to the USFL. The front office thought the offense would do just fine with new QB Paul McDonald. You remember him: the guy who handed off to Charles White in the Rose Bowl and then played after Sipe and before Bernie.

62. Gary Jeter. Cathedral Latin grad was an All-American at Southern Cal and played 13 years at defensive tackle, recording 52 career sacks, after being a first-round draft choice of the New York Giants in 1977.

61. Jimmy Bivins, The world light-heavyweight champion during World War II, this Clevelander fought most of the top heavyweights of his day. His title defense against Lloyd Marshall was a brawl, with Bivins going down in the seventh for a two-count, Marshall decked in the ninth for a nine-count and spilled again at the 12th-round bell and finally knocked out in the 13th.

60. Larry Nance. Acquired for Mark West, Tyrone Corbin, Kevin Johnson, a No. 1 draft pick and two No. 2s, the "Highatollah of Slamola" (a nickname gained in his triumph in the first-ever NBA Slam-Dunk Contest, beating Dr. J, among others) was worth all that. A top shot-blocker, dunker and rebounder, Nance benefited from assistant coach Dick Helm's teaching and made himself into a deadly wing shooter as well.

59. Clark Kellogg. The greatest hooper from Cleveland, he scored 51 points for St. Joseph in a loss in the state finals. Not Jerry Lucas, not LeBron, not nobody, not no how, has topped Kellogg's performance in the OHSAA finals. He would have been a ten-year All-Star (as it was he made the All-Rookie Team) in the NBA had he not hurt his knee with the Indiana Pacers. Later became CBS-TV's top in-studio analyst for college basketball. We love how he says "Buck-eyes."

58. Frank "Gunner" Gatski. He came out of the hollers and hills of West Virginia to earn a nickname reflective of his blocking ferocity. This Hall of Fame center on the Browns' AAFC and early NFL dynasty teams simply blew people away. He never missed a game, scrimmage or practice, even though he began playing in West Virginia with one shoe that was size 9 and one that was a 10?. After retiring, Gatski returned to his roots, living with no phone so deep in the woods that he found out he had made the Hall of Fame by reading about it in the local paper. "Where I'm from, they put a note on an arrow and shoot it into your door," he said in his induction speech.

57. Early Wynn. "Burly Early" went 23-7 for the '54 Indians' record-setters. He won 20 games four times on his way to winning exactly 300 over his career, hit as high as .317 and was sometimes used as a pinch-hitter. This Hall of Famer would throw at anybody, even his grandmother. "But only if she was digging in," he said. When a Detroit pitcher threw at Larry Doby in 1949, Wynn knocked the hurler down during his next at-bat on four straight pitches. "You hurt Doby, you hurt me," he said. "I had to teach him some manners."

56. Jack Lambert. Called "Count Dracula in cleats" because his four front upper teeth were knocked out playing basketball, he could've given hockey players lessons in disagreeable dentition and malevolence. A second-round draft pick of the Pittsburgh Steelers, he first played linebacker at 204 pounds. Never really big enough for the position, he compensated with a raging competitive fire, best exemplified when he spiked the Cowboys' taunting Cliff Harris after a missed Steelers field goal by Roy Gerela in the first of the teams' three Super Bowls against each. A native of Mantua in Portage County, Lambert was NFL Defensive Player of the Year in 1976 and a key member of Kent State's only Mid-American Conference football championship team in 1972.

55. Tim Mack. A journeyman pole vaulter for years, Mack was able to read the riddle of the air in a glorious 2004 season, using meticulously compiled performance data to determine the right pole for the correct height and the prevailing wind. In first making the U.S. Olympic team, and then in winning the gold medal, both on his third attempt at the bar—the latter at an Olympic record height 19 feet, 6¼ inches, the pole vaulter from St. Ignatius and Westlake gained propulsion from the power of self-belief. Jumped 6 meters (19-8¼) late in 2004, the metric measure of greatness in the event.

54. John Hicks. The right tackle form John Hay High went on to become one of OSU's finest linemen ever. Hicks won all the collegiate lineman awards in 1973, the Lombardi and Outland trophies. And he nearly became the first interior lineman to be designated as college football's best player, finishing second to Penn State running back John Cappelletti in the '73 Heisman vote. He split votes with Archie Griffin (fifth) before Archie's two-year run to the little stiff-arming statuette.

53. Robert Smith. A consistent force in the NFL who would have put Minnesota in the Super Bowl in 1999 with his gutty running between the tackles had kicker Gary Anderson not gagged a late field goal in the NFC title game, Smith was one of the great high school players in local history at Euclid. He evoked O.J. Simpson comparisons in college, but left Ohio State after two years, passing up the Heisman he seemed certain to win.

52. Stella Walsh. Her family moved to Cleveland from Poland when she was three months old. With a name Anglicized from Walasiewicz to Walsh, she won the women's 100 meters at the 1932 Olympics while representing Poland. She was the silver medalist in 1936 at Berlin. After Walsh was slain as a bystander to a robbery in Cleveland, an autopsy revealed she had male genitalia and possessed chromosomes of both genders. We chose Jesse Owens to run the 100 meters on our all-time track team list, but Walsh belongs in this "century" of great athletes. The Stella Walsh Recreation Center stands on the grounds of South High School.

51. C. C. Sabathia. Sorry, John Beckett. It's a regular-season award. Carsten Charles' 2007 Cy Young Award was won on merit, as he persevered through his teammates' hitting famines without complaint and became a team leader. So desperate were the times offensively that serious fans wondered if Eric Wedge would consider C.C. as a pinch-hitter. It is a very great mistake to look at Sabathia's pear-shaped physique and conclude he is not a fine athlete.

50. David Albritton. One of three East Tech athletes to crack the Top 100, Albritton became the first black man to hold a world record in track and field, the first practitioner of the straddle style in high jumping and the silver medalist at the 1936 Olympics in Berlin.

49. Desmond Howard. The St. Joseph (now Villa Angela-St. Joseph) product was the first receiver to lead the Big Ten in scoring (23 TDs, including 19 TD catches) as he won the 1991 Heisman Trophy at Michigan. He had wings on his helmet and on his feet on the transcendent, diving, fully extended, fingertip catch of high school teammate Elvis Grbac's throw in fourth-and-inches to beat Notre Dame. He had the punt return and Heisman pose to beat Ohio State. In the pros, he was the MVP of Green Bay's Super Bowl victory over New England with a 99-yard kickoff return just when the Pats had drawn close and had all the momentum.

48. Tom Weiskopf. Benedictine's finest won the British Open in 1973, played on two Ryder Cups and had a swing out of a instructional DVD, plus length off the tee that sent his ball flying past Jack Nicklaus' boomers. Yet, we still wanted more because of his four seconds in the Masters and another runner-up finish in the U.S. Open. Nevertheless, he gave us plenty.

47. Hector Marinaro. The top scorer in indoor soccer history drove home the game-winning goal against St. Louis in 1994, giving the Crunch an MISL title and Cleveland its first pro championship of any kind in 30 years. He was part of three championship teams in Cleveland. Soccer, whether outdoors or on a rug inside, is all about the goal. So was Marinaro.

46. Gaylord Perry. So what if a foul ball off one of his offerings one night in Arlington, Tex. hit the press box window and left a slick smear on the glass? Spitballer or not, he won the first of his two Cy Young Awards (the other was in 1978 in the NL with the Padres) by going 24-16 with a 1.92 ERA and a save for the 1972 Indians. The Hall of Famer did more with less help from teammates than anyone but LeBron James. Well, okay. The K-Y lubricating jelly helped too.

45. Sandy Alomar Jr. Hit a homer to the opposite field off Mariano Rivera when winter was five outs away, after hitting the All-Star Game game-winning homer in Cleveland—what a Joe Hardy year 1997 was for the 1991 Rookie of the Year. Sandy took less money for years so the Indians could stay contenders, then got traded in what signaled the end of Camelot for the Tribe.

44. Bernie Kosar. Embraced the city when it needed a hug, then courted it by manipulating the supplemental draft when most players shunned it. Kosar dominated the 1980s in Cleveland in a way that not even LeBron matches today. Bernie novelty songs on the radio. Number 19 jerseys flying off the racks. The Cowboys' Tony Romo gets all the pub today as a resourceful quarterback who makes plays with unusual releases. Bernie, side-arming and three-quarter-arming, standing 6-5 and fearless in the pocket with the thunder of pass rushers raging all around him, was Romo without the quickness to find an escape route.

43. Johnny Kilbane. The Cleveland featherweight held the title from 1912-23, the longest in division history and second-longest ever in any division behind Joe Louis' heavyweight title run. He became such a by-word for fistic fury that, when baseball player Ty Cobb attacked a heckler in the stands in 1912, it was written that Cobb had "johnnykilbaned" the critic.

42. Glenn Davis. A Barberton hurdler who was Edwin Moses before Edwin Moses, Davis became the first man to win the 400-meter hurdles gold medal at two Olympics—in Melbourne in 1956 and Rome in 1960. A great sprinter and hurdler at Ohio State, Davis sometimes outscored opposing track teams at Barberton all by himself in the sprints and hurdles.

41. Gene Hickerson. Before he joined the Browns, only seven men had rushed for 1,000 yards in a season. The Browns had one in nine of this Hall of Famer's first 10 years. A former "messenger guard" used to bring in plays, Hickerson quickly advanced to making them. He was Jim Brown's bodyguard during his seven 1,000-yard seasons, but did not really gain the fame he deserved until he ushered Leroy Kelly into the same club after Brown retired. Five straight years an All-NFL first team selection, Hickerson started in four championship games.

40. Herb Score. Not that long before Score was hit in the face by Gil McDougald's line drive, he failed to cover first on a grounder because his pitching motion caused him to roll his eyes toward the sky and lose sight of the ball off the bat. It was a flaw that would prematurely cripple a career that could have made him the Sandy Koufax of the American League. Herb then became the "Voice of the Indians." He had some flaws behind the mic, too. But he remained one of the most beloved Indians ever—for his good humor amid some very black days on the mound and in the booth, for his knowledge of the game and for never, for one moment, complaining.

39. Austin Carr. A solid pro career was slowed by injuries with the Cavs. Carr is now a part of the Cavs' TV broadcast team, and nobody on the floor wants them to win as much he does. A.C. had one of the smoothest strokes ever. At Notre Dame, he had a scoring average for seven NCAA Tournament games of 50 points. Untouchable, unreachable, unthinkable.

38. Gary Collins. He would be in the Hall of Fame if he played with a powerhouse team and had a last name that personified a receiver's grace. A name like, oh, "Swann" comes to mind. The Browns' career leader in receiving touchdowns snagged 13 scoring passes in 1963, breaking Dante Lavelli's team mark of nine that had stood since 1947. (The mark lasted until 2007 when Braylon Edwards caught 15 TD passes in 16 games—two more than Collins played.) Collins also led the NFL in punting with a 46.7-yard average in 1965. He went on to become the team's second most prolific receiver, behind Ozzie Newsome in yards, and caught three touchdown passes in 1964 against the Colts in the last championship game the Browns won. His pet play was to run a receiver into the goal post, which was located on the goal-line then, using it like a screen in basketball. He scored many touchdowns on this literal "post pattern."

37. Denton True "Cy" Young. Just wondering, but why are his victories in the Gaslight Era still counted as the modern record? It's inconceivable that anyone will come close to his 511 victories in the modern game. Get 20 wins for 20 straight years and you'd still be 111 short. "Cyclone" played from 1909-11 for the Cleveland Naps and he's the guy for whom the game's top pitching award is named. Little-known bit of Americana: the old Cy Young and the young Woody Hayes were friends in Newcomerstown.

36. Madeline Manning (Mims). The first great American female middle distance runner, this John Hay graduate extended the Tennessee State Tiger Belles' track dominance beyond the sprints. She won the 800-meter gold medal in the 1968 Olympics by 10 meters and dominated the distance enough in the USA to make four Olympic teams, although the 1980 boycott limited her to running in only three.

35. Denny Shute. The long-time pro at Portage Country Club won two PGA Championships in the 1930s when they were man-killer match-play events and also claimed a British Open title.

34. Elmer Flick. Once known as a trivia question (for having the lowest league-leading batting average of .308 in 1905 until Carl Yastrzemski in 1968), Flick also led the league in slugging and RBI. He led the league twice in stolen bases and three times in triples. The Hall of Famer was born and raised in Bedford.

33. Joe Sewell. All this 5-6, 155-pound shortstop had to do was step into the line-up at the most important defensive position in 1920 after Ray Chapman had been killed by Carl Mays' pitch, with the Black Sox scandal erupting and the Tribe in a desperate pennant race. Sewell responded by hitting .329 with 12 RBI in 22 games. His incredible batting eye let him pick out, he claimed, the individual seams on a thrown ball. He struck out only 114 times in a 14-year career with the Indians and Yankees, a record for anyone who played very much.

32. Manny Ramirez. The best hitter on the great 1990s Indians was only tangentially connected to reality. He asked two beat reporters for $10,000 for a motorcycle, left his paychecks in his glove compartment and once, after observing the O.J. Simpson Bronco chase on TV, said: "Why are people mad at Chad (Chad Ogea, the Indians pitcher)? But he was an RBI machine (165 in 1999), who could hit with power to all fields. In his last at-bat in 2000, he had a "Kid Bids Adieu to Hub" moment, smashing a line drive over the wall in center field.

31. Dante Lavelli. You want big-game performance? "Gluefingers" scored twice and caught a then-record 11 passes, including the game-winner, in the first NFL Championship Game to lead the Browns past the Rams for the title in the franchise's first year in the league. And all this with only three games experience in college at end, a position to which Paul Brown, a fellow who knew a thing or two about his personnel, moved Lavelli at Ohio State. A Pro Football Hall of Famer, Lavelli emerged as one of the most outspoken critics of Art Modell after the move of the team.

30. Bill Willis. Along with Marion Motley, this Hall of Famer helped break the color barrier in pro football. A 210-pound defensive lineman, Willis was so explosive, he changed the way football plays actually begin. His presence led centers to begin placing the ball far in front of them to create space, so Willis couldn't crash into them after the snap and before they could react, sending send both the center and the quarterback tumbling like bowling pins. When he ran down Gene "Choo Choo" Roberts, cruising downfield on a 44-yard gain with a blocking convoy, at the Browns' three-yard line in the playoff for the division title in 1950, he saved a touchdown and forced the Giants to settle for three points, the only ones they scored in the 8-3 contest. It was the only win in three tries over New York for the Browns that year, but, without it, the last-gasp defeat of the Rams the next week and the dynasty reputation might never have gotten off the ground.

29. Addie Joss. The only player in the Hall of Fame to have the ten-year rule of service qualification waived, Joss played with the Indians from 1902-10. He pitched a perfect game against the White Sox and Hall of Famer Ed Walsh in 1908 and conventionally no-hit the Chisox in 1910. His career ERA of 1.89 rates as the second lowest of all-time and his walks-and-hits-per-inning-pitched ratio remains history's best. Joss had five sub-2.00 ERA seasons and won 20 or more games four times. After Joss died at the age of 31 of tubercular meningitis in 1911, his fellow players organized the first All-Star, played over the protests of AL President Ban Johnson, to benefit the Joss family.

28. Stan Coveleskie. One of the great spitballers and a stalwart of the 1920 World Series champion Indians, Coveleskie won three games in the Fall Classic, all five-hitters. He had an ERA of 0.67 that could barely be seen with the naked eye. A great control pitcher, "Covey" once went seven innings without missing the strike zone or having a pitch hit, even for a foul tip.

27. Vic Janowicz. The Elyria native was probably Ohio State's greatest player. He won the 1950 Heisman and might have repeated had this Hayes guy not taken over and decided the forward pass was a known carcinogen. His field goal in the "Snow Bowl" game against Michigan in 1950 is considered the greatest play in OSU football history.

26. Fred Glover. When the NHL consisted of the Original Six, the American Hockey League champion was usually called the seventh-best team in hockey. That was the Barons in 1954, 1957, and 1964. Glover led them to the Calder Cup each time. He played 15 years in the AHL and retired as its second-leading goal-scorer and assist man.

25. Butch Reynolds. It is unfortunate that his long battle with track authorities over a probably botched drug test took attention away from his 43.29-second 400 meters. Such a time was unheard of until Butch posted it at the Weltclasse meet in Zurich in 1988, and only Michael Johnson has gone faster since. If the race had been 401 meters long, Butch, his eyes pinched nearly shut, his face a mask of pain, his long strides devouring the ground off the final turn, would have won the gold and not the silver in Seoul.

24. Kenny Lofton. Arms pumping, legs digging, Lofton went flying around third and streaking home, covering about 175 feet of Kingdome vinyl grass on a lowly passed ball to score the clinching run as the Indians won the 1995 pennant, their first in 41 years. The Indians hit a lot of walk-off homers in the 1990s, but this was the most exciting play of the decade, as well as perhaps the wildest run outside Pamplona.

23. Albert Belle. Would rank higher, except he was a poor with the glove, did not hustle all the time and was the most ornery person in the big leagues since Ty Cobb. He alienated teammates as well as journalists, and his constant tantrums and suspensions hurt the Indians' chances to win. But, good Lord, he could hit. Belle clobbered 50 homers and 50 doubles in a short, 144-game season in 1995, when his failure to win the MVP award was based solely on personal dislike by the baseball writers who voted. He seldom missed a mistake pitch.

22. Jim Thome. Apparently, beached the canoe for Moses Cleveland, erected the Soldiers and Sailors Monument and still had time to become the most prolific home run hitter in Indians' history. On the night he set the franchise record for homers, future Hall of Famer Thome solemnly said: "The biggest thing is, I did it with one team." Nobody ever said he was a genius, too.

21. Brad Daugherty. In one of the best Cleveland trades ever, the Cavs gained the right to grab Daugherty with the first overall pick in the 1986 NBA draft for only Roy Hinson and cash. Daugherty was not an extremely athletic center. But he had the last of the old-time hook shots, painstakingly learned at the knee of assistant coach Dick Helm. He was also an extraordinary passer for a big man, and he joined the team as a North Carolina graduate at age 21. He should've lasted into the current century, but a bad back cut him down.

20. Mark Price. Pat Riley said he was the best in the NBA at "turning the corner," meaning getting into the lane and creating havoc. He was also twice the best three-point shooter in the All-Star Game Shootout, and, if the Cavs had ever gotten past Michael Jordan, he and Brad Daugherty would be as famous for their version of the pick-and-roll as Utah's John Stockton and Karl Malone.

19. Omar Vizquel. Didn't need a glove and, in warm-ups, this ex-soccer player didn't even need hands. Made the game fun to watch because it was obvious he was having such fun playing it. Seeing Vizquel at the Rock 'n' Roll Hall of Fame for the 1995 World Series party, dressed in a canary yellow outfit that only he could wear with style, was like seeing the sun king of Cleveland in his suit of light.

18. Ozzie Newsome. Revolutionized the tight end position, along with Kellen Winslow Sr. The Wizard blocked adequately, played like a split end with lineman size, and had the hands of a magician. Incompletions disappeared around him.

17. Bob Lemon. The Hall of Fame pitcher started as an outfielder who couldn't hit and a third baseman whose throws across the diamond had enough "late life" (to use the term for a fastball's movement) on them to rival Lazarus. Affable and easy-going, "Lem" won 207 games and lost 128 for the Tribe and was at his best in big games. He also hit 37 home runs, second-best ever for a pitcher.

16. Paul Warfield. The Warren native played on ball-control running teams, both with the Browns and Dolphins (after the Art Modell brain burp that sent him to Miami for the draft pick that became Mike Phipps). Therefore, this Hall of Famer's career numbers are not overwhelming. But he had that great football last name, yoked to a game of speed, elusiveness, and grace. His average of 20.1 yards per catch ranks among the best ever.

15. Earl Averill. He was a 27-year-old rookie when he broke into the Indians' line-up. The 1930s were an offensive era, and Averill provided more of it than most. A Hall of Famer, the center fielder hit better than .300 his first six seasons with the Tribe. The '90s Indians were an offensive machine, but when you check the team record book for career RBI, runs, triples and total bases, "Averill" is the name next to the marks. Averill's 1937 All-Star Game bullet broke Dizzy Dean's toe, which led to the end of Dean's career.

14. Rocky Colavito. His signature gesture was pointing his bat straight at the pitcher, who turned quite frequently into aspic at the sight. Colavito had an arm that made baseballs subject to ballistics testing. He led the Indians in homers and RBI in 1958 and '59, and in batting average in '58. Unfortunately, when he was traded for Harvey Kuenn before the 1960 season, many fans put the bat to Cleveland and GM "Trader" Frank Lane. Rocky became a part of the many "curses" invoked to explain failure.

13. Larry Doby. A racial pioneer, Doby made us look at the man beneath the skin. The two-time AL home run champion played out of position and still was glorious. He arrived in Cleveland only six weeks after the carefully prepared introduction of Jackie Robinson broke the color barrier in Major League Baseball. But while Robinson had a spot waiting for him in the Brooklyn Dodgers lineup, Doby had to fight his way into the lineup for the Tribe at first base, since Joe Gordon was the incumbent at his natural position of second. Doby hit 5-for-32 and played only six games in the field in 1947. He could have been broken by his early struggles, yet went on to a Hall of Fame career. His hug with white teammate Steve Gromek in the 1948 World Series, after Doby's homer provided the winning run in the fourth game, was shocking at the time. Today, we see it as an ebony-and-ivory moment, showing that in a world often divided, sports could create perfect harmony.

12. Leroy Kelly. Once upon a time, the Browns didn't have to wait 20 flipppin' years between 1,000-yard rushers (the span between Mack/Byner and Reuben Droughns). Back in the days of the shorter 14-game seasons, when Jim Brown quit the Browns to film *The Dirty Dozen*, Kelly stepped into his spot and led the league in rushing yards in 1967 and '68. He ended up with over 12,000 all-purpose yards and 90 touchdowns, making six Pro Bowl squads and into the Hall of Fame. He followed Jim Brown like Pestilence following Famine, or maybe Death on the heels of Destruction for opposing defenses.

11. Lou Boudreau. The Indians player/manager in 1948 gained American League Most Valuable Player honors when he hit .365 that year, Boudreau not only carried the biggest bat in the one-game playoff against the Red Sox, he is the last Indian manager to bring home the title. The Hall of Famer endured second-guessing after games from owner Bill Veeck, who had tried to trade him the year before, and GM Hank Greenberg. It would have frazzled a weaker personality.

10. Harrison Dillard. Went to East Tech, just like Jesse Owens. The inspiration of his life came when Owens winked at him and some buddies and said: "Hi, kids" as they stood at E. 63rd and Central during Jesse's post-Olympics victory parade. Dillard did not qualify in his specialty, the 100-meter high hurdles in London in 1948, so he won the 100 instead, then came back and won the hurdles at the next Olympics in 1952, the only man to turn that double.

9. Napoleon Lajoie. Can you imagine an NBA team named the Cleveland LeBrons? Such was the case when Lajoie played second with the Cleveland baseball club called the Naps. One of the great players at the turn of the last century, this Hall of Famer hit over .300 nine times with the team that was later known as the Indians, five times besting .350. A defector from the Phillies in the National League, Lajoie was enjoined from playing for the Philadelphia A's in the AL and signed with the Cleveland team because the legal ruling had no effect in Ohio.

8. Tris Speaker. His stats, well, speak volumes. This Hall of Famer played the shallowest center field of any era, making six unassisted double plays after grabbing sinking liners on the run and sprinting to second base to double up base runners. He managed and hit the Tribe to the 1920 World Series title, while coping with the on-field death of teammate Ray Chapman, the suspicions from the tainted World Series of the year before (which led to the suspension of the star players of the White Sox late in the season), and a livelier ball. A member of the Ku Klux Klan as a young man, Speaker worked with Larry Doby in spring training in 1948, turning him into an All-Star outfielder.

7. Marion Motley. Old-timers say he was the greatest fullback ever. Sports Illustrated's Paul Zimmerman said he was the greatest player he ever saw. More to the point, so did Blanton Collier, coach of the Browns' last championship team. Motley, a Hall of Famer and racial pioneer, averaged a breath-taking 8.4 yards per carry in his first season in the AAFC. When the Browns entered the NFL, Motley, who was bigger than many of the linemen of the time, led it in rushing in 1950. He was a great linebacker, Otto Graham swore by him as a pass blocker, and he combined power with speed. He made the trap play a pitfall for almost every defense

6. Lou Groza. Far more than "The Toe," Paul Brown's favorite player prided himself on making the tackle on kickoffs, too. In addition to serving as placekicker, he started at left tackle most of the first decade that the Browns were in the NFL. Groza's late field goal gave the Browns the 1950 league title in their 30-28 victory over the Los Angeles Rams, the team that deserted the city. Since title game losses in 1951-53 followed, it also kept the team from being the 1950s version of the Buffalo Bills.

5. LeBron James. The most famous basketball player in the world while still in high school, the most publicized rookie ever in the NBA, James proved to be so precocious, showed such an unprecedented combination of speed and power, heart and head, and got so good, so fast, that the only proper response to his breathtaking career is to ask: "What hype?"

4. Otto Graham. This Hall of Famer was born too soon. Before Bo Jackson and Deion Sanders received so much publicity for participating in two sports, Otto Graham earned first-team All-American honors in basketball and finished third in the Heisman Trophy voting in football during his senior year at Northwestern. He had been recruited to football when coach Pappy Waldorf got a load of his arm in leading Delta Upsilon to the intramural baseball championship. In his first year as a professional, he played basketball on the championship team in the National Basketball League (an NBA forerunner), baseball for the Rochester Royals and football for the Browns. He then concentrated solely on football and led the Browns to ten straight championship games. He also played the oboe, English horn, French horn, piano, cornet and violin. Was he sports' greatest player? Or its greatest Renaissance man?

3. Bob Feller. Not only the top Indian, this Hall of Famer is one of the top Americans of his time—just check his war record. He won 266 games and would have won 300 in a snap of his curveball had he not lost 3½ years to World War II in the prime of his career. As the sole support of his family, he did not have to enlist, but did because he felt it was the right thing to do. He was the first LeBron James, striking out 17 Philadelphia A's while he was still in high school. He threw three no-hitters and 12 one-hitters. "Bullet Bob"— whose fastball was once timed at 107.9mph—had a high leg kick because he intended to cover so much ground in baseball history.

2. Jim Brown. Amazingly, when he retired at the age of 29 to go to Hollywood to kill Nazis in *The Dirty Dozen*, Brown was already acclaimed as the best there ever was— and he remains so today. He held the all-time yardage and touchdown records, despite playing less than a decade during the era of 14- or even 12-game seasons. The Pro Football Hall of Famer still boasts the career mark for yards per carry (5.2). He did it with an unprecedented and still unmatched combination of speed and power. Brown won practice sprints against Bobby Mitchell, a Big Ten sprint champion and one of the fastest men of his era. His huge, chiseled frame could "make it hurt when they tackle you." The nine-time Pro Bowler arose slowly after every tackle—not to keep the opposition from knowing when he was tired, as many thought, but to make sure no one was lurking, waiting to step on his hands as he got up. It was a brutal sport then, and Brown was one of the top merchants of pain—though he didn't have to resort to stepping on anyone's hands, needing only to lower his shoulder to dish it out in heaping portions. Want more? The National Lacrosse Hall of Fame says Brown, who was an All-American in the sport at Syracuse, also rates as the best lacrosse player of all-time!

1. Jesse Owens. He literally ran Adolf Hitler's Master Race theories into the ground in Berlin at the 1936 Olympics, winning four gold medals, in what has to be the greatest performance under pressure in sports history. Seen in the context of what was to come—World War II and the ghastly horrors of Hitler's Final Solution—it was the most powerful drama in sports history. It resonates still in track and field, the political arena and the human heart. At Ohio State, Owens set three world records and tied another in 45 minutes at the 1935 Big Ten track meet in Ann Arbor. His long jump mark at Ann Arbor lasted for 25 years, or longer than Bob Beamon's. His high school long-jump mark, set at East Tech, lasted 44 years. Jesse Cleveland (J.C., hence "Jesse") Owens was so far ahead of his time, he needed to cross the International Dateline every day for decades to get back. It is a disgrace that the statue of him in downtown Cleveland is tucked into a small park on W. 3rd and not proudly displayed on Public Square. He was the greatest, and still is the greatest.